*Nathan
Söderblom
and the Study
of Religion*

Studies in Religion

Charles H. Long, Editor
Syracuse University

Editorial Board

Giles B. Gunn
University of California at Santa Barbara

Van A. Harvey
Stanford University

Wendy Doniger O'Flaherty
The University of Chicago

Ninian Smart
University of California at Santa Barbara
and the University of Lancaster

Nathan Söderblom (1866–1931)

Nathan Söderblom and the Study of Religion

Eric J. Sharpe

The University of North Carolina Press

Chapel Hill and London

© 1990 The University of North Carolina Press
All rights reserved

Library of Congress Cataloging-in-Publication Data

Sharpe, Eric J., 1933–
  Nathan Söderblom and the study of religion / by Eric J. Sharpe.
    p. cm.—(Studies in religion)
  Bibliography: p.
  Includes index.
  ISBN 9780807865941 (pbk. : alk. paper)
  1. Söderblom, Nathan, 1866–1931—Contributions in history of religions. 2. Religion—Study and teaching—History—20th century. I. Title. II. Series: Studies in religion (Chapel Hill, N.C.)
BL43.S67S53 1990
284.1'092—dc20   89-34138
                                                            CIP

It is a fearful thing to fall into the hands of the living God.
—Hebrews 10:31

The scientific approach to the study of religion—or of anything else—does not rest on the absence of personal conviction, least of all on the absence of a religious conviction. The scientific approach is tested by its results; it rests upon scientific competence and a love of truth.

The requirement that the theologian should possess a feeling for religion or a definite religious conviction or belong to a religious community is implied, to the extent to which it is justified, in the general scientific requirement of familiarity with the object [studied]. Thus it lies in the nature of the case. Should the requirement be made in any other sense, it would be incompatible with the nature of science.

Therefore science cannot recognize any difference in principle between the science of religion and theology.
—Nathan Söderblom, 1907

I know that God lives. I can prove it by the history of religion.
—Nathan Söderblom, 1931

Contents

	Preface	xi
	Introduction	xv
1	Antecedents	1
2	Student in Uppsala, 1883–1892	12
3	Discovering Iran, 1892–1894	35
4	The Paris Years, 1894–1901	49
5	Professor in Uppsala, 1901–1912	94
6	Leipzig, 1912–1914	134
7	Toward a Phenomenology of Religion	150
8	Archbishop and Scholar	172
	Postscript	201
Appendix 1	To the Students of Theology	215
Appendix 2	Method in the History of Religion	219
Appendix 3	Söderblom on His Father	223
Appendix 4	Söderblom's Honorary Doctorates	225
	Notes	227
	Bibliography	245
	Index	253

Preface

In December 1973 the History of Religions Project of the American Council of Learned Societies met in New York to discuss the preparation of a series of books in English on persons of importance in the history of the discipline, persons who it was felt were insufficiently well known, other than as names, to present-day students. A straw vote was taken as to which scholars ought to be given priority if the project were to come to fruition (it did not, though that is neither here nor there). Two names tied for first place: Rudolf Otto and Nathan Söderblom, with thirty-four votes each. There followed Gerardus van der Leeuw, Friedrich Max Müller, Raffaele Pettazzoni and Max Weber, with votes ranging between twenty-six and fifteen. The original intention, incidentally, was to devote one-third of each volume to a biographical introduction and the remaining two-thirds to selections—in translation where necessary—from the works of the scholar in question.

Of the two who came highest on the list, Otto and Söderblom, the former is accessible to the English-speaking student as the latter is not. All of Otto's major works have been translated into English, and in any case, German is acquired as a matter of course by graduate students.

In Söderblom's case access is far more difficult. His earliest scholarly publications appeared in French, and some of his later work in German translations. Most of the remainder is in Swedish—a vast "remainder," since throughout his life Söderblom was a prolific, not to say a compulsive, writer. In English we have only the handful of articles Söderblom wrote for Hastings's *Encyclopaedia of Religion and Ethics* before the first world war, and the book by which his name is chiefly known today, *The Living God* (which appeared in 1933, two years after his death). Bengt Sundkler's biography of Söderblom appeared in 1968 in English; timed to coincide with the Uppsala Assembly of the World Council of Churches, it quite naturally concentrated on Söderblom's role as a world church leader, and passed over the scholarly contribution of the years between 1901 and 1914 fairly quickly. Whoever reads Swedish, on the other hand, very soon finds that there is an *embarras de richesses* in the Söderblom literature and archives. Some of that material I shall attempt to translate and interpret in what follows.

A personal word about how this study came to be undertaken may not be out of place. In the fall of 1958 I attended my first seminars, under Carl-Martin Edsman, in the medieval building in Uppsala which once had served as an apartment for Söderblom's widow, and which housed his personal library. One of the other participants in these seminars was Söderblom's youngest granddaughter. I had neither the time nor the competence to begin writing about Söderblom at that stage; I did, however, begin to assemble my own personal collection of his writings, which were cheap and plentiful in Swedish secondhand bookshops. Twenty years later, for a few months I occupied the tower room set up by Anna Söderblom as a shrine to her late husband. Söderblom's letters and papers had long since been removed to the university library, but there remained his books, many of them with his personal annotations, his desk, his blotter, his photographs and memorabilia (among them an elephant tusk, the gift of Albert Schweitzer). Two cramped attics contained even more books, journals, newspapers, and unclassifiable oddments; downstairs there was a collection of practically everything that Söderblom had ever published. But with one or two exceptions, the researchers who might have been expected to besiege this treasure-house of scholarship were conspicuous by their absence. And early in 1981 part of its contents had to be removed, since the Uppsala Cathedral authorities who owned the building needed extra office space! The tower room and library remained, but were effectively sealed off. I was thankful for the time I had been able to spend there, but I have not been back since.

That I have undertaken this task now, almost thirty years after first making Söderblom's acquaintance, is a direct consequence of a visit paid to Australia in 1983 by Charles Long. He left Sydney carrying a tentative proposal for a Söderblom study; it was accepted in principle, and the result is contained in what follows.

It is, I fear, not in my nature to write other than biographically. I have never been capable of (or indeed much interested in) "systematic" studies unrelated to time and place, personalities and pressures. I have written chiefly of Professor (rather than Archbishop)

Nathan Söderblom, that is, what we might call "the early Söderblom" in the years prior to 1914, though with a chapter on what came later, notably his encounter with Sadhu Sundar Singh in 1922 and his Gifford Lectures of 1931.

Even so, Söderblom's was a life of such extraordinary richness as to make a coherent chronological narrative of even part of it practically impossible to carry through. I do not pretend to have covered more than a few aspects of that life. I have not had access to all the relevant firsthand material, and often I have had the dismal feeling that to give even an outline of Söderblom's scholarship is bound to fall so far short of the man himself as to be almost a species of sacrilege. Perhaps, though, to have too much material is as dangerous as to have too little. In any case, my many Swedish friends have the Söderblom literature close at hand as the English-speaking student of religion generally does not. Let what follows, then, be seen as a modest work of translation aimed at a non-Swedish readership, though a translation that at the same time attempts to be something of a portrait of a man, a country, and an age.

Since most of the sources on which this study has been based are in languages other than English, a good deal of direct translation (chiefly from Swedish) has been necessary along the way. For most of these translations I am myself solely responsible, though in the very few cases where English texts have been available I have used these. I have tried not to overload the text with references that would be of very limited value to the English-speaking student, though I do of course identify the sources of direct quotations.

I should like to thank my teachers of many years ago in Uppsala,[1] chiefly Carl-Martin Edsman and Bengt Sundkler, for first awakening my interest in Söderblom; *Nathan Söderblom-sällskapet för religionshistorisk forskning* for electing me in 1976 a "corresponding member"; the Swedish Institute for a grant to enable me to do archive work in Uppsala in the spring of 1985; the manuscripts department of Uppsala University Library for many courtesies; and Charles Long for providing the necessary catalyst to set me to work. Margaret Gilet has typed and word-processed several drafts; my thanks for her patience and efficiency. Lastly I must thank my wife Birgitta (née Johannesson). A quarter of a century ago, when we were both students in Uppsala, I used to promise that some day I would write a Söderblom book on the typewriter she had bought a couple of years earlier. Perhaps, therefore, she will accept the fulfillment of the promise as a belated silver wedding present.

Eric J. Sharpe
Sydney, Australia
Easter 1989

Introduction

The phenomenological treatment of the greater part of the history of religion," wrote Gerardus van der Leeuw almost half a century ago, "lies still in the future." To cite names of scholars in the immediate past who had contributed to that "treatment" van der Leeuw found difficult; therefore, "rather than cite many, I select here the great name of Nathan Söderblom. For without his acute insight and his deeply penetrating love of what 'appears,' we could not advance another step in our territory; and the change of direction in the history of religion, plainly set forth in the current phenomenological viewpoint, finds its symbol in this thinker's name."[1]

The German original of van der Leeuw's book *Phänomenologie der Religion* had appeared in 1933, only two years after Nathan Söderblom's death in Uppsala at the relatively early age of sixty-five. Also in 1933 there was published, posthumously, the only one of Söderblom's larger studies ever to appear in English, *The Living God*.

According to his son-in-law Yngve Brilioth, who supplied *The Living God* with a biographical introduction, on his deathbed Söderblom had said (though these were not his last words, as some have since supposed): "There is a living God, I can prove it by the history of religions."[2] What Söderblom actually said on this solemn occasion—for he knew that he had little time left—might better be translated: "I know that God lives. I can prove it by the history of religion." The verbal difference is slight; the difference in meaning is not insignificant. "The history of religions" suggests an academic subject as studied in a university, but that was not what he meant. What he *did* mean will, I trust, emerge in due course.

Söderblom's words have since been repeated by perhaps everyone who has ever written or spoken about him. Over half a century later they still have a curious and a tantalizing ring. In these days we are uneasy about "proofs" of the existence of God, and doubt very much whether, if proofs are to be had, they are ever likely to emerge out of the relativities of history, even out of the history of religion. We may be left with little more than the sad feeling that dying archbishops, like living mystics, must be permitted their visions, but that we must seek elsewhere for our certainties.

There remains the problem of how the testimony "that God lives" relates to Söderblom's role as, in effect, the father of the phenomenology of religion—an approach which we have generally come to associate with the suspension, rather than with the affirmation, of belief. One cannot read far in the Söderblom literature, however, before discovering that the suspension of belief, or the exercise of a phenomenological *epoché*, was not part of his approach to the study of religion. True, he always treated that in which he did *not* believe with the most scrupulous fairness; never, on the other hand, did he conceal or "bracket" that in which he *did* believe. He was little of a philosopher, and would seem not to have read Husserl; even during his professorial years, only while in Germany from 1912 to 1914 was he without pastoral responsibilities as a Lutheran minister. And in 1914 he became archbishop of Uppsala.

Thus we appear to be faced with a man having two identities: a holder of dual citizenship, one in the world of scholarship, the other in the world of faith. Others have found themselves in a like predicament, if indeed it is a predicament. How Söderblom resolved the tensions this undoubtedly brought upon him will be one of the major themes of this study. For the moment it will be enough simply to state that during his most active years, he was by no means alone in carrying the burden of dual identity; nor was he alone in being criticized from one wing for being too Christian to be scientific, and from the other for being too scientific to be Christian. Nor has the controversy subsided even in our day—for which reason the retelling of the Söderblom story might be of more than historical significance.

From 1914 until his death in 1931 Nathan Söderblom was archbishop of Uppsala and primate of the Church of Sweden. In Swedish terms, the country's one and only archbishop is first and foremost an ordinary diocesan bishop and a primus inter pares, judged chiefly by the way in which he operates within his diocese and within Sweden. Circumstances made of Söderblom something more: Sweden's first *international* churchman. This many Swedes found hard to understand and appreciate. At home he was seen as the extroverted, somewhat flamboyant figure who was seldom out of the public eye; to the conservative majority in the churches, a reputation as a dangerous liberal had dogged him ever since before the turn of the century. In 1931 his academic past was all but forgotten outside the little world of Sweden's universities.

On his death, many tributes were paid to his life and work. It could not be forgotten that he had been one of the eighteen members of the Swedish Academy or that he had been awarded the Nobel Peace Prize in 1930 for his work of postwar reconciliation among the nations. Before the year 1931 was out, several short biographies and memoirs had appeared in Swedish and other Scandinavian languages; there was also a 450-page *In Memoriam* volume. Three other volumes of personal reminiscences appeared shortly afterward, containing 138 individual tributes in all. It was the second of these that startled Sweden, made up as it was of seventy personal tributes by non-Scandinavian writers—churchmen and churchwomen, ecumenical leaders, scholars, authors, artists, musicians, politicians, and friends—from no less than twenty-one different countries.

Reviewers of this collection were impressed by two things. First, each individual had something different to say about Söderblom: of pious rhetoric and vain repetition there was little trace. Apparently there had been many Söderbloms; while this would have been remarkable in anyone, in a churchman it seemed almost beyond belief. An English theologian, Father Gabriel Hebert, put it in a nutshell: "We [in England] should count it a remarkable thing if, two years after the death of an Archbishop of Canterbury, a volume of reminiscences were published contributed by seventy foreign writers, representing practically all the nations of Europe, and the United States, and all the churches, including the Church of Rome. It seems scarcely possible. Yet such a book has just appeared."[3]

Secondly, however, of all these many tributes, relatively few looked back to Söderblom's pre-1914 academic career. Academic contributions were made chiefly by Germans—Adolf Deissmann, Johannes Hempel, Gerhard Kittel, Paul le Seur, and others—and related mainly to Söderblom's two years as a professor in Leipzig, from 1912 to 1914. Swedish academics of course contributed to other volumes. The overall impression, however, was that the *international* Söderblom was a churchman first and a scholar only incidentally, or at least that, in the eyes of Sweden, his scholarship in his own major field of the history of religion was of interest and concern only to a very few.

But there was that larger and more lasting problem which Söderblom in a manner of speaking bequeathed to his successors. Is it possible for the same person to sustain two identities, one within a community of faith and the other apparently outside it, and if so, how? Bearing in mind the course of Söderblom's own career, one might be tempted to speak of an "earlier" and a "later" Söderblom, one an academic historian of religion and the other a theologian and ecumenical churchman. In my view, however, to do so would be a serious distortion. That there were tensions in Söderblom's personality is one thing: he *was* versatile, many-sided, and capable of switching from one role to another as the occasion demanded. Some of his contemporaries wondered where, if anywhere, the "real" Söderblom might be hiding. Nevertheless there was a scarlet thread running through the whole of his work and helping to shape his character, bringing together what to a later age often appear as incompatibles: the world of religious faith and the world of scientific inquiry. That thread was in place from the moment when, as a young student of theology, he first encountered Harnack and Ritschl and woke up to the importance of history in the world of religion.

In March 1920 Söderblom, by then archbishop of Uppsala, addressed an audience of Danish students on "science as a way of life" (*vetenskapen såsom livsform*). "Most of my spiritual strength," he said, "has been spent in the study of religion. No part of my far too diverse, and yet, perhaps, basically concordant work has given me a purer sense of satisfaction."[4] Later in his address he asked his audience whether they had ever seen a real scientist at work, and went on:

> Sometimes I come across him. I sit and listen as the problem he is tackling becomes more and more complex. It may come to seem hopelessly involved, in measure as he really is dedicated to the investigation of the tiniest of details in the secret of nature, and will be satisfied with nothing less. I hear how necessity becomes the mother of invention. How as his work proceeds, his method is sharpened and refined, how he discovers ways to make pathological changes in the organism

stand out under the microscope, how new, entirely unexpected factors break in and complicate everything, perhaps at the very moment he thought a plausible and simple solution to be possible. He is not satisfied with an abstraction that permits him under certain conditions to achieve a given result; he wants to get to the living root of the matter. It is as though one had been initiated into a mystery, and in the end, when I analyze my interest, I find a fair proportion of reverence in it. It was the scholar himself who had inspired it. Scientific method to him had the effect of a strict asceticism. There is a sanctity about his work, irrespective of its object, and that sanctity comes from his own person, from the purification that his working methods have effected in his soul.[5]

As with the natural scientist, he continued, so with the historian. The historian, too, is inspired by the same ideal—not that of forcing material into the straitjacket of artificial laws and generalizations, but of facing up to events, situations, and personalities as aspects of one kaleidoscopic reality. Even so, once one's crutches have been discarded and one has learned to walk on one's own in the jungle of history, patterns emerge—not the convenient patterns of the textbooks, but a pattern that is human and moral in equal measure. First, though, one must learn to observe, even when one recognizes that one can discern only in part. And having observed, one may evaluate. But then, Söderblom goes on:

Does such a superiority in observation and judgment not run the risk of becoming indifferent to the fates and sufferings of human beings, or at least of becoming hard? And does it not lead one astray when it refuses to take sides for or against, or when its contrariness leads immediately, over against every cut-and-dried judgment, to the seeing of the other side of the question? Were one to talk here of method, that would mean making one's task still more difficult. The scientific ideal is an ideal that grows and becomes more inaccessible, the closer one comes to it. Similarly with moral judgment. The foundations on which one relies are torn down. Reality emerges without any protective shell of false imagination. Nevertheless it is a source of strength and comfort to hear people speak.[6]

What, then, did Söderblom mean by "science" or "scholarship" (*vetenskap*) in this connection? Later in his Copenhagen address he described it: "For science does not of course mean knowing a great deal about something, but that our knowledge is organized, not haphazardly, but organized into a chain of cause and effect, in a necessary connection."[7]

The scholar's task therefore is threefold: first, to observe what is actually there in the world of religion—in which connection Söderblom did not shy away from using the word "reality" (*verklighet*); secondly, to establish cause-and-effect relationships; and thirdly, to attempt a moral evaluation.

It was the first of these aims, that of observing what is *there* (as opposed to what the textbooks claim ought to be there, or might be there) that impressed Gerardus van der Leeuw, and earned Söderblom his place among the founding fathers of the phenomenology of religion. But all three desiderata have their place in the phenomenological scheme of things, as observation leads on to "understanding" (*Verstehen*) and "attestation" (*Bezeugen*).

However, we must not make Söderblom into more of a phenomenologist than he was, or force him into the wrong kind of phenomenological mold. He was not in any sense a representative of Husserlian phenomenology. Nor would we be justified in speaking in Söderblom's case of the application of a phenomenological *method*. He had no such method. Ideals were another matter entirely, and in Söderblom's case, he was motivated by two sets of ideals, one inherited from the Christian tradition and the other learned from his mentors Harnack, Ritschl, Fehr, Hjärne, Sabatier, Bergson, and others. He was convinced that the two were entirely compatible, but still they needed to be justified in their interrelations, not least in face of those who were equally convinced of their incompatibility.

In his 1968 biography of Söderblom, Bengt Sundkler stated at one point that the theme of "Nathan Söderblom, Professor," might well be made the subject of a lengthy study, "dealing with Söderblom's academic contribution to Religionsgeschichte and the history of ideas."[8] Although this is substantially what I am setting out to do in these pages, it would perhaps be as well to make it clear from the very beginning that Söderblom's "academic contribution to Religionsgeschichte" cannot be evaluated other than in relation to his theology. Leave theology out of the reckoning (as one might well be tempted to do in our present-day climate of opinion), and it becomes practically impossible to grasp why Söderblom ever took up the comparative study of religion, or what he did with it.

Today there are those who speak of what it has become somewhat fashionable to call a "crisis of identity" in the study of religion, a crisis precipitated by the lack of understanding shown by two blocks of scholars for one another's positions. Up to a point the two are in general agreement, that what Söderblom would have called the "body" of religion is to be studied minutely and as dispassionately as possible for the sake of the light that can be thrown on the intricacies of human behavior. At that point, however, the ways part. The "empiricist" insists that that is *all* that the academic study of religion can investigate, and that whatever else there may be in the world of religion should be left to communities of faith to deal with on their own principles. To introduce "faith" into the debate distorts, if it does not destroy, the scientific principle of observation and verification. To this the opposing camp—for which it is hard to find a name, though "theological" and "transcendentalist" are often used—responds that if religion has no transcendental point of reference, it could well be left to the sociologists, anthropologists, and psychologists to study in their way. This position may be "theological" in the sense that it affirms—or at least does not go out of its way to contradict—some dominant religious tradition. Or it may be "transcendental" in that it attempts to look beyond traditions to some ultimate reality. It will accept the findings of the empiricists for what they are worth, but where the empiricist stops, refuses to "speculate," and indicates that transcendental meanings are a matter of private concern, the transcendentalist (or whatever else he or she may be called) peers beyond those findings to their ultimate significance.

A century ago, the problem was still that of admitting empirical research on historical and "scientific" principles into the vicinity of the sanctuary, and of convincing a community of faith that such research was an imperative necessity. Söderblom's community of faith was Lutheran, Protestant (in Continental parlance, Evangelical), Christian, and "religious," moving outward in concentric circles from a point which for Söderblom was a personal encounter with "the living God." Our problem is in a sense the opposite, since our style is to begin somewhere on the behavioral periphery and generally to stay there, conducting ventures into the interior only rarely and with great caution. But at least the "transcendentalist" believes there to be a center, the "empiricist" meantime maintaining an official agnosticism on the subject.

Still, a review of what a Christian made of the wide-angle study of religion in the thirty or so years before the first world war may be of interest. I would not for one moment wish to suggest that a study of the Söderblom generation—for Söderblom was by no means the only liberal Christian scholar of his day to grapple with "the problem of religion"—will resolve whatever "crisis of identity" there may be today. One does not attempt to reawaken the past merely to find ready-made solutions to contemporary problems. In this case, however, mutatis mutandis, the problem has shown itself to be one of extraordinary tenacity. Söderblom was a theologian, and no amount of interpretative ingenuity will make him into less of a theologian than he was. But we have to take seriously the extent of his "academic contribution to Religionsgeschichte" and the vast amount of energy he devoted to the attempt to arouse his community of faith to the need to acknowledge the "scientific" principle.

At the beginning of the third chapter of his celebrated book *The Idea of the Holy*, Rudolf Otto made what to most readers still seems the extraordinary request that whoever had never experienced "the numinous" should read no further, since they would be unlikely to grasp what he was saying.[9] Later we shall have occasion to record precisely such an experience in Söderblom's own life. It happened in 1893.[10] One may place whatever interpretation one wishes on this event, but to Söderblom himself it gave his life a focal point in the sense of having been grasped and overwhelmed by *den levande Guden*—"the living God." Thereafter he could be a historian, but not a historicist, an empirical student of religion, but not an empiricist. Most of his writings on "holiness" predated Otto's *Das Heilige* by several years; his meetings with Otto took place later than the 1893 experience. This is not to say that Otto was directly indebted to Söderblom for his "holiness" idea. That is not the point at all. The point is that to Söderblom, the issue was not between two species of intellectual theory, one operating within and the other outside a community of faith (which is the way much of the present-day debate operates). It was not, in other words, between "theology" and "the science of religion" as antithetical approaches to the same body of material.

In the preface to his 1907 book *Studiet av religionen* (The study of religion), Söderblom stated categorically that "science cannot recognize any difference in principle between the science of religion and theology."[11] Theology may on the other hand do so, to the extent that it insists (if it insists) on dictating the terms on which the study is carried out. But that would not have been Söderblom's theology. Should science make similar claims, that would not have been Söderblom's science. Clearly, then, everything rests on what, to Söderblom, was religion, what theology, and what science. It is to be hoped that this study, short as it must necessarily be, will show some of the steps by which he came to his own unique synthesis, and how, throughout an academic career lasting from 1883 to 1914—and indeed down to his death in 1931—he was never other than a student of religion and never other than totally possessed by the living God.

*Nathan
Söderblom
and the Study
of Religion*

1

Antecedents

Lars Olof Jonathan (Nathan) Söderblom was born in the country parish of Trönö, in the north central Swedish province of Hälsingland, on January 15, 1866. His father, Pastor Jonas Söderblom, had been assistant minister (*komminister*) in Trönö since 1864. His mother, Sophie (née Blume), had been born in Sweden of Danish parents. At the time of their eldest son's birth his father was already forty-two years old, his mother twenty-seven.

On his father's side, Nathan Söderblom was descended from a long line of independent farmers. As late as in the 1930s it was recorded with pride that the family farm in Orsta had never been sold, and there was reason to believe that it had passed from father to son in the same family ever since the land had first been cleared. Before the mid-nineteenth century names were passed on in a similar fashion, eldest sons alternating between Jon Olsson (or Olofsson) and Olof Jonsson, generation after generation.

Nathan Söderblom's paternal grandfather maintained this tradition. Jon Olofsson (1789–1871) was a solid, pious farmer, a churchwarden, and a man of great dignity and integrity. It is recorded that his wife, Margta Olsdotter, was of a more lively temperament. Both were deeply influenced by a wave of revivalism which swept over Hälsingland between about 1820 and 1840.

Revivalism is a complex element in Sweden's church history, on the one hand because, in a period of poor or nonexistent communications, what was happening in one province had comparatively little effect in another, and on the other, because its expressions, too, varied greatly. In the far north of Sweden, revivalism could take on an ecstatic form, perhaps not unconnected with Lappish and Finnish traditions, while elsewhere, for instance on Sweden's west coast, the pattern was rigidly moral and ethical. Some revivalists and their followers broke away or were expelled from the Lutheran church, while others worked from within. This was all the more necessary since in the nineteenth century there were still in Sweden strict (though not always applied) "conventicle laws" which forbade the holding of free religious gatherings outside the established church. In the early 1840s both kinds of revivalism—independent and internal—were represented in Hälsingland, the independent type by the followers of Erik Jansson (who were soon to migrate en masse to Illinois, where their leader was murdered), the internal by the solid majority, among them Jon Olofsson. In 1844 we find him writing with some satisfaction to his son Jonas, Nathan Söderblom's father, that the atmosphere in the church was quieter since the Janssonites had been excluded.[1]

The Lutheran confessional form of revivalism in Hälsingland had much in common with that of the "old readers" of Norrland ("reader," in Swedish *läsare*, refers of course to the practice of Bible-reading in private, in the family, and in small conventicles of the faithful, as well as in church). The Bible was central. For its interpretation, the "readers" relied upon Luther's commentaries and sermons (*postilla*) and such devotional writers as the German Johann Arndt and the Swede Anders Nohrborg. Within the Bible, theological convention dictated that Paul's letters to the Galatians and Romans, with their distinction between the law and the gospel, provided the key by which all else was to be understood. The work of Christ took precedence over his person, his divinity over his humanity, his death over his life. Each individual had first of all to be brought face to face with his or her own sinful nature, and with the ruthless judgment of God over all sin. The world was under the sway of "the prince of this world," the devil (and his minions), but each individual might be set free from that inborn subjection by reliance on the efficacy of the atoning death of Christ. In order to prevent "backsliding," those thus set free from the guilt and power of sin were to be gathered together into small companies of the faithful, conventicles, with a standard of faith and conduct different from that of the world outside. But where a congregation as a whole moved in this direction, then the church and its sacraments would serve as bulwarks against the corruption of the world. Liberation for the individual could, however, come only after having passed through the terrors of the law, and having faced the condemnation of God over against all sin. In not a few cases, the fear of condemnation far outweighed the assurance of salvation—a situation to which natural Swedish pessimism must often have contributed.

Jonas Söderblom was one who all his life wrestled with this problem.[2] Born on November 8, 1823, he was deeply gripped by the seriousness of the Hälsingland revival, which was at its height during his impressionable teens. Not being the eldest son in the family, he was free to study, and it was as a young student that, in accordance with the custom of the time, he changed his name from Olofsson to Söderblom ("Söder" from the parish name of Söderala; "blom" from *blomma*, "flower"). Ascetic, disciplined, strict with himself and his family, he was at times subject to fits of depression (to which his son, appearances to the contrary, was no stranger either). A deep religious crisis in his teens is said to have brought him to the verge of insanity, but he emerged to become an admirable, if somewhat fierce and intimidating, country minister. To Jonas Söderblom, religion was the one thing requisite in life—religion with all its demands and all its renunciations, religion untouched by any milder southerly wind. At the same time, he had considerable intellectual gifts. When he went to Uppsala in 1862 to take his ordination examination, his examiners were startled to hear that he had read the entire Old Testament in Hebrew, and subsequently he was offered a lectureship at the university, which he declined.

At this time Jonas Söderblom was in his late thirties, still unmarried and a curate in the town of Hudiksvall. It happened that in Hudiksvall there was a Danish doctor and his family, Dr. Laurentius Ribe Blume, one of whose daughters became in 1863 Jonas Söderblom's wife.

A more complete contrast between the Olofsson-Söderblom family and that of the Danish doctor would be difficult to imagine. Dr. Blume (1810–1900) was descended from worthy burghers of Copenhagen, prominent, comfortably-off, socially respected; so too was his wife, Johanne Koefoed (1807–61), the daughter of a minister of the Danish church. That Dr. Blume was working in Sweden was the direct result of a request for young doctors to help out during a cholera epidemic in 1834. He had come and he had stayed. He was cheerful and popular, and his family was relaxed and cultured. He had three sons and three daughters; all three sons became sea-captains. It was his daughter Sophie, born in 1838, who married the strange Söderblom—a man of whom Dr. Blume evidently did not greatly approve, thinking him fanatical and tightfisted, and likely to work his daughter to death. Why he gave his consent is not at all clear, except perhaps that Sophie—"quiet and gentle, bright and cultivated, introspective and dreamy"[3]—was already showing signs of a deafness which in time was to become total, and might otherwise have been condemned to a life of spinsterhood. They married in 1863, and in the following year Jonas Söderblom became *komminister* in the parish of Trönö, where Nathan was born three years later.

Arguably the marked contrast between the two sides of Nathan Söderblom's personality in later years can without too much difficulty be attributed to the hereditary factors coming from his father and his mother respectively. From his father came his deep religious seriousness, his incredible capacity for hard and sustained work, his powers of concentration and perhaps also a certain tendency toward depression (though a tendency of which the world around him remained for the most part unaware). From his mother came the "Danish" side of his personality, an expansiveness in public, an ability to make friends quickly and easily, an attraction to (and capacity for) music and the arts, and a love of company.

Nathan Söderblom was born, as we have said, in the Trönö manse on January 15, 1866, and was baptized Lauritz Olaus Jonathan—Lauritz from his Danish forebears, Olaus from his father's family, and Jonathan (always shortened to Nathan) his own personal name.[4] The first seven years of his life—generally happy years, it would seem—were spent at Trönö. Both parents taught their son (and in course of time a growing company of smaller sisters and brothers), the mother apparently being the more effective teacher of the two: "Mother's calm and clarity made her into an excellent teacher. . . . My father's teaching was more forceful than methodical. His worry that I would not have time to learn Latin began when I was five years old, and resulted in my absorbing a certain undigested Latin vocabulary."[5] Evening prayers were said by Jonas Söderblom's side. Sermons were listened to (if seldom understood) beneath his pulpit.

Trönö church life left a lasting impression on the child. Writing as archbishop in 1923, Söderblom acknowledged that he was too young to appreciate the beauty of the church and its natural surroundings. But, he went on, "it was great to sit in the little church, filled as it was from floor to ceiling. The adolescent boys looked down from the uppermost balcony. And because, fortunately, there were so many other things to look at and listen to, only occasionally, with fearful curiosity, did one's eye need to glance at that intimidating painting to the right of the chancel window, depicting the open jaws of the dragon and the human bodies toppling into it."[6] This was the young Nathan Söderblom's first introduction to the mysteries of death, judgment, and the future life—to eschatology, in the technical language of theologians. This was the theme to which he was to devote his doctoral dissertation in 1901, and one which was never far from the center of his concerns.

In 1873 the Söderblom family left Trönö for Bjuråker, a parish farther north. There they remained until 1882. "It was there that my father gave of his best," wrote Nathan Söderblom years later. "What attracted people to him? The answer is not far to seek. His burning, sincere concern for souls confirmed what Lars Landgren had said about him. The Rural Dean of Delsbo was asked about the other two ministers involved in the election, and spoke with appreciation of both, but added, 'If you want someone who can show you the way to heaven, vote for Jonas Söderblom.' "[7] In 1882 a further move took place to Hälsingtuna, partly, it would seem, for reasons connected with local politics. There was considerable tension at the time between the farming community and at least some of the local landowners, and Jonas Söderblom had taken the farmers' part. Pressure mounted and another move became necessary. The Hälsingtuna experience was short and not altogether happy, and in 1886 Jonas was appointed, at the age of sixty-two, vicar (*kyrkoherde*) of Norrala, not far from Trönö and a little to the north of the town of Söderhamn. There he was to remain until his death in 1901. This final appointment was made in the year in which Nathan Söderblom began to study theology, and thus it was to Norrala that he had to return every summer to work in the fields and, as it transpired, to face his father's growing disquiet at the direction in which his eldest son's ideas were beginning to move.

The years between 1875 and 1883, from the age of nine to seventeen, Nathan Söderblom spent at school in the coastal town of Hudiksvall, at the district *läroverk* (grammar school). His father having bought a small house for the purpose, during these years several of the Söderblom brothers and sisters eked out a spartan existence under the supervision of a maid, Karin Gisselsdottir ("Tadda"), returning to the family home only during holidays. Of home comforts there were few enough. Furnishings were rudimentary, and the children's diet was made up chiefly of porridge, herring, and "cinnamon tea" (an infusion of cinnamon in hot water).

There is little enough that need concern us about this period in Söderblom's life. Clearly he was a good—and even then a versatile—student, extroverted, physically energetic, interested in practically everything he came across, and capable of achieving high marks with little apparent effort. He was always close to the top of his class, and it is reported that one lasting friendship developed out of a fistfight with his closest competitor for top place—one Herman Palmgren, with whom he was later to share a student room in Uppsala. No single one of his teachers would seem to have had a lasting influence on him, at least not an influence in any way comparable to that of his father. When the time came for him to graduate, it was a matter of some surprise that he achieved only the lowest mark (*godkänd*) in three subjects: Swedish, Latin, and French. It has been supposed that he may have been suffering from some temporary indisposition, though in the case of French at least his knowledge was still fairly rudimentary in 1890. The low marks in Swedish and Latin are harder to explain.

In common with practically every other Swedish grammar school of the period, the senior students had their own literary society for the cultivation of good fellowship, patriotic sentiment, and letters, more or less in that order. The Hudiksvall variant carried the name *Rimtussarna*—a play on words: in the Edda "frost-giants," here "verse-giants"—and from its papers Tor Andrae has extracted this character sketch of Söderblom at the time of his graduation. Söderblom

> was known to be a versatile youth. Having a genius capable of penetrating the most complex questions with ease, he familiarized himself with every conceivable subject. Musician, poet and composer, student of Latin and Greek, Hebrew, mathematics and philosophy—and all this at the age of eighteen [*sic*: actually he was only seventeen at the time]. Furthermore he was of a pleasant, respectful and helpful nature, to which no

one could take exception; apart from his frequent childish sense of fun and mischief, he was an admirable youth.[8]

This was the first more or less public acknowledgment of Söderblom's versatility in matters academic. It was not to be the last.

We may also note in passing that Söderblom was not at this early stage consciously preparing himself for the ministry of the Church of Sweden. Clearly he could have moved in any one of a number of directions professionally and academically. But at the same time his father was evidently hoping that his eldest son would follow in his footsteps. The decision, however, came later.

School holidays were spent at home, and there is no lack of testimony from his brothers and sisters that when Nathan returned to the vicarage, the gloom lifted. "He kept his father's house bright with songs and laughter."[9] Jonas Söderblom, however, would seem not to have joined in either the songs or the laughter. He was taking his eldest son somewhat more into his confidence, seeing in him a spiritual heir and perhaps already assuming that he would follow him into the ministry. But where the salvation of souls was concerned, there was no room for levity.

In daily life Jonas Söderblom was a hard taskmaster. Disciplined almost to the point of fanaticism, he was incapable of treating his children in any other manner. In those days a country parsonage had attached to it a small farm. Generally the minister would lease it out to a local farmer, but not so Jonas Söderblom. His smallholding he worked himself, with a minimum of assistance, mostly provided during the holidays by his children. Jonas genuinely loved farming; Nathan did not. As a student he would much have preferred to have been at his books, but was forced instead to spend long and hard hours—especially during the short summer months—in the fields, behind the horses, building barns, whatever needed to be done. It may be that Jonas's educational methods extended to the need for hard physical labor as a corrective to intellectual pride. Certainly some of his parishioners thought it improper that the minister's children should be forced into such hard manual labor—especially so in Nathan's case. But in the long term the policy paid dividends.

One of the chief difficulties which faced European Protestantism in the late nineteenth and early twentieth centuries was the gulf which was opening up in these years between the church and the working classes. Most ministers—especially in the growing cities—led sheltered and privileged lives, associating only with their own kind. Academic theologians were if anything still better insulated from the world of manual labor. Between the ecclesiastical establishment and the working classes there was, it is true, a buffer zone occupied by the faithful laity, but these—again especially in the cities—belonged to the middle rather than to the working classes. In the country parishes there was still a large measure of trust and understanding, but these parishes were already beginning to decline under the pressures of rural rationalization, urbanization, industrialization, and in Sweden's case migration to North America. This is not the place to enlarge further on this question, except to say that Nathan Söderblom certainly was never one who considered himself to stand apart from the working classes, or who regarded their movements toward greater freedom and independence as a threat. The reasons were certainly connected with his knowledge of the conditions of manual labor: he knew what it was to be a worker with hands and arms and back. As long as he was a student—and this extended to his years in Uppsala—at home he shared the life of the workers. Visiting the parish of Norrala in 1924 as archbishop, he took part in a dinner in a barn pressed into service for the occasion, and one of the things he said was: "I never thought that our barn would make such a fine banqueting chamber when I was helping to build it."[10] Söderblom's subsequent involvements with Social Christianity, chiefly during the late 1890s, may be seen as a logical consequence of his background, his father's training, and his natural affinities with a class too often ignored by his ecclesiastical and academic contemporaries.

This is not to say that Söderblom was in any way pulled in the direction of socialism at this early period in his life. To have been a socialist at the time would have meant to have harbored a measure of resentment at the workers' lot, but of this there would seem to have been no trace in Söderblom's makeup. On the contrary, memories of him from his youth generally emphasized his unforced happiness and spontaneity, especially when in company. A good singer and musician, he was easily persuaded to be the life and soul of any party he attended. A fellow farm worker of the early 1880s, in conversation with Tor Andrae many years later, stressed this side of his nature, but told the story of one such occasion, a wedding party, at which Nathan had entertained the assembled company—until his father entered the room, at which point he became abruptly and totally silent.[11]

Nathan Söderblom's relationship to his father opens up vast possibilities for psychological investigation.[12] Although posthumous psychoanalysis is a dangerous pastime, there were certain characteristics of this relationship simply too obvious to be overlooked. Jonas Söderblom, a formidable and uncompromising figure, and a man of iron will, clearly expected of his eldest son everything he expected of himself. He would do everything in his power to "mortify the flesh," his own and his family's, and to emphasize the one thing needful, the soul's relationship to God. Where he saw weakness, he would institute measures to overcome it. His children's fear of darkness he attempted to "cure" by making them take turns to ring the church bells—mounted in a separate steeple, which was also used as a temporary mortuary chapel prior to funerals. The darkness was one thing; the presence of an unburied corpse quite another. No bodily comfort was admitted into Jonas Söderblom's scheme of things, and in religion, no compromise with the conditions on which salvation might be obtained. Paul's words, "But I keep under my body, and bring it into subjection: lest that by any means, when I have preached to others, I myself should be a castaway" (1 Cor. 9:27, KJV), express his attitude with complete accuracy. Why should any of those close to him be satisfied with less?

In such circumstances, children can do one of two things. They can launch into out-and-out rebellion, go their own way, and cope with the resultant sense of guilt as best they may. As Olov Hartman has rightly said, "The process of emancipation is always attended by feelings of guilt, and if the final result is spite or even hate, the sense of guilt can be overwhelming."[13] Or alternatively, they can attempt to meet the father's demands, imitating and obeying as far as they are able—though often with the underlying fear that the demands are too huge ever to be actually attainable. It is surely significant that of all the Söderblom children, Nathan was the only one to follow in his father's footsteps as a churchman (to which we might add that only one of Nathan Söderblom's eight sons entered the church, though all three of his daughters married ministers). He was the Elisha on whom the mantle of Elijah was to fall—and from his school days he knew that it must be so.

Although this is to anticipate, a certain amount of what was to happen later in Nathan Söderblom's career will perhaps be understood better if his relationship to his father be borne in mind. As a theological student in Uppsala, he was pulled in two directions: by filial piety (and a measure of fear) toward an individualist form of Lutheran orthodoxy, and by intellectual integrity toward social liberalism. He knew in his Uppsala days that his early theological explorations were leading him into paths of which his father could not possibly approve—and indeed, Jonas was convinced at the time that his son was well on the way toward becoming a "freethinker."[14] The son's exhilaration over new discoveries in the areas of religion and theology was, one feels, constantly tempered by the thought of his father's intense disapproval at the direction his thought—and by implication his faith—appeared to be taking. But that he hoped to be able to persuade even his father that he had not abandoned the faith, that he hoped still at the last moment to be able to win his father's approval, seems, if not obvious, at least conceivable. Possibly Nathan Söderblom could have become a full-fledged liberal only had he been able fully to dismiss from his mind's eye the vision of the gaunt figure in the Hälsingland rectory. But this he could not do. And when, his professorial years behind him, he was faced with the onerous task of steering the Church of Sweden through the shoals of wartime crisis, it was fully characteristic that he should have devoted part of his Pastoral Letter to the memory of his father. It was no less characteristic—though less obvious—that he should have chosen for the day of his consecration as archbishop the eighth of November, his father's birthday.

Söderblom's first (and still in many ways his best) biographer, Tor Andrae was himself well versed in the intricacies of psychology, and clearly had reflected on the father-son relationship. Andrae saw the potential conflict, the son's evident desire to measure up to the father's demands, even after the father had been long in his grave. But he saw more: he saw a direct inheritance and a community of personality. He wrote:

> Between father and son there is in many ways an astounding similarity. In some cases this extends even to small details. But

this similar and common temperament is elevated in the son's case to a different level, where it is transposed to the service of genius. The restless desire always to be active, the impatience, the impulsiveness, the ascetic discipline of the will, the inclination to do the remarkable and the unexpected, which in the father's case leads to constant excesses, bizarre and often ridiculous, becomes productive originality in the son.[15]

If we accept Andrae's view that temperamentally the two were very similar, then their dissimilarities might consist less in any fundamental cleavage in principle than in the fact that the expansive, emotional, intuitive side of the personality, violently suppressed in the father's case, in the son came to its full flowering. Nathan had opportunities which never came Jonas's way. He lived in an age in which intellectual and spiritual freedom was greater. He moved in an immeasurably wider world. But he possessed his father's iron will and incisive mind, and however different their respective fields of activity—narrowly circumscribed on the one hand, worldwide on the other—they did what they had to do in basic harmony.

2

Student in Uppsala, 1883–1892

Nathan Söderblom, then only seventeen years old, signed the register of *Gästrike-Hälsinge nation* and became a student of the University of Uppsala on September 19, 1883. His connection with Uppsala thereafter was to last, with only brief interruptions, for the better part of half a century. His first three years in Uppsala were spent in the faculty of arts, from which he graduated in 1886 with the degree of *filosofie kandidat* (B.A.). In that year he entered the faculty of theology, completing his *teologie kandidat* (B.D.) degree in December 1892. Ordained in March of the following year, he spent approximately a year, still in Uppsala, as a hospital chaplain before being appointed pastor to the Swedish legation in Paris. Söderblom's first Uppsala period therefore lasted from the fall of 1883 to the spring of 1894. His second period lasted from the summer of 1901 to his death in July 1931, with a two-year intermezzo in Leipzig from 1912 to 1914.

There is little in Söderblom's first three Uppsala years that need concern us. He was still, after all, only a teenager, an academic adolescent, spending most of his life in industrious isolation. After 1886, on the other hand, he was to enter more and more fully into the controversies of the time, playing an increasingly active role in academic and university life and developing a distinctive profile as a writer and later as a public speaker. By the standards of the place and the time he did so as a "liberal," though as we shall see, while liberal in some ways he always remained remarkably conservative in others. That peculiar tension is one of which we shall have frequent occasion to be reminded in what follows.[1]

By the late 1880s, religious liberalism in Sweden seemed almost a spent force.[2] Never numerically strong, in the earlier part of the century it had nevertheless had some outstanding representatives in and around the universities. Still very much active at the time Söderblom began to study theology were the philosopher Carl Pontus Wikner (1837–88) and the polymath Viktor Rydberg (1828–95). Wikner was a Christian Platonist, serious and devoted, critical of both sides of the debate between orthodoxy and free thought, and highly regarded by the student generation immediately preceding that to which Söderblom belonged. But the idealism he represented was beginning in the 1880s to come under heavy fire from a new type of radical intellectualism that claimed to trust only in that which is empirically, scientifically verifiable. In 1882 the "culture-radicals" had banded together in the *Verdandi* society—*Verdandi* being the name of one of the Norns, or Fates, in Old Norse mythology—and under this kind of empiricist pressure, idealism began to crumble. In 1883, a very young Söderblom was one of only eight students who attended Wikner's last course of lectures in Uppsala, and who heard him observe wryly that in former years, his lecture room would have been full.[3] In 1884 Wikner left Uppsala for Oslo.

Viktor Rydberg is more difficult to characterize.[4] For many years he was a writer on the staff of a Gothenburg newspaper, but after 1884 became a lecturer in the Stockholm college that some years later was to become the University of Stockholm. His subject there was the history of art and culture. Chiefly Rydberg was known as a poet, a novelist, and an essayist—inviting comparisons with Emerson, Ruskin, and Andrew Lang—but he was also a considerable scholar in his own right, and a self-taught amateur theologian. His faith was that of the pious rationalist, and in his religious writings he followed the liberal tendency to emphasize the humanity rather than the divinity of Christ, the relativity of all doctrinal statements and creeds, and the pressing need to democratize the church. By the generation of students to which Söderblom belonged, Rydberg was read assiduously and regarded with great reverence; one of his most celebrated books did much to help provide Söderblom with the subject on which his doctoral dissertation was eventually to be written.

Over against the liberalism of Wikner and Rydberg and the out-and-out radicalism of *Verdandi*—and leaving aside for the moment the winds of theological change blowing out of Germany—the Uppsala faculty of theology was solidly conservative, and in danger of being stranded altogether in the thought forms of an earlier age. The historian of the University of Uppsala has recorded that in the late nineteenth century, the faculty of theology "presented a rather shabby appearance," having "no outstanding or leading personalities in the sphere of scholarship or in the Church of Sweden."[5] This is perhaps a little unfair: by the accepted standards of the time the professors of theology in Uppsala exercised their functions adequately. What they did not and could not do was (as they saw it) to trim their sails to every change in the direction of theological thinking that happened to come along. Their conservatism was not identical in every case. Some were more, and some less, pietistic. Some held a higher view of the church than did others. All, however, were agreed as to the foundations of Christian faith and practice: the witness of Holy Scripture as mediated through the cumulative tradition of the Protestant Reformation on its Lutheran side. Paul had interpreted Jesus; Luther had rediscovered Paul after centuries of neglect; the witness of Luther had been established and codified by Melanchthon and the orthodox writers. The confessional documents spoke with one voice on the question of the scriptures in the Christian scheme of things. The *Formula Concordiae* stated that "We believe, confess and teach that the sole rule and standard according to which all teachings and all teachers must be regarded and judged, is nothing other than the prophetic and apostolic writings of both the Old and New Testaments."[6] The orthodox pattern was one in which a series of doctrinal statements, having been constructed out of the Bible, were subsequently tested by reference back to the same Bible, making of the Bible a supremely authoritative doctrinal sourcebook, a code of law, precept, and example for everything having to do with the Christian life. It was massively solid, and at best created deep and serious devotion. But it permitted no flexibility.

Nineteenth-century theological liberalism as a rule was by no means disposed to discard the Bible, or to deny its authority. What it did do, on the other hand, was to rearrange the sequence in which the various books of the Bible were read, and hence their relative value. To orthodoxy, every part of the scriptural record was treated as possessing equal authority—at least in theory. The Old Testament was read in the light of the New, Jesus in the light of Paul. To the liberals, there were two overriding concerns, one to apply the searchlight of historical scholarship to the whole of the biblical record, the other to bring Jesus out from under the shadow of Paul. On the first count, the effect was to reaffirm that although the Old Testament as a historical record might be regarded as a *praeparatio evangelica*, much of what it contained could and indeed should be discarded, with the notable exception of the Prophets. On the second, the effect was less to devalue Paul than to restore the person and teachings of Jesus to their rightful place at the heart of the Christian faith. To this, orthodoxy reacted with nervous fear, for a mixture of reasons.

Chief among those reasons was the fact that to orthodoxy, having pinned the whole of its faith to the affirmation of the authority of the whole of the Bible, those who questioned that authority in any way or in any part could hardly be seen other than as a danger to the church. Once begun, where was the process to stop? Begin by questioning miracle, and one must end by calling in question the very possibility of salvation. Question the testimony of Genesis, that the earth had been created in six days, and the result must be the same. Elevate the teachings of Jesus the man over the work of Christ, and one is left with an example to follow; what one may have lost is a savior. That there were those outside the church who by the 1880s had pressed these questions to their limit simply made matters worse. One may take up arms against an enemy outside the walls. The enemy within the gates is the more dangerous—for which reason conservative Christianity has generally reserved the full force of its condemnations for those of its own community who have moved away from what a given age has decreed to be theologically normative.

Unlike orthodoxy, theological liberalism can never be finally pinned down under a single set of norms and categories. Its very nature decrees that it be open and flexible to whatever is most compelling in its day, and therefore it may alter its stance repeatedly. The liberalism of the 1890s had practically nothing in common with that of the 1980s save in its openness and flexibility. Also it is greatly variable. An individual may be liberal in some ways and not in others. He or she may very well undertake a long and solitary voyage of intellectual discovery, only to arrive in the end at a position very similar to that from which he or she initially set out.[7] What will be different in such a case will be less the final affirmation than the arguments by which it is supported. In all essentials the affirmation is that of orthodoxy, but the supporting arguments are entirely different. In 1917, surveying Sweden's theological literature of the period 1901–15, Edvard Rodhe drew attention to the curious combination of "traditional orthodoxy and modern biblical scholarship" in a collection of sermons published in 1910 by one of Söderblom's closest friends, Samuel Fries.[8] Much the same might well have been said of Söderblom himself. The voyage of intellectual and spiritual discovery he began in 1886 under the guidance of those who were not his "official" teachers did not so much lead him away from the position from which he started as provide him with a new arsenal of arguments to use in its support. Rejecting those arguments, his opponents (and they were many) refused to accept his bona fides as a pastor, as a professor, and ultimately as an archbishop.

The process of intellectual adjustment through which Söderblom passed between 1886 and 1894 was not a smooth and painless transition from one habit of mind to another. On the contrary, it was both exhilarating and traumatic: exhilarating in the vistas that were being opened up almost daily, traumatic in the brutality with which old certainties were uprooted under the impact of new methods and new approaches. Those who suppose the 1890s to have been an age of secure and even smug faith have not looked at the records. Personal documents of the time repeat the story over and over again: of the collapse of certainties, personal crises of faith in cramped student rooms, fresh courage in some cases and the abandonment of religion in others, others again retreating behind high confessional walls as a condition of religious survival. Many years later, Söderblom recalled the atmosphere of those days: "We were struggling with the fundamental problem. . . . No one could give us guidance, or clarity, or absolution. We were told simply to pray, to wrestle individually with God in prayer; He would have to help us, when the theory of the truth of Christianity tottered or fell apart. And in later years, when we saw how another, better informed generation seemed able to take such questions as these in its stride, we may even have felt a sense of sacrilege."[9]

Söderblom's years as a theological student were years during which the student community in Sweden (and of course elsewhere) shaped itself into fellowships, fraternities, societies, and clubs as a matter of course. Most important were the regional fraternities, or "nations," to which every student had to belong as a condition of university membership. The smallest was the dining club, or *matlag*, entirely unofficial and with perhaps only half a dozen members. In between there were clubs and fellowships to suit every taste and meet every interest. Söderblom being an eminently clubbable person, at various times he was deeply involved in numerous such societies. There was his regional fraternity, *Gästrike-Hälsinge nation*, of which he eventually became "first curator" (student president). For one year he was president of the student body as a whole. On the musical front he was a member of that most exclusive male-voice choir *Orphei Drängar* (the Servants of Orpheus). Among Christian groups there were several to which he belonged, and attended regularly. Three in particular helped shape his thinking.

Teologiska föreningen (the theological association) was the chief forum of public discussion among students and professors of theology, and it was in its meetings that the waves of controversy between conservative and liberal approaches ran the highest. From these encounters Söderblom and his friends learned what was to be expected from the Uppsala theological establishment.

Studentmissionsföreningen (the student missionary association) was a society primarily for the study of Christian missions over against the religions and cultures of the world at large. Founded in Uppsala in 1884 in close association with similar movements in other parts of the world—including the YMCA, with which it overlapped at a number of points—it created relatively few active missionaries. It did on the other hand stimulate an active and intelligent interest in the encounter of religions and cultures in the world. For Söderblom's part, it has often been claimed that it was his involvement in this association which first turned his attention toward the study of the religions of the world, and helped make of him the outstanding internationalist he was later to become.[10] This being so, we shall have much more to say about the student missionary association shortly.

Most important of all was a tiny and entirely informal group of students of theology who in the spring of 1888 began to meet together on Sunday afternoons to read and discuss their favorite authors—Ibsen, Goethe, and especially Viktor Rydberg. Initially it had only four members, Nathan Söderblom, Samuel Fries, N. J. Göransson, and Samuel Freidenfeldt, together with their respective fiancées, charmingly called, after Ibsen, "pillars of the fellowship" (*Samfundets stötter*). Freidenfeldt died early, at the age of only thirty-two. The other three formed a formidable trio. "We solved the riddles of the world, until our next meeting, when we tore everything up and solved them afresh. But not Sam [Fries]. He had his principles clear from the beginning. We were very different from one another. Our friendship became all the stronger for that. When [Rydberg's prose-poem] *Vapensmeden* [The Swordsmith, 1891] came out, we called our fellowship *Fritt ur hjärtat*."[11]

Fritt ur hjärtat is strictly impossible to translate: literally it means "freely from the heart," but what it actually implies is "free speech," tending in the direction of "no holds barred." As Söderblom wrote, he, Fries, and Göransson were very different types. We shall return to Fries, but for the moment we may say that he was choleric, aggressive, and usually sure of his own abilities and the rightness of his own increasingly radical position. Göransson by contrast was quiet and somewhat introverted, philosophical in every sense of the word. Tor Andrae took up their own half-ironical description of themselves as "Thesis" (Fries), "Antithesis" (Göransson), and "Synthesis" (Söderblom), comparing them to Handel, Bach, and Mozart—power, depth, and proportion. Often in later years it was Söderblom who had to function as peacemaker between the other two. Fries he admired; Göransson's judgment he trusted, and in his letters to Göransson he revealed most of himself.

For a quarter of a century—to the time of Fries's premature death in 1914—the *Fritt ur hjärtat* guild gave Söderblom the sense of deep and sympathetic support he so seldom encountered in the higher echelons of the church to which he belonged. To the beleaguered Fries the fellowship was if anything still more important. Often in his letters he addressed Söderblom as "comrade-in-arms" (*vapenbroder*): adequate testimony to the way he generally felt. Göransson, too, spent many years in academic exile in parishes up and down Sweden before gaining recognition and an Uppsala chair. Fries's troubles will call for special treatment later.

Although in the late 1880s Söderblom was moving in some ways toward theological liberalism, there always remained within him a solid core of personal Christian devotion. A struggle between the liberal and conservative elements in his own makeup there certainly was, and it was to come to a head in 1890. Up to that time, however, though he was reading Harnack and Ritschl, his deepest involvement outside the lecture room was with the student missionary association, which was hardly a nest of extreme liberals.

At home in Hälsingland Söderblom had grown up in an atmosphere of missionary concern, and had met many missionaries on "deputation work." Thus it was only natural that he should gravitate to those in Uppsala who shared a like interest. The student missionary association was an admirable antidote to the ingrown life of a small and remote university, opening up as it did the widest of world perspectives. Exploration was opening up the world; colonialism was doing its best to exploit it; mission was bent on bringing it under subjection to "the Kingdom of Christ." As yet there was little thought of how discovery, conquest, and mission might be related. Even in Uppsala, on the other hand, there was a growing desire to know more about the world outside the frontiers of the West, and this desire the Christian students of Uppsala, like those of Connecticut and Massachusetts, set themselves to satisfy.

Some of the missionary enthusiasm of the time was supplied by the North American–based Student Volunteer Movement for Foreign Missions. Germany supplied another impulse, the desire to learn, classify, analyze, and reduce to principles—in short to create a "science of mission" (*Missionswissenschaft*). Here the great name was that of Gustav Warneck, founder in 1874 of that most admirable journal *Allgemeine Missions-Zeitschrift* and author of a five-volume *Missionslehre* and a history of Protestant missions.[12] The Uppsala society absorbed rather more from German *Missionswissenschaft* than it did from North American enthusiasm, and in later years Söderblom was to recall an occasion in the fall of 1883 when he had heard a Norwegian missionary, Lars Skrefsrud, on being asked what was the first qualification for a good missionary, answer: "Not to have a head stuffed full of porridge."[13]

The leader of the Uppsala group was Karl Fries (no relation to Samuel Fries), who translated Warneck's history of Protestant missions into Swedish, and who in 1888 was instrumental in launching a Swedish-language journal as a modest counterpart to the *Allgemeine Missions-Zeitschrift*. It happened, however, that at precisely that time Fries was appointed YMCA secretary in Stockholm. In the event, the editorship was offered to, and accepted by, Söderblom, and it was in the first issue that there appeared his first printed essay. He was twenty-two years old.

Entitled "On Sweden's first Christian teacher" (*Om Sveriges förste kristne lärare*), Söderblom's paper had begun life as a lecture delivered to the student missionary association on November 26, 1888.[14] Its subject was the life and work of Ansgar, the first missionary to Sweden in the ninth century. Mostly it was as unremarkable as one would expect from a young student of theology. However, in one passage there was a touch of a style and angle of approach that was entirely characteristic of the later Söderblom. Throughout his life the highest accolade Söderblom could bestow on anyone was the label "genius" (in Swedish, *snille*). To be a genius in Söderblom's eyes was to be preeminent as a human being in one's occupation and calling, whether a prophet, mystic, artist, writer, or scholar. Over the years he was to respond deeply and instinctively to genius, whenever and wherever he believed that he had found it. Rimbert's *Vita Ansgarii* hardly provided the material for the answering of the "genius" question, but that did not prevent Söderblom from asking "Was Ansgar a great man? *One* type of greatness no one can deny him: that moral greatness which lies in a pure, pious life, a life devoted to God. But did he possess that originality, that breadth of ideas, that power, that consistency in carrying them out, which marks a great soul? Did he possess genius? Was he not rather, for all his devotion and his piety, an insignificant personality?"[15] Söderblom's answers were of no consequence. The question "Did he possess genius?" was of more than passing significance. So too was the fact that he was prepared to approach historical—in this case fairly remote historical—material with this question in mind.

Söderblom's interest in missionary questions was never to leave him. He was of course never himself a missionary, and was to leave the frontiers of the geographical West on only one occasion, to attend a conference in Constantinople in 1911.[16] But he was to write and speak on missionary subjects on many later occasions, and after 1914, when as archbishop of Uppsala he became chairman ex officio of the Church of Sweden's board of missions, he was to be deeply involved in missionary practicalities in Africa and South and East Asia. That is not a matter we can discuss further here. We may merely note that it was his early involvement with the student missionaries that began to turn his thinking away from a narrow-angle approach to the study of religion, and helped to provide a Christian justification for a wider study. When in December 1892 Söderblom graduated in theology and chose a field for postgraduate study, he settled upon comparative religion partly out of the need to place Christianity among the religions of the world. He might not have done so without this particular impulse.[17]

In 1923, as archbishop of Uppsala, Söderblom had occasion to write to the seventy-two-year-old Adolf von Harnack on matters ecumenical. He began his first letter: "When as a young student reading the first edition of your *Dogmengeschichte* I became not only enthused but, I might claim, intoxicated, and for the first time grasped the nature of free scientific research, I could never have dreamed that one day I would make your personal acquaintance."[18]

The first edition of Harnack's *Lehrbuch der Dogmengeschichte* had begun to appear in 1886, and must therefore have been read very early in Söderblom's period as a theological student. There were of course excellent historians in Uppsala at the time—chief among them Harald Hjärne, historian of the Reformation, with whom in after years Söderblom was to develop a warm friendship. Among historical theologians, however, Harnack in the 1880s and 1890s occupied a practically unchallenged position as the theological Ranke, vastly erudite in the history of the early church, scientific up to a point and challenging beyond it, the living embodiment of late nineteenth-century German religiohistorical scholarship at its most profound. This is not the place to enlarge on Harnack's achievements, save to say that he taught the young Söderblom to appreciate history as an approach and a technique. For Harnack's liberalized version of contemporary Christianity Söderblom had, it must be admitted, less appreciation. When Harnack's Berlin lectures on "the essence of Christianity" (*Das Wesen des Christentums*, 1900; English translation, *What is Christianity?*) were translated into Swedish, Söderblom dutifully supplied them with a foreword, though without real enthusiasm.[19] But in 1886 or thereabouts, the young Söderblom needed to be taught what conscientiously applied historical scholarship could achieve in the study of religion, and this Harnack taught him.

At about the same time, Söderblom discovered Ritschl and the Ritschlians (one of whom was Harnack). Again to quote Söderblom's later reminiscences:

> I for my part date a new insight back to an evening about thirty years ago [again probably in 1886] in Uppsala, in the reading room of the students' union ... when I happened upon a review in *Theologische Literaturzeitung*. I did not understand all of it. But the Kingdom and the work of God were placed in the center. The room in which I sat lit up, and a wave of joy swept over me. We did not need to rely on a book, because God had founded his Kingdom through Christ. The origins of the Bible were part of that work of God. Christianity was no longer only a book-religion, but a historical revelation, brought to completion in Christ. However obvious this may seem today, then it was a new discovery.[20]

The review was not by Ritschl but by one of his disciples, Julius Kaftan, who had been a professor in Berlin since 1883.[21] The message, however, was liberating. Revelation comes not through the human record *about* Christ, which is important, but can never be infallible; it comes through Christ himself, to whom history can provide access, and whose mission was that of the establishment of the Kingdom of God.

On the biblical front, although in the 1880s and 1890s students in Uppsala were taught the appropriate languages to a high degree of proficiency, textual interpretation was fitted into the pattern laid down by the Lutheran confessional writings. In 1878, however, Julius Wellhausen had published the first edition of his *Prolegomena zur Geschichte Israels* (2d ed. 1883, translated into English under the supervision of W. Robertson Smith as *Prolegomena to the History of Ancient Israel*). Wellhausen was not on any official Uppsala reading list. He had argued that Moses could not have written the five books of the Pentateuch attributed to him, that the religion of Israel had begun, not with a sublime revelation, but with something as crudely unpleasant as bull worship, and that the Bible's earliest narratives were to be seen more as myth, legend, and folklore than as revelation. Yahweh had been a primitive war god, whose characteristic sphere of activity was the battlefield. Wellhausen had maintained that the ancient Hebrew sources should be read purely as history. Having been painted over by generations of piously tendentious interpreters, the specific character of Israelite history had altogether been lost sight of—which character Wellhausen had set himself to restore.[22]

Orthodox Protestantism reacted with fury against Wellhausen, and subsequently against those who allowed themselves to be convinced by his arguments. In Scotland, one such was William Robertson Smith, dismissed from his post as professor of Old Testament studies in the Free Church College in Aberdeen for following closely the Wellhausen line. Another was the young Samuel Fries in Uppsala. Fries could not be dismissed from a teaching position he did not hold; he could, on the other hand, be prevented from ever getting one.

Fries, "the mighty Sam," was a year younger than Söderblom, and had been a student in Uppsala since 1886. Like Söderblom he was the son of a minister in the Church of Sweden, and we have already mentioned his name as one of the founder-members of *Samfundet fritt ur hjärtat*. From the first moment of his arrival in Uppsala, he had set himself to become a professor of Old Testament exegesis. Had he been more cautious and moved ahead with more circumspection, very likely he would have achieved his aim. Had he been born a quarter-century later, his "radicalism" would perhaps have mattered less. His trouble was his enthusiastic adoption of the Wellhausen position. In October 1889 he wrote to his fiancée that the historical and critical study of the Old Testament

> is in fact too little known—please forgive me if I say that I imagine that I know it better than anyone else; up here [in Uppsala] practically no one knows what excellent results modern scholarship has achieved—for the learned gentlemen to be able to discuss these matters. . . .
> Among the theologians up here the name of Wellhausen, thanks to their ignorance, has frightful overtones. They think that he is a kind of antichrist. Personally I am of the opposite opinion, believing him to be one of the greatest geniuses of the century.[23]

Certainly at the time Fries did know more about Wellhausen than anyone else in Uppsala. A few miles to the south, in the capital city of Stockholm, there was, however, another Wellhausen enthusiast in the person of Pastor Primarius (then the virtual equivalent of bishop: there was no bishop of Stockholm at the time) Fredrik Fehr.[24]

Fredrik Fehr (1849-95) had for a time held a lectureship in Hebrew in Uppsala, and had been appointed to his high office in 1884 at the unusually early age of thirty-five. Fehr was the most gifted, and in the eyes of orthodoxy the most dangerous, man in the Church of Sweden at the time when Söderblom and Fries were students of theology. He was a liberal in a conservative age, a disciple and a friend of many of the most radical of Germany's theologians. Young as he still was in the late 1880s, he had presence, authority, and a brilliant mind, and was acknowledged as an outstanding preacher and teacher. Fehr knew Wellhausen and Harnack, and Harnack had pointed him in the direction of Albrecht Ritschl. In the late 1880s and early 1890s, therefore, Fehr—who was not a university teacher—was Sweden's most outstanding liberal theologian, and a man to whom the young liberals in Uppsala naturally turned for guidance and moral support in their own private war with theological conservatism. Wellhausen had suggested an approach to the biblical documents, but it was in Ritschl that there was to be found a *theological* program to which they could give their support.

In Sweden, as the nineteenth century drew to its close, the name of Albrecht Ritschl (1822-89) stood for either the great liberation or the great apostasy in Protestant theology and the life of the Protestant churches.[25] To those set free by Ritschl and his "school" from a narrow biblicism, Ritschl was the great liberator. To the conservative majority, knowing of Ritschl only at second-, third-, or fourth-hand, he was the most dangerous of heretics. What he had done in his massive works was to rearrange the priorities of Protestantism, to point beyond Paul to Jesus, beyond justification by faith to the Kingdom of God, beyond individualism to the social life of the community, beyond the transcendent to the immanent, most of all beyond the Bible to the person of Jesus of Nazareth.

Before Fehr, few in Sweden had heard the name of Ritschl. But in 1886-87, Fehr's advocacy of the Ritschlian cause made the name "Ritschlian" practically synonymous with "heretic." The reason was trivial enough: that in 1886 Fehr took it upon himself to publish—for the best of pedagogical reasons—a "Family Bible" from which a considerable amount of "difficult" material had been amputated. There was a storm of protest from the Swedish clergy. Petitions were signed. Fehr acquired a reputation as a theological troublemaker only two years after having been appointed to the highest church position in the nation's capital. Other controversies followed, notably in the wake of an objection on Fehr's part to a necessary revision of the Swedish hymnal, on the grounds that many hymns in the new book had kept the worst and most sentimental features of Catholic "mystical" theology (Fehr, like his mentor Ritschl, disliked "mysticism" intensely). But to the young theologians in Uppsala, Fehr was less a troublemaker than a role model. They were reading Harnack, Wellhausen, and Ritschl; Fehr had actually met these giants. They were fulminating uselessly against the shortcomings of their teachers; Fehr filled the highest pulpit in the nation's capital. After 1891 there was a closer and more personal contact.

This is to anticipate somewhat, but in the fall of 1891 a young lady, Anna Forsell, transferred her student enrollment from Stockholm to Uppsala.[26] Born on September 24, 1870, Anna Forsell had grown up in a liberated home, and having once heard Fredrik Fehr preach, had without much difficulty persuaded her parents to allow her to study for confirmation under him. This was irregular, since the Forsells did not live in Fehr's parish, but it was arranged. Many years later she described the life of a Stockholm schoolgirl of the 1880s, and what it was like to be a confirmation candidate under "Primarius" in 1886–87:

> The teaching we were given came out of the hard-won experience of a manly, struggling soul, and was therefore reassuring and genuine at every point. Between us and our teacher there was a great distance, which there were no out-of-class contacts to lessen. The whole of our relationship to him was marked by great respect. What a little confirmation candidate who had not done her homework once said—"I get so frightened when Primarius looks at me"—applied in varying degrees to all of us. But we had the encouraging feeling that this powerful spirit had been through spiritual struggles before us, and that he had found a treasure for us. We could rely on his word.[27]

To have been one of Fehr's "confirmands" was a high qualification. But there was more, since Anna Forsell had also studied for a time under none other than the great Viktor Rydberg himself.[28] In October 1891, at the age of twenty-one, she became one of the very few women students in the University of Uppsala (20 out of some 1700), and met Söderblom for the first time. Part of their first conversation consisted of a question from Miss Forsell whether Söderblom had ever heard of Wellhausen. Seventeen years after Söderblom's death she recorded his answer: "What are you talking about? You historians come and ask us theologians whether we have ever heard of Wellhausen!" But, she added, "it was a start."[29] On November 30, 1892, Nathan Söderblom and Anna Forsell were engaged. They were married—by Fredrik Fehr—in the spring of 1894.

Bengt Sundkler has pointed out that "Söderblom was not so much the *Religionsgeschichtler* who happened to make certain excursions into the field of Christian theology, but rather the Biblical scholar and church historian who also studied the history of religions."[30] This is undoubtedly correct. It does not lessen his significance as a historian of religion, but it does indicate the angle from which his contribution must be approached, and the terms in which it should be estimated. Down to 1893 he was a historically minded student of theology, and no more—or less—than that. It is rather too easy to form an impression of Söderblom's professors of theology in Uppsala as a group of conservatives from whom he had little to learn. This was not altogether the case. That they were theologically conservative was one thing; so too was Söderblom in all essentials. But quite apart from this, there was much to absorb, historically and textually, as part of the theological craft, and this they were fully capable of teaching him. There would, however, be little point in passing the whole of the Uppsala faculty in review. Most are scarcely remembered, even in Sweden, and few did more than provide Söderblom and his generation with the straw out of which to make their own bricks in their own way. Three names only may be mentioned.

Söderblom's teacher in church history was the dean of the cathedral, Uno Robert Sundelin. Hardly in the Harnack class, nevertheless Sundelin had some grasp of scientific historical method, and would willingly have seen Söderblom appointed as his assistant, had he chosen that particular path.[31]

In 1887 there was appointed to the curiously named chair of theological propaedeutics and theological encyclopedia (virtually a chair of "Christian apologetics") Johan August Ekman. Notably less orthodox than most of the other members of the faculty, Ekman was a cautious supporter of the group around Söderblom and Fries, and also hoped that Söderblom might become his assistant. It is doubtful whether Söderblom ever learned anything of importance from Ekman. His subject, on the other hand, embraced in principle a measure of comparative religion, and on graduation, it was to Ekman that Söderblom turned for postgraduate supervision (of a kind). We shall have much more to say on this subject later.

Waldemar Rudin had been lecturing in Uppsala since 1872, and had been professor of biblical exegesis since 1877. Rudin's element was spirituality rather than scholarship, and he was by far the most pietistic member of the faculty at the time. Almost alone among the Uppsala theologians, he had read and written on Kierkegaard—who otherwise had been far too antichurch to win orthodox approval. From Kierkegaard Rudin's reading had expanded to take in many of the classical mystics of the Western tradition—Richard Baxter, Madame Guyon, Fénelon, Teerstegen, and Boehme, as well as the Lutheran devotional writers Spener, Francke, and Arndt. Rudin was in many ways a religious romantic, being instinctive and personal, and never far from *Schwärmerei*. In Söderblom's opinion—and in due time Söderblom was to write a book on Rudin[32]—his best work had been that on Kierkegaard: "the most congenial description we have of the greatest writer and most powerful disciple of Christ to come out of Scandinavia in recent years."[33] Otherwise Rudin's medium was the devotional sermon rather than the scientific study of the biblical text.

Söderblom and Fries were of opposite opinions about Rudin. While Söderblom in time came to see in him a genuine continuation of the Western mystical tradition, was a frequent visitor to Rudin's home, and almost regarded him as a spiritual director, Fries very soon lost patience with Rudin's total indifference to questions of critical scholarship where the Bible was concerned. Fries was never a person to mince his words, especially in his letters, and in the 1890s was to heap scorn and abuse on Rudin, whose style he once described as enshrining "the most thorough superficiality and the most superficial thoroughness."[34] In the end, it was said that Rudin would not willingly enter any room in which Fries happened to be.

Student in Uppsala

Rudin lived to see Söderblom become archbishop, and missed no opportunity of hearing him speak.[35] He would not have crossed the road to listen to Fries.

Previously we have mentioned the impact on the young Uppsala theologians of the reading of Wellhausen, and the vast enthusiasm with which Samuel Fries had embraced the Wellhausen position on the critical study of the Old Testament. It would seem that it was only in 1888 that a single copy of Wellhausen's *Prolegomena* (published ten years earlier) was brought to Uppsala from Germany by a returning student. Previously it had been an entirely unknown quantity. Söderblom too read it, and it threw him into a crisis of faith from which he did not manage to extricate himself for two more years.

We have Söderblom's own description of the resolution of the crisis, though not of the doubtless complex causes that had brought it about. Lecturing in America in the 1920s, he described (in the third person) the uprooting of certainties, the anxiety and unresolved guilt, the hopeless prayers for release, the concealing of his state from those closest to him, that the crisis had brought with it. Then a coincidence took place. "Was it a coincidence? A pious countrywoman lent him a book, a book of conventional revivalist piety. In that book the student read—as he had read many times before in the third chapter of John—about the serpent that was lifted up in the wilderness, so that the sick Israelites might gaze upon him and be healed. Now it struck him. Had he been blind before? Before him he saw Jesus on the cross, as never before. In some strange way he looked into the eyes of the Savior, and he was healed."[36]

The book in question remained unidentified until Bengt Sundkler published his Söderblom biography in 1968. Now we know it to have been a Swedish translation of a book by W. P. Mackay, entitled *Grace and Faith*.[37] Insignificant in itself, the book accomplished on the level of personal faith precisely that which Ritschl had urged as a matter of theological principle: the centrality of an atonement brought about through the person and work of Christ, and not through dogmatic statements about him.

Sundkler has also suggested that there was more involved here than a religious conversion, however deeply felt. Late in 1889

Söderblom's relationship with his father had reached crisis point. Jonas Söderblom was gloomily convinced that his son was well on the way to becoming a "freethinker," due to the books he was reading and the company he kept. Christmas 1889 might have been a dismal, tense, and argumentative time, with his mother, perhaps, suffering worst of all. But his forebodings were not realized. The details must always remain obscure, but in Sundkler's words, "The conversion, while understood by Söderblom as a return to the Heavenly Father, was just as much a reconciliation with the earthly father. It might well be argued which of these came first. It is quite possible . . . that the reconciliation with Jonas Söderblom signified the opening of the sluicegates, and the Pietistic conversion at the reading of Mackay's tract followed."[38] At all events, it lifted a great burden from Söderblom's mind. Already 1890 promised to be an exciting year. Now he was able to enter into it with fresh confidence.

In the fall of 1889, Sweden was visited by a young American, James B. Reynolds of Yale, who had come to Europe to invite a few nominated students from Britain and the Continent to the next of Dwight Moody's Northfield student conferences, which was to be held in the summer of 1890. Thanks to Karl Fries, secretary of the Stockholm YMCA, Söderblom was proposed as the representative of the Swedish student Christian community.

Writing to Karl Fries in October, Söderblom sounded both enthusiastic and nervous: "You must understand that a trip to the great, powerful republic, for which in spite of everything I have *a great deal of enthusiasm*, means to me a rare, unique opportunity for widespread perspectives and educating, awakening influences. And I want to thank you from the bottom of my heart." There might, on the other hand, be problems with his studies. He had too many irons in the fire already—added to which, he did not trust his ability to communicate in English: "Perhaps I might accomplish something small at home here in my room, but over there—oh no!"[39]

The summer's Northfield conference was scheduled to take place between June 28 and July 9. Moody would be there and would speak every day, in addition to which there would be missionary subconferences under R. E. Speer and R. P. Wilder, and on the fourth of July there would be a "jovial celebration." There would be 370 students present, but only four from continental Europe: two Frenchmen, one German, and Söderblom from Sweden.

Söderblom kept a detailed and exuberant diary of his travels, long extracts from which were published after his death by Anna Söderblom.[40] They provide fascinating and often highly entertaining reading, though hardly relevant to a study of this kind. Söderblom—who had never previously been farther south in Sweden than Stockholm, and had never before left the country—traveled by way of Denmark, Germany, and France (a landfall at Le Havre, where he was arrested as a suspected Prussian spy, and narrowly missed being jailed). He enjoyed shipboard life enormously, and on arrival in New York was introduced to the YMCA, before moving on to New Haven and Yale University. At New Haven he found a charming and cultivated English tutor in the person of a Mrs. Campbell, noting in his diary that "the educated American woman is perhaps America's most unique and advanced asset."[41] Then came the Northfield conference itself, where two persons made a deep impression on him. One was the young John R. Mott, with whom in later years he was to have far more to do than he could possibly have anticipated. Chiefly, though, he was impressed by Dwight Moody.

At first Moody was a disappointment, seeming crude and unsophisticated. But very soon Söderblom came to recognize in him a quality that may well have reminded him of his own father: a childlike immediacy under a rough-hewn exterior, a deep and genuine devotion without the slightest trace of guile. In 1890 Söderblom was still a country boy at heart, who was only beginning to come to terms with the larger world. In Moody he recognized a kindred spirit. His description of Moody is worth recording:

> Love is and always has been the driving force in his life, love of God and all those who, like him, have been redeemed by God, a love the unselfishness of which not even the bitterest enemy of Christianity who has encountered him can deny. And Moody is a child, a true child of God. This is his first and last characteristic. He is childlike in his simplicity. One notices that he feels it to be his important and sacred duty to say precisely what he has to say. When he speaks, one recalls the words, "If I were to keep silent, the stones would cry out." A

word carried by such a deep and burning conviction of its importance and truth does not return in vain. Is he not a child, sitting there and listening to Sankey's passionate singing, and shaking his head in conviction when he hears his friend sing a verse about his favorite theme: atonement in Christ? It is as exhilarating as cold spring water in an indifferent and sullen time to come into contact with such childlike faith and such childlike spontaneity.[42]

With one or two adjustments, these words might serve equally well as a characterization of Jonas Söderblom, and, cast in academic language, as a description of a "saint"—a subject to which Söderblom was to return again and again in later years. There had been his father; in Uppsala there was Waldemar Rudin (with temporary reservations); a few years later, in Paris, there was to be Auguste Sabatier; now for a few brief days there was Dwight Moody. All in varying degrees possessed "genius" in the life of the spirit.

This is not meant to be a study of Söderblom's contribution to Christian unity. Nevertheless it would be less than just to omit another entry made by Söderblom in his diary during his few days in New Haven, which read: "Lord, give me humility and wisdom to serve the great cause of the free unity of Thy Church."[43] He did not know which church Moody represented, if indeed he belonged to a church at all. It did not seem to matter. In Sweden, church problems tended to fill the greater part of everyone's field of vision, but in the freer atmosphere of the United States there were more important issues. In later years, although Söderblom was never one to forget the church to which he belonged, or to minimize its heritage, he always sought for that which belongs rather to religion as such than to any local variant of it as the ground of unity. On this occasion, that must suffice. A quarter-century was to elapse before Söderblom actually found himself in a position to do something to further this "great cause"—ironically enough, as a more or less direct result of certain events in Russia involving another delegate to Northfield 1890, John R. Mott.[44] That, however, is another story.

Following his North American adventure, Söderblom became a more and more frequent traveler. In the following year, 1891, he took part in an international YMCA conference in Amsterdam, and in 1892 he had advanced to the role of a conference speaker, this time at a Scandinavian student Christian conference in Norway. In

Uppsala, while pursuing his studies to good effect (though how remains something of a mystery), he was becoming a celebrity in the exclusive student world, first as president ("first curator") of his regional fraternity, then as vice-president and finally as president of the Uppsala student body as a whole. He chaired the local YMCA. And after 1890, perhaps as a result of the confidence his American trip had given him, he began to emerge as a brilliant public speaker, to the initial surprise of some of those closest to him. If anything in his strenuous life could be spoken of as relaxation, music served that function. Always an excellent musician with a fine tenor voice and a good keyboard technique, he was studying piano, organ, harmony, and counterpoint (one of his hymn tunes, that to the words "I denna ljuva sommartid . . ." is still today one of Sweden's most widely sung). And in 1891–92 he found his life's companion in the person of Anna Forsell.

Still there was no particular indication of any special interest on Söderblom's part in the serious *comparative* study of religion. His scholarly interests were laid down for him by the syllabus on the one hand, and by the struggle of the new Ritschlian liberalism to gain breathing space in the faculty of theology on the other. What developments there were in his thinking were taking place mainly on this latter front.

Important in this connection was a visit paid by Söderblom and Fries to Fredrik Fehr in Stockholm, on Good Friday 1892. The day began with a service in *Storkyrkan* (to all intents and purposes Stockholm Cathedral, though it did not have that name), where Fehr was preaching. Fries was overwhelmed, and wrote to his fiancée to tell her so: "What a glorious voice, what a *calm* devotion to the subject, and what content! I have never before heard such a sermon. . . . Fehr's theme was: 'The supreme revelation of the divine love and the fulfilment of human faithfulness.' A genuinely Ritschlian idea. I wept, it was so beautiful."[45]

In the afternoon, the two students were invited to Fehr's home for dinner, simple but substantial, and spiced with "pleasant, lively conversation about our teachers of theology, whom neither we nor Fehr held in particularly high esteem."[46] The conversation continued after dinner. Fries and Söderblom were promised whatever help they might need, and hints were dropped that they in their turn might help Fehr in one or another of his literary enterprises—which both must have found flattering. Fehr showed them his portrait gallery of famous German theologians, with that of Wellhausen in the place of honor, the autograph book in which they had written their polite phrases, and his doctoral diploma, in which he had been praised as, among other things, Sweden's chief contact with German theology! Fries and Söderblom left knowing that they had an influential friend and ally in high places.

A few days later, Fehr came to Uppsala to be present at a public academic disputation. A student, Hjalmar Danell, was defending his dissertation on—and obviously to a certain extent in opposition to—the theology of Ritschl. (The conservative Danell was subsequently to be one of Söderblom's most consistent opponents.) On this occasion Fehr came, urged by Söderblom, with the express purpose of defending Ritschl by means of an "extra opposition" from the floor—an entirely normal procedure in the old-style academic disputation. The result was an embarrassment to everyone. The student being examined refused to concede a single point, and replied to Fehr in a tone which Fehr heard as arrogance, however it may have been meant. Fehr lost his temper. There was an outburst of hissing and stamping from the largely student audience (evidently they were enjoying themselves considerably). The chairman failed to intervene as he should have done, whereupon Fehr stormed out of the room, deeply offended. Fries and Söderblom hurried to the railway station to catch Fehr and attempt an apology, but it was too late. Fehr had never had much liking for Uppsala theologians, and what had taken place had further widened the gulf between them, now with an added factor of personal resentment to add to the ideological bitterness.[47]

Although this is Söderblom's story, and not that of either Fehr or Fries, much of the suspicion with which Söderblom was regarded from the conservative (largely clerical) wing of church opinion in Sweden will be clearer if his association with Fehr and Fries be borne in mind. Matters came to a head in the spring of 1894, and this is a good opportunity to look forward to that occasion, since the storm began to build in November 1892.

At that time Fries (still a student of theology) was asked by his tutor in Semitic languages, Herman Almkvist, who was not a theologian and indeed was generally regarded as a "freethinker," to consider writing a modern history of Israel in which he would place the results of recent scholarship before the Swedish public. He accepted with a certain solemn sense of destiny, and after a year's remarkably concentrated writing—during which time he had also begun to give a few university lectures in Uppsala—the book was published early in 1894. In 1894, too, Fries was ordained and through Fehr's good offices given a curacy in a Stockholm church. This was poorly paid, and he was eking out his income by doing a little teaching in the girls' school once attended by Anna Forsell. After half a term, he was summoned to the office of the headmistress, and told that if he had written that dreadful book on the history of Israel, he was not a right and proper person to teach religion to impressionable young ladies. Ordained minister or not, he was fired on the spot. Fehr was outraged, and wrote to the papers in Fries's support. There followed a frantic debate in the press, while from Uppsala there came a pained and solemn letter from Waldemar Rudin, informing Fries that if these were the practical public consequences of his scholarship, there could be no question of his ever being permitted to teach ministerial candidates in Uppsala.[48] Nor did he. He did his utmost in later years to convince his opponents by the sheer weight of his learning, but all in vain. The writing of *Israels historia* had cut him off from the very preferment he had believed to be inevitable. He was to die in 1914, the most brilliant biblical scholar of his generation in Scandinavia, still only the vicar of a Stockholm city church.

Söderblom's temperament was not that of Fries. Still, his reputation was to suffer a certain "guilt by association" with the controversies surrounding his friend. Fries's chief fault lay in his aggressiveness and his inability to compromise, neither of which were Söderblom's characteristics. There was little of the Pietist in Fries, nor did he have a feeling for mysticism. Fries could see little in Waldemar Rudin, and very probably would have been repelled by Moody. One feels that he was more interested in principles and problems than in persons, and certainly he knew nothing of the art of diplomacy. Had he possessed a measure of flexibility, there would have been less reason to write of his career as a tragedy— which in the end, inevitably, it was. He almost pulled Söderblom down with him.

3

Discovering Iran, 1892–1894

The history of religion as a branch of late twentieth-century scholarship has well-established conventions which decree, among other things, that the advanced student should have a specialist field within which he or she can move freely. There are languages to be learned (if not always altogether mastered), texts to be read, secondary literature to be combed, monographs to be written in accordance with the strict standards of the guild. During the student's time of apprenticeship, premature synthesis is discouraged. The general history of religion will have been tackled first as a means of learning one's way about among the religious traditions of the world, and the student will have been exposed at an early stage to a wide range of methods and approaches. But in most cases graduate work proper will be sharply and narrowly defined, and it is in the student's best interests to remain within its guidelines—as most of course do.

In the 1890s in Sweden there was no academic discipline corresponding to what we today call the history of religion. The historical approach to the late Judeo-Christian tradition was gaining ground, though slowly and amid bitter controversy, in the Uppsala faculty of theology. But to do advanced linguistic and historical work on any religious tradition outside the Judeo-Christian borders it was necessary to cross into the faculty of arts. There one could acquire a training in Semitic and Indo-European languages, read texts, and construct histories—as in the case of Samuel Fries's ill-fated history of Israel, commissioned outside the faculty of theology and immediately rejected by it. Similarly one could become an Arabist or a Sanskritist. One could not on the other hand relate the one to the other, or either to theology—at least not on any official academic level. Within the faculty of theology there was one professorial chair, the occupant of which was expected to pay a certain attention to non–Judeo-Christian material, and we shall have more to say about this narrow opening shortly. But in comparison with Holland and France in particular, the machinery for training historians of religion in Sweden was not yet in place. Least of all was it in place in the vicinity of the faculty of theology.

However, although little of the general history of religion was being taught in Uppsala in the early 1890s, a certain amount of material was filtering through from Germany, France, Holland, and Britain. We shall return to the German *Religionsgeschichtliche Schule* later. For the moment it will be enough to observe that the "school" was made up of theologians bent on tackling the question of the historical origins of Christianity; that in it, the historical question led inexorably to the question of the nature of revelation; and that it was beginning to take shape from about 1890 on.[1] In France there was the Protestant faculty of the Sorbonne, transferred from Strasbourg a few years earlier and maintaining admirable relations between "science" and theology. In Holland there were the giants, C. P. Tiele and P. D. Chantepie de la Saussaye, working along similar lines in "secular" faculties. And in Britain, a variegated company of gifted individuals were pursuing comparative studies in various ways, though with little institutional support. Between the "nature-mythologists" and the "evolutionists" there was being waged tireless war over the question of the origins of religion and mythology—again a question with obvious theological implications. In Sweden, however, little of this had made an impression in 1892.[2]

With Söderblom's background and the range of his involvements and interests thus far, he might have been expected to have chosen as a field of graduate study either church history or a subject within the biblical field. He completed his theological degree (*teologie kandidat*) in December 1892, with a high distinction in church history, distinctions in comparative religion, ethics, and New Testament studies, and credits in his remaining subjects.[3] Three months later, on March 5, 1893, he was ordained by Bishop Gottfrid Billing into the ministry of the Church of Sweden, and appointed chaplain to Uppsala's mental hospital, where he also lived for the next year or so: an abrupt change of milieu for such a student celebrity as Söderblom had become. But there is no indication that it ever did him any harm, and it had at least one great advantage: apart from holding services in the hospital chapel, his duties were not onerous, and he had ample, distraction-free time to devote to his continued studies.

To a certain extent those studies followed the biblical and especially the theological line that he had been establishing over the past five or six years, but now with the difference that his work was beginning to appear in print more frequently. During 1893 he published a series of summer lectures, at first separately and then together, under the title of *Den lutherska reformationens grundtankar* (The fundamental ideas of the Lutheran Reformation). Also in 1893 there appeared a sixty-four-page translation from the French, *Ritschls åskådning af kristendomen* (Ritschl's view of Christianity). The author of the original, Ernest Bertrand, had published *Une nouvelle conception de la rédemption, la doctrine de la justification et de la réconciliation dans le système théologique de Ritschl* in Paris in 1891, and it had been well received in Germany. At the time there was practically nothing either by or about Ritschl in Swedish, and Söderblom took it upon himself not only to translate the first part of Bertrand's book, but to go through Ritschl's writings and supply it with accurate references. This work had been done before his graduation, however, and represents the high point of Söderblom's Ritschlianism, since over the next few years he was to become more critical of the master. And as we have seen, to be too Ritschlian in Sweden was not without its risks.

The preface which Söderblom wrote to his translation was dated New Year 1893, from his parents' home in Norrala. By that time he had made up his mind not to pursue a *directly* Ritschlian line in his graduate work, but to apply Ritschlian insights to a problem in the history of religion. From among a number of potential supervisors in Uppsala, any one of whom would have welcomed him with open arms, he had chosen J. A. Ekman in "apologetics" (the history of religion, or comparative religion, as viewed from a Christian angle). His chosen subject was the relationship between Iranian and Judeo-Christian eschatology. Both choices may be seen as the products of a number of factors acting together.

Chief among them was sheer interest in the emerging question of whether the religion of the Old and New Testaments had in fact been influenced by the religion of Iran, particularly in its eschatological conceptions. But beyond this there were certain practical considerations. Söderblom wished to qualify himself for a teaching post at the University of Uppsala, and such posts were few and far between. His chances might have seemed better in a less heavily populated field, and Ekman would certainly seem to have encouraged him to believe that he had a future in comparative religion.

What we are here calling "comparative religion" went under another heading entirely in the Uppsala of the 1890s. The professorial chair within which comparative studies played a modest part actually had been established by Bishop Kalsenius as far back as 1754 with the stated intention of defending the Christian faith against the errors of "atheists, naturalists, deists, antiscripturalists, and indifferentists."[4] At various times during the nineteenth century the field to be covered by this teaching post had been redefined, and in 1877 had crystallized as *teologiska prenotioner och teologisk encyklopedi* (theological propaedeutics [i.e., preliminary investigations] and theological encyclopedia), at which time the first full-time full professor was appointed.

This was K. H. G. von Schéele, whose previous work had covered such areas as the ontological proofs of the existence of God, rationalism in theology, and church catechetics.[5] He occupied the chair for eight years, 1877–85, before becoming Bishop of Visby—the first of five successive occupants of the chair to be elevated to the Lutheran episcopate. Von Schéele would seem not to have been greatly impressed by nature-mythological or evolutionary theorizing about such matters as the origins of religion. He did, however, publish an essay on the position of pre-Christian Scandinavian religion in the history of religions generally, and by 1880 was lecturing modestly on a few subjects connected with the comparative study of religion.

His successor (appointed in 1887) was Johan August Ekman, and during his incumbency the Uppsala chair moved a little further in a comparative direction. In 1888 he had published a book entitled *Den naturalistiska hedendomen eller lägsta stadiet av humanitetsidéns utveckling* (Naturalistic heathenism, or the lowest stage in the development of the idea of humanity), which may well have been written expressly to qualify him for the chair, since his previous work had been entirely in biblical studies and church history. It did not advance the study of the subject in any way and, although noteworthy as the first book written in the field of comparative religion in Swedish, is otherwise best forgotten.

In 1892, therefore, what comparative religion there was in Uppsala's faculty of theology was limited to general lectures on the religions of the world, and was seen in the light of a necessary exercise in Christian apologetics. Ekman's book had been designed to show that "heathenism" was in error on every important point, and that in the absence of direct divine revelation, had fallen into the grossest moral turpitude. According to Tor Andrae, its angle of approach and method was that of K. F. A. Wuttke's *Geschichte des Heidentums* (History of heathenism, 1851), a Hegelian theory of religious development translated into terms of strict Lutheran orthodoxy; Ekman's book Andrae considered to be out of date at the time of its publication. Andrae concluded that Ekman and Söderblom were generations apart: from Ekman, Söderblom "learned nothing and had nothing to learn."[6] Ekman did, on the other hand, lecture on the history of religions (still, let it be remembered, only part of the professorial duties of that particular chair) in 1888, and again in 1892–93—lectures which Söderblom undoubtedly attended, adding to the informal studies being carried on at the same time within the student missionary association. But in either case the aspect of Christian apologetics was prominent. The religions of the world, past and present, were not being brought under review for their own sake, but for the sake of the relationship in which they stood to Christianity, in history on the one hand, in the modern world on the other.

The word "apologetics" in these days has a somewhat dismal sound, suggesting as it does special pleading, if not outright dishonesty in the putting forward of only those arguments that suit one's own cause and further one's own sectional interests. And certainly apologists have been known to be special pleaders. Some such exercise is, however, necessary and indeed inevitable in any society that does not exist in complete isolation from all other societies. Given the encounter with "the others," one must form theories to account for them, their beliefs and practices, their works and ways. And in the last two decades of the nineteenth century, with the Western world brought more and more into contact with peoples elsewhere on the globe and, through the developing sciences of history, archaeology, and anthropology, with its own past, explanations had to be sought and found. Söderblom was involved in the "apologetical" quest on both levels—as a matter of contemporary concern and as a historical puzzle. Within a nineteenth-century faculty of theology only the latter was open to academic investigation.

The problem that had forced itself on Söderblom's attention by the time of his graduation concerned the historical roots of the Old and New Testament traditions. Were those traditions the unambiguous products of a single continuous process of divine revelation, as an earlier apologetical tradition had unhesitatingly affirmed? Or were they in actual fact the composite products of many independent influences, some of them "primitive," others emanating from Near Eastern nations far more powerful than tiny, oppressed Israel—from Babylonia, from Persia, from Egypt, from Greece, from Rome? We shall have more to say on this subject later; for the moment it will be enough to say that in none of these cases could the scholar estimate the extent of outside influence on the world of the Bible without first sitting down and examining the sources—all the sources—and that among the problems confronting the historical wing of the apologetical enterprise, none was more tantalizing than that having to do with the possible extent of Iranian (Persian) influence on the Old Testament, and hence indirectly on the New.

In the early 1890s, a few scholars were beginning to assume there to have been such influence, and therefore were starting to examine the Iranian and Jewish material in search of resemblances between the one tradition and the other. This was largely the approach of the German *Religionsgeschichtliche Schule*, though the members of that "school" generally moved only within the world of Greco-Roman antiquity. Resemblances were often taken as evidence of influence, on a *post hoc propter hoc* basis. Sometimes this conclusion was justified. Almost always it was desperately difficult to prove the matter either way.

But there were other reasons for Söderblom's sudden shift away from church history and into historical comparative religion. In 1892–93 Zoroastrianism was hardly one of Christianity's chief rivals for the religious allegiance of the modern world. The prophet Zoroaster/Zarathustra himself was another matter entirely. The Old Persian sources which reproduced his teachings were being edited and translated, and given Israel's links with Persia (about these at least there was no question) there were those who were prepared to suggest that Zoroaster and his followers had (however indirectly) taught Israel much of importance in the area of eschatology.

The Iranian field, however, was still poorly defined. For one thing, the oldest Iranian sources were written in an obscure and difficult language, Zend, or Avestan, for which at the time there was not even an adequate dictionary—none was to be available until 1904, when Christian Bartholomae published his *Altiranisches Wörterbuch*. Translations of the Zend-Avesta there had been nonetheless: first in 1771 by Anquetil Duperron, in the 1880s by James Darmesteter and L. H. Mills in the *Sacred Books of the East* series,[7] and by de Harlez of Louvain. A few years later Darmesteter produced his French version, *Le Zend-Avesta* (3 vols., 1892–93). It would seem to have been the reading of Darmesteter that convinced Söderblom that if he were to proceed further in the Iranian field, he should do so in Paris.

There were other impulses. In 1883–84 Friedrich Nietzsche had published his celebrated *Also sprach Zarathustra* (Thus spake Zarathustra), and this had been much discussed in student circles. Most important of all may well have been, however, the appearance in 1886–89 of Viktor Rydberg's two-volume *Undersökningar i germansk mytologi* (Investigations in Germanic mythology), which contained many comparisons between Germanic and Iranian ideas.[8] We have no further need to elaborate on the extent to which Söderblom and his circle idolized Rydberg; here we may merely note that Rydberg's work was to be quoted frequently in Söderblom's own doctoral dissertation of 1901.

The final circumstance would appear to have been a sheer coincidence. It did not affect Söderblom's decision to do graduate work in comparative religion, since it took place after that decision had been made; it did, however, confirm his resolve and give him, if not a field, at least an angle of approach. In December 1892, only a few days after his graduation in theology, Söderblom, together with his new fiancée Anna Forsell, paid a courtesy call on Fredrik Fehr in Stockholm. There he was lent a recent copy of an English-language periodical, *The Thinker*, which contained an article on "Zoroaster and Israel" by a writer previously unknown to Söderblom, James Hope Moulton (1863–1917).[9]

In 1892 Moulton, still not thirty years old, was no more than a hardworking schoolmaster at a Wesleyan Methodist school, The Leys, in Cambridge, England. Three years Söderblom's senior, he was still almost as much a beginner in comparative religion as was Söderblom. In after years, the two men's careers were to run on similar lines for a decade or so: Söderblom was professor in Uppsala from 1901 to 1914, Moulton in Manchester from 1904 to his tragic and premature death in 1917. In 1904 Moulton described the course of the development of his studies in these words: "My work has been slowly shifting its centre of gravity for years. I was, of course, a comparative philologist at Cambridge, a classic mostly for teaching purposes, a N.T. student from the grammar side . . . , and a Zendist as a philologue originally, finally a disciple of [J. G.] Frazer from the growing taste for comparative religion."[10]

Moulton was one of the most brilliant Indo-European philologists of his generation, and it is to do Söderblom no injustice to say that his respect for philology notwithstanding, neither his training nor his inclinations were such as to place him in Moulton's class. Theologically, on the other hand, the Lutheran and the Wesleyan occupied very similar ground. Neither was an extreme liberal; both were, one might say, "progressive conservatives." In Cambridge, Moulton had studied Sanskrit and Avestan (Old Persian) under the Orientalist E. B. Cowell (d. 1903), a man described as "a simple, convinced, humble believer in the faith which is in Jesus Christ"[11] —which words might well be taken to apply to Moulton himself, or to Söderblom for that matter.

Moulton's 1892 article on "Zoroaster and Israel" was designed to demonstrate the very great *improbability* of Persian influence on the religion of the Old Testament, on the grounds that by the time of the Jewish-Persian contacts in the time of the Archemaenids, Zoroaster's *Gatha* hymns and the younger Avesta were largely unknown. He concluded that "no doctrine of Zarathustra's—under which head is included the belief in immortality—can possibly have reached the Jews as early as the reign of Xerxes."[12] Therefore it might be concluded that the most essential doctrine of the Bible, namely, that of the resurrection of the body, either had been communicated directly by God or, failing that, had arisen by a process of independent development within Israel itself. There was no *historical* evidence that it had been "borrowed" from Iranian sources. From that fact the Christian might draw whatever conclusions seemed appropriate. Or, as Moulton put it, "historical considerations" need not trouble the Christian: "for I do not think that there is any reason why such a theory should trouble the firmest believer in a unique revelation to the Hebrew people."[13]

The vistas opened up by this angle of approach impressed Söderblom as overwhelming in their breadth and possibilities. Thus far critical historical study of the Bible had generally appeared to the faithful as a threat to the integrity of Christianity, relativizing the absolute and humanizing the divine. But suppose that good history—history, that is, worked out according to the strictest scientific standards of accuracy and impartiality—were to prove to be not the enemy but the ally of true religion! This would still be apologetics of a kind, since it would be engaged in the intellectual defense of truth. But it would not be the old apologetics, arguing from infallible sources to unavoidable conclusions. Rather it would be scientifically inductive, piecing together the history of religion from all the available evidence, a little at a time, motivated (on the ideal level at least) by no more than the desire to know *wie es eigentlich gewesen ist*, "what really happened."

Early in 1893 Söderblom threw himself into the study of Old Persian, convinced that in a year or so he would be able to produce a dissertation professional enough to qualify him for the position as *docent* (lecturer or assistant professor) in apologetics he believed would soon be open. On February 18, 1893, he wrote to Göransson:

> I am in Iran and Persia, still barely able to find my way about. It may seem a little strange and unpractical for me to be researching for my *docent* dissertation in such a new area, when I am so well qualified already in the history of doctrine, for example. But if I keep at it, perhaps I can do something useful. I regard it as a happy complement to use the scientific confidence and joy which Ritschl has given me, by pointing to our prophet as the greatest, to Christ as the Only One, to work among the other revealers of God, who gave to others their solution of the problem of religion. If I were able some day to obtain a concrete picture of the history of religion, I would have reached my life's proudest goal. Dreams, you say, Göran. Happy dreams, I reply.[14]

How far and how fast Söderblom was able to proceed with his Iranian studies at this stage is open to question. That he was working immensely hard to master Avestan is abundantly clear; whether he ever achieved anything more than an average working knowledge of that language is a matter of some doubt, on which opinions still differ.[15] But as the previous letter shows, it was never his intention to become an Iranist in the narrower specialist sense; rather his aim was to acquire expertise sufficient to enable him to speak with confidence of one prophet (Zoroaster) in relation to another (Jesus Christ), and of Iranian ideas in relation to those of the Judeo-Christian tradition.[16]

Previously we have spoken of the profoundly liberating influence on Söderblom of an experience through which he passed in 1890, almost a classical conversion experience which turned him from a book to a person, from the Bible to Christ. A second such experience followed in 1893—though precisely when is not clear from the sources. In Söderblom's own words, again expressed in the third person:

> One Sunday, he had held his service as usual. When he returned with a close friend [Anna Forsell, his fiancée] to his room, there came over him what might be called a direct perception of the holiness of God. He understood what he had long felt indistinctly, that God was far stricter than he could imagine or than anyone can really comprehend. God is a consuming fire. This apprehension was so powerful, so shattering, that he was unable to stay on his feet. Had he not collapsed into a chair with his head on the table, he felt that he must have fallen to the floor. He moaned and groaned under this mighty grasp. Slowly he recovered and calmed down. But for the rest of his life, for decades these two experiences [in 1890 and 1893] have been firm points of departure or, rather, irrefutable experiences, fundamental to spiritual life, incomparable in their meaning, the incomprehensible means of mercy: the cross, the miracle of God's mercy. Man's nothingness, broken-heartedness, trembling, his faith *quand même*. Since then he has been unable to doubt God in spite of everything.[17]

This was not a comforting assurance of salvation through Christ, as his experience in 1890 had been. Rather it was a sense of the *mysterium tremendum*, the holiness, the otherness of God, of that *sensus numinis* on which Rudolf Otto later was to base his interpretation of religion in *Das Heilige* (1917; English translation, *The Idea of the Holy*, 1923). But this was least of all an "idea." It was a presence and a pressure, overwhelming in its intensity, paralyzing in its impact. But it was not without mercy. Söderblom's first experience in 1890 doubtless made him into more of a Christian than he had been previously, but the second gives us the better clue to an understanding of how he approached religion as a field of study. "It is a fearful thing to fall into the hands of the living God" (Hebrews 10:31). Not without reason, almost forty years later, did Söderblom entitle his last major work *The Living God*, and subtitle it "basal [*not* "basic"] forms of personal religion." The terms on which such a book might eventually be written were established in his twenty-eighth year, before he had even begun to make the smallest inroads into the academic world.

On September 5–7, 1893, there was celebrated in Uppsala the three-hundredth anniversary of that council through which the Protestant Reformation became firmly established in Sweden—Sweden's own "Reformation Day," in fact.[18] King Oscar II came from Stockholm with a large retinue including a number of foreign royalty, among them Grand Duke Karl Alexander of Sachsen-Weimar. After a solemn service in the cathedral on the morning of September 5, it was the turn of the Uppsala students to greet the assembled celebrities in song and rhetoric. The song was provided by the students' male-voice choir, the rhetoric by Pastor Nathan Söderblom as chairman of the student body.

To King Oscar he spoke in Swedish. Immediately thereafter he addressed the noble German guests, in German, with a special word to Grand Duke Karl Alexander as representative of that university from which the waves of the Reformation had spread. The grand duke, delighted, proposed to bestow upon Söderblom the Order of the White Falcon there and then. He sent for Söderblom, who by that time was otherwise occupied and could not be found. In the interval the Swedish nobles had persuaded the grand duke that the award might be premature; therefore it was never made.[19] But on that day Söderblom had for the first time emerged as a public personality, expansive and self-assured, anything but overawed by the immensity of the occasion.[20] Just the opposite was the case: whatever inward doubts Söderblom may have had about his abilities, and whatever depressions he may have suffered in later years, always thereafter he remained the consummate public performer, somewhat in the manner of a great musician or actor. Some always disapproved. Swedes—and particularly Swedish churchmen—are not generally noted for extroversion, and in later years there were not lacking those who were only too prepared to add Söderblom's public performances to his liberal reputation as foci of disapproving criticism. One suspects, however, that often disapproval was a thinly disguised envy.

Söderblom spoke on one other occasion during the celebrations, at a public meeting in the Botanical Gardens on September 7. Although brief, his speech was full of characteristic touches. Olaus Petri, Sweden's Reformer (born one hundred years before the Council of Uppsala), he praised as a great man, a masterly interpreter of the Bible, and a historian outstanding in his day. The modern historian, he pointed out, views the Swedish Reformation other than through rose-tinted spectacles and sees more than the simple fulfillment of noble ideals: "When history paints with its incorruptible brush, the picture shows not ravishing beauty and harmony, but rugged, rough figures and a strange mixture of odd, ugly colors, which may perchance drive the occasional admirer away, scared or disillusioned, from the object of admiration." But it would be foolish to complain, "for that is the way history develops and the condition of human life. Whoever looks more deeply and understands what he sees, finds at the deepest level the power of truth."[21]

The message of Uppsala 1593 was one of liberation, he continued: "spiritual freedom: freedom in face of opinions—the most modern opinions can be no less tyrannical than the old and discarded ones—freedom in face of people, freedom in face of oneself. But freedom presupposes liberation. Only a power greater than we can liberate us. . . . Faith gives freedom. We need such a faith on the dizzying heights where we falter and are overwhelmed by the new perspectives opened up to our gaze by scholarship."[22]

Today doubtless we should be less confident than was Söderblom as to the incorruptibility of the historian: historians we know to be eminently corruptible, given certain conditions. What we cannot dismiss so lightly is the ideal of a historian who actually sets out to cut through the sentimental, the inaccurate, and the subservient, states what he or she finds, and emerges not a cynic but a convinced believer in the liberating power of truth. Even then it is arguable that Söderblom's favorite biblical verse was "you will know the truth, and the truth will make you free" (John 8:32). This certainly was the spirit in which he embarked on his career as a scholar in 1893. It was this attitude which, in Gerardus van der Leeuw's estimation, made him the father of phenomenology in the study of religion: a passionate commitment to that which is actually *there* in the records of past and present alike.

At the time, Söderblom was contemplating the rapid completion of a dissertation which would qualify him to teach in Uppsala. However, at precisely this time another possibility was opening up that would take him out of Uppsala for a few years—a pastorate in Paris.

Shortly before the Reformation celebrations, Söderblom had been to Stockholm to discuss matters of protocol with King Oscar II. It happened that another Swedish churchman, Professor H. W. Tottie, was also waiting in the antechamber to see the king, and in conversation happened to mention that a vacancy existed for a Swedish pastor to the legation in Paris, with subsidiary duties in the channel ports of Calais and Dunkirk. Söderblom had been ordained for less than six months. Whether or not it was actually suggested at the time that he ought to approach the archbishop in Uppsala with a view to asking to be considered, Söderblom was greatly attracted by the possibility, first, because it would mean having a church of his own far sooner than he had any right to expect, but secondly, because having made up his mind to pursue graduate studies in the history of religion, he saw Paris as the ideal place in which to qualify himself for—in the long run—a professorial chair in Uppsala.

Letters written by Söderblom—chiefly those to N. J. Göransson—in the fall and early winter of 1893 hint at his progress and his uncertainties. Early in September he was divesting himself of his responsibilities in the student community. "It is a good feeling to be able to leave it [the Uppsala student] and enter a new phase of my life—though at the same time I am bound to my time in Uppsala by the bonds of gratitude, whether it continues or comes to an end."[23] Later in the month he was reading Darmesteter with admiration for his boldness and clarity.[24] In October he was expressing his confidence in the emergence of a freer, more historical theology in Uppsala, and reassuring his friend that his real goal was less to become a professional academic than to proclaim the Christian message.[25] And in December: "My plan to write a dissertation in the history of religion is not without risks. It is extremely time-consuming. As you know, I have had to cope with a new language and a new field." He added: "I do not know what will happen about Paris, though I am sure I stand little chance. The archbishop is of the opinion that the appointment cannot be combined with studies."[26]

More than twenty years later Söderblom published his own account of how he finally overcame the archbishop's doubts and secured the Paris appointment, partly, as he put it, to lay to rest a "legend" that had been in circulation for many years—presumably that he had been sent off to Paris to cool his heels and correct his theology. Learning about the Paris vacancy, he wrote, had left him no peace:

> The need for an independent active field of practical work had become strong, and I had to confess that I was also attracted by the rich possibilities for the comparative study of religion that Paris would provide. When I went to see the archbishop, he discouraged me. The stipend had been reduced as a result of the poor state of the church's finances, and I had my academic plans as well. But he gave me time to talk things over with those closest to me. When I went to see him again to say that I would be grateful for the appointment, he asked me again about my academic plans. I was honest enough to say that I intended to complete my studies alongside my real task in the church and among the seamen in the ports. . . . He smiled doubtfully, and said that he thought that this was an illusion on my part. For a long time he sat in silence, looking at me, and then he promised me the post with a hearty handshake.[27]

Söderblom was realistic enough at this stage to recognize that what Archbishop Sundberg had said—that he would not have time to study in Paris—was very probably correct. The appointment was officially confirmed at the end of January 1894. The question now was whether a Swedish-language dissertation on Iranian and Judeo-Christian eschatology could be completed before leaving for Paris.

4

The Paris Years, 1894–1901

Söderblom had tried to explain to Archbishop Sundberg in Uppsala that one of the main reasons for his interest in the legation pastorate in Paris was the opportunity it would give him to continue his Iranian studies. Like his "brothers-in-arms" Fries and Göransson, he had his sights set on a professorial chair in Uppsala, and where the subject of comparative religion was concerned, Paris in the 1890s had resources unmatched by any other city in any other part of the world.[1] There were the scholars of the École Pratique des Hautes Études of the Sorbonne, among them the Iranist Darmesteter, under whom Söderblom particularly wanted to study. In Paris there was the Musée Guimet, transferred in 1888 from Lyon. From Paris there was published what at the time was the only major journal in the field, *Revue de l'Histoire des Religions* (since 1880). And at the Sorbonne there was at the time a Protestant faculty of theology which was notably less conservative than its Uppsala counterpart. Had the Paris vacancy not appeared at this time, then very likely Söderblom would have been content to remain in Sweden to complete his studies. But the opportunity being there, he saw no reason not to make the most of it.

He had no intention of remaining abroad for any longer than was necessary, however. Paris would be an academic finishing school which he could attend parallel with his practical work in the church. On first hearing from the archbishop that he would be appointed to Paris, he had written to Göransson to reassure him that he was leaving Uppsala only reluctantly, adding that "I intend to come back."[2]

But before leaving Sweden there were two important things to do. One was to marry, the other was to complete his dissertation on Iranian eschatology and make arrangements for its publication. On April 29, 1894, Nathan Söderblom married Anna Forsell in Stockholm. Naturally the wedding was conducted by the patron of *Samfundet fritt ur hjärtat*, Pastor Primarius Fredrik Fehr.³

The dissertation was another matter entirely. Certainly it was finished by March, and in the spring and early summer the manuscript was sent to the printers, where at least part of it was set in type. However, it was to be part of a scientific monograph series, and its final acceptance was conditional upon the approval of three assessors. Obviously Söderblom would not have begun the printing had he not believed that it would be approved for publication. In the event, it was not—though the real reasons behind the decision remain obscure. Certainly Söderblom had been working on the Iranian material for only a very short time, less than two years, and had begun the study of the Avestan language no sooner than the beginning of 1893. Arguably, therefore, it was rejected for purely scholarly reasons, as a premature statement based on inadequate preparation. It is, on the other hand, at least equally possible that the veto was applied for personal reasons by only one—the most influential—of the three assessors. Further than that, in the absence of positive evidence, we are not able to go.[4]

The news that his dissertation would not be published did not reach Söderblom, other than by way of rumor, until August 1894. He was of course annoyed and upset, not least at the thought of the money he had wasted on the useless printing. In actual fact its rejection was a blessing in disguise. Although it had been called "a remarkable achievement, both intellectually and physically" by a modern Iranist,[5] it could not under any circumstances have won him the international recognition that was to come his way seven years later on the publication of *La Vie future*. Söderblom's pride had been hurt by this, his first (and only) academic failure. But little else suffered, and on the surface at least the episode was soon forgotten.

Söderblom's first few months in Paris were trying in many ways. He found the city oppressive in the summer heat, and its pace—at least in contrast to sleepy Uppsala—overwhelming.[6] His church duties were more extensive, and more difficult, than he had imagined. The Swedish church on the Boulevard Ornano was a long way from the tiny "bird's nest" on Rue de Maleville in which he and Anna lived. Sunday services were poorly attended, chiefly by people for whom the intellectual problems of Uppsala belonged to another world. The demands made of the pastor were of a different order altogether. Many wandering Scandinavians gravitated to Paris in these years. Some—among them August Strindberg—were writers, others artists, sculptors, musicians. Few had a history of church involvement, but many were prepared to make an exception in Söderblom's case, and over the next few years he found many firm and lasting friends in the Left Bank community. Far more were poor: the struggling servant girls, the sick, the bereaved, the Nordic flotsam and jetsam of Europe's gilded age, any one of whom might call for their pastor's help at any time. Beyond Paris there were the channel ports of Calais and Dunkirk, and there Söderblom had his other congregation, if the comings and goings of Scandinavian seamen can be held to form a congregation. He visited Calais regularly, living in a shed and (for a time at least) dressing in the garb of a French workingman when not on duty—blouse, straw hat, and clogs. The style was that of a young Swedish Tolstoy. It was not, on the other hand, a pose, for as we shall see shortly, the precept and example of Tolstoy was only one impulse helping Söderblom in these Paris/Calais years to turn in the direction of Christian Socialism. The process of adjustment began almost from the moment of his arrival in France, and reached its fullest flowering in 1897–98.

Initially, however, Söderblom felt himself to have been violently uprooted from his native soil. His duties, he wrote in August 1894, were much more onerous than anything he had anticipated; furthermore, "In many ways they are so unlike those of my former life that I have sometimes felt myself to have been torn out of the soil in which I can grow."[7] But he was young, his health was good, and he was determined to succeed in his parallel worlds of church and scholarship.[8]

In the fall of 1894 Söderblom became a postgraduate student of the Protestant theological faculty of the Sorbonne, after which time his academic work began to take shape afresh, and his sense of disorientation diminished rapidly. However, he had one initial disappointment. In looking to Paris, he had most of all anticipated working in Iranian studies with James Darmesteter.[9] But Darmesteter died in October, only a few weeks after Söderblom's enrollment, and this may have had a rather important effect on the direction his work was to take in the next few years. Under Darmesteter, Söderblom might have turned into more of an Iranist than he was eventually to become. As it was, although he continued his Avestan studies under the guidance of Meillet, and comparative religion under Léon Marillier, a far greater influence was exercised on him over the next few years by the two theologians, Ménégoz and Sabatier. As a fellow-Lutheran, Söderblom found Ménégoz both friendly and congenial; his fullest allegiance, however, went to the dean of the faculty, Auguste Sabatier, with whom he developed almost a father-son relationship in the best sense of the term.

Born of a Huguenot family near Marseilles on October 22, 1839, in 1870 Sabatier had been appointed professor of (Reformed) dogmatics at the University of Strasbourg. After the Franco-Prussian War, during which he served as an ambulance officer, the transfer of Alsace to Germany brought his Strasbourg career to a premature end. Hostile to the new German regime, he refused the offer of a chair in the reconstituted university and left for Paris, where for some years he supported himself chiefly as a free-lance writer. In 1877 the Strasbourg faculty was transferred to Paris as the Protestant faculty of theology of the Sorbonne, and Sabatier again became professor of dogmatics; in 1895 he became dean of the faculty.[10]

During this time Sabatier had moved away from his earlier orthodoxy to occupy a position which was critical and historical while at the same time remaining deeply pious on the individual level. Humanity, he maintained, following a pattern not greatly different from that of Comte, had passed through three stages in the course of its development, from a mythological stage, that of ancient paganism, by way of a dogmatic stage, that of the Catholic and Protestant systems alike, to the final stage of historical, critical, and psychological reflection. In religious terms, this developmental scheme reached its highest point in a notably undogmatic Christianity centered on the faith and experience of the individual believer, and it was this individual, experiential side of Christianity that appealed most strongly to Söderblom at this time. He was not altogether uncritical in his acceptance of Sabatier's "fideism," and in later years was to draw attention to Sabatier's exaggerated respect for the immutability of the laws of nature.[11] But in 1894 he was captivated by Sabatier's personality, by the elegance of his style, and by the breadth of his culture.

At this stage Söderblom was much in need of an "elder brother," a person to look up to and respect, spiritually and intellectually. This need was to become all the more pressing a few months later, in consequence of Fredrik Fehr's unexpected death in May 1895. That person would above all have to demonstrate that the way of Christian devotion and the way of modern critical scholarship were not irreconcilable opposites, but that on the contrary, the two together provided the *only* way forward for the church in the new age. Sabatier was not a comparative religionist, and in the area of scholarly specialization could contribute little to Söderblom's development. But he contributed all the more to his religious outlook.

By the end of 1894 Söderblom was getting to know Ménégoz and Sabatier. To both he gave high marks as modern, historical theologians and as admirers of Adolf Harnack—though apparently not of Albrecht Ritschl: "Their writings are clear, to the point, fearless and competent—and masterly as literature. They stand at a very high level in one respect. They know the age they live in and are determined not to lose touch with contemporary ideas."[12] But, he went on, "they are not *germaner*"—a slightly odd and slightly chauvinistic comment. He did not mean that they were not Germans—obviously they were not—but rather that they were not sufficiently inspired by the "Teutonic" or "Germanic" spirit of scientific inquiry. He continued: "We *germaner* are the most advanced race of our day. Will we have the power and originality to create the new religion that the times demand?"[13]

Söderblom began attending Sabatier's lectures, and was much impressed. One of his obiter dicta he passed on to Göransson: "Go forward in faith and with a love of truth. Do not ask where you are going. God will look after that."[14] Soon he was calling Sabatier "the most outstanding French-speaking theological thinker and scholar of the present day" and "the best academic lecturer I have ever heard." "Move him to Uppsala!" he added.[15] As well as listening to Sabatier, Söderblom was of course also reading his numerous books. In 1895 he noted in his diary a point that Sabatier had made in his book on Paul about the importance of mystical fellowship with God.[16] This is worth bearing in mind in the light of the investigations into mysticism that Söderblom was himself later to undertake. In 1897 he was able to persuade Sabatier to come to Sweden to attend the Stockholm Congress of the Science of Religion—of which more later. In the same year the appearance of Sabatier's

Esquisse d'une philosophie de la religion excited Söderblom. Incredibly, in view of all his other commitments, in the following year Söderblom was able to publish a 380-page translation into Swedish. And in 1901 Söderblom's dissertation, *La Vie future d'après le Mazdéisme*, appeared with a dedication to Sabatier.

In Sabatier, Bengt Sundkler has written, Söderblom "met one of those who influenced him most: Auguste Sabatier, with his experience of the frontier situation of Strasbourg prior to 1871; his literary and esthetic activity and journalistic contribution to *Le Temps, Journal de Genève*, and *Revue Chrétienne*; Sabatier, the orator and preacher . . . ; Sabatier, the author writing in lucid French; and finally, Sabatier, Söderblom's personal friend."[17]

One has the impression, as previously hinted, that Söderblom's developing reverence and affection for Sabatier went some way toward compensating for a serious blow that took place in the spring of 1895, with the unexpected and premature death of Fredrik Fehr in Stockholm at the age of only forty-six. It had been Fehr who had through his personal support helped launch Fries and Söderblom on their path of religious reform. He had received them graciously, serving as a personal link with the great men of German scholarship, Wellhausen, Harnack, and above all Albrecht Ritschl. He had served in a manner of speaking as their man in high places. He had confirmed Anna Forsell and had married the Söderbloms little more than a year earlier. On May 14, 1895, he died, almost certainly of a heart attack. Söderblom expressed the feelings of the whole of the fellowship when he wrote to Fries: "My pen has no words to describe how I felt and feel, since reading the news of his death last Saturday. . . . He was our incomparable friend and in human terms the only support for our work."[18] Fries immediately launched into the preparation of a biography, which appeared in the following year.

However, the courtesy that decrees that one should not speak ill of the dead did not apply for others in Fehr's case. What transpired following Fehr's death might appear to have little enough to do with Nathan Söderblom's scholarly career. Let it be remembered, however, that what Fries, Söderblom, and (to a lesser extent) Göransson most of all desired was to win a firm place for scientific scholarship, not in opposition to the church but as an acknowledged part of the church's accepted teaching role. And this, in the eyes of the church's compact conservative majority, was totally unacceptable. To the conservatives, the archenemy was Ritschl, and in Sweden Ritschl's errands had been run by Fehr and his young men, Fries and Söderblom. Söderblom's move to Paris had taken him out of the firing line; in any case, he was generally of a less aggressive disposition than Fries, but that he was capable of writing polemically when the occasion demanded was amply demonstrated at this time.

It all began with a lecture delivered in the summer of 1895 by a conservative churchman, one E. D. Heüman, on the subject of "Ritschlianism and the Church, or Heathenism in the Sanctuary."[19] The burden of Heüman's message was that the pernicious errors of the liberals must be eliminated from the church at all costs. This new heathenism was "far more seductive and satanic than the heathenism of antiquity ever was," since it was operating *within* the church. "Ritschlianism"—a catchall term for every teaching diverging by one hairsbreadth from confessional orthodoxy—must be destroyed. Ordinands infected with the Ritschlian bacillus must be refused ordination and prevented from enrolling for higher degrees. In short, "a Lutheran faculty should be the church's guarantee of the confessional orthodoxy of the ministry." And for Sweden's part, the source of the infection, transmitted of course from German liberals, had been the late Fredrik Fehr.

Söderblom sat down in his Calais shack and wrote an enraged reply to this blasphemous attack, as he saw it. Heüman he accused of hysteria, confusion, ignorance, prejudice, and bigotry, calling him "a copy in Falkenberg of the pope in Rome." What right had Heüman to attempt to dictate to the church what ministers might and might not study? Söderblom concluded that Heüman knew practically nothing of either Ritschl or Fehr in their real teachings, and what little he knew, he had misinterpreted.[20]

The first version of this outburst he sent to a Swedish newspaper (*Göteborgs Handelstidning*). Fortunately, perhaps, the editor refused to print it. Subsequently Söderblom rewrote it, though his wife even then was forced to censor its contents, and printed it as a pamphlet. It did him rather more damage than it did Heüman. Most Swedish churchpeople were still solidly conservative, Bible Christians, and greatly suspicious of the works and ways of the young liberal theologians, especially those who happened, like Söderblom, to be known to be dabbling in "heathenism." Söderblom's growing involvement with Christian Socialism simply fueled the fires of controversy, since socialism (of whatever sort) was even then appearing as the sworn enemy of true religion, whatever its advocates might claim. Journals and church newspapers began to reject his contributions, forcing him to rely more and more on the secular press and cutting him off more and more from those he most wished to influence. In a word, following his attack on Heüman he was no longer thought to be "sound," and his future prospects as a professor of theology in Sweden began to appear gloomy. Thirty years later Söderblom was able to look back on this tense period with a certain detachment, and see it with more equanimity than he felt at the time: "I was suspected of various heresies. Now it seems more amusing than it did at the time, that those innocent (theologically, if not in other respects) Swedish, Norwegian, Danish, and Finnish servant girls in Paris should have been made to suffer for the real or supposed shortcomings of my theology."[21] At the time it was anything but amusing for him to be thought an enemy of true religion, when his own deepest convictions were precisely the opposite: that if there were enemies of true religion anywhere to be found, they should be sought deep in the conservative confessional trenches, and not out in the high country of European scholarship.

Exactly one year after Fehr's death, Samuel Fries published his biographical study *Fredrik Fehr, hans verksamhet och betydelse som teolog* (Fredrik Fehr, His work and significance as a theologian, 1896). The biographical part of the book took up 133 of its 213 pages, the remainder being a study of the theological background against which Fehr's work should be seen, concentrating particularly in the post-Schleiermacher period in the history of Protestant theology. The study is still well worth reading. However, it was in a review of Fries's book that Söderblom revealed what to him was its message to Swedish scholars and theologians. In Sweden, he wrote,

> we have never seen, and perhaps never will see the makers of great theological systems, but our philosophy bears comparison with any contemporary philosophy, and therein lies our

strength. In modern theology there runs a strain of the history and philosophy of religion. It is on this that we should concentrate our effort. Let England gather religiohistorical material from the hidden places of the world's archives; let Holland, France, Germany and Switzerland edit this material into a history—we shall interpret the meaning of that history! And should this be our destiny in terms of the science of religion in our time, which is a period of transition, religiously, politically and socially, still we have a great and sacred duty to perform.[22]

Let the British collect the material, let the remainder of Europe edit it into a history; we in Sweden will tell the world what it means! But who in Sweden were "we"? Clearly Fries, Göransson, and Söderblom—*Samfundet fritt ur hjärtat*—thesis, antithesis, synthesis; Fries the beaver, Göransson the brake, Söderblom the interpreter.

During his Paris years, Söderblom was able to establish personal contact with numerous European scholars in his own and related fields. The first of these contacts (Parisians excepted) was with the Iranist de Harlez in Louvain, who as well as being a profound student of Iranian religion was also a Roman Catholic churchman, comparable in many ways with his disciple, that other scholarly prelate Louis Charles Casartelli in Salford, England, who had a decade earlier, in 1884, presented for his Louvain doctorate a dissertation on *La Philosophie religieuse du Mazdéisme sous les Sassanides* (English translation, 1889). In October 1895 Söderblom wrote to Göransson about his meeting with "old Monseigneur de Harlez, a high prelate and a famous scholar—one of the most open-minded men I have ever met. At the same time he is the church's foremost supporter of Belgium's Christian Socialist (workers') movement. . . . He has nurtured a *small* elite group of scientific theologians . . . among the bigoted priests of Belgium and the Catholic scholastic theologians of Löwen [Louvain]."[23]

Three years later, in 1898, Söderblom visited Holland and met the two most outstanding Dutch comparative religionists of the day, P. D. Chantepie de la Saussaye in Amsterdam and C. P. Tiele in Leiden.[24] Both he found most congenial, establishing particularly good personal contacts with the younger of the two, Chantepie. But it was the meeting with Tiele that was to lead, a couple of years later, to the most permanent consequences and to a lasting link between the names of Tiele and Söderblom. In the spring of 1900, his Sorbonne dissertation not yet completed, Söderblom was surprised and flattered to be approached by the publisher of the German edition of Tiele's comparative religion textbook, *Kompendium der Religionsgeschichte*, with the request that he prepare the third edition. Tiele in 1898 was approaching his seventieth birthday, and was only too willing to turn over the hard grind of textbook revision to a younger and more energetic man. There were times over the next few years when Söderblom wished that he had been less accommodating, work on the *Kompendium* taking up valuable time that he felt could have been better spent. But that this helped establish his reputation in the German-speaking world cannot be doubted.[25]

Another important contact established by way of the Dutch connection was between Söderblom and the Danish scholar Edvard Lehmann, a close friend of Chantepie de la Saussaye and a fellow-Iranist. However, Söderblom and Lehmann would appear not to have met personally until after Söderblom's return to Uppsala in 1901. From that time, however, they corresponded voluminously, and met whenever the opportunity presented itself, while their careers and interests followed remarkably parallel courses, as we shall have occasion to be reminded in what follows.

In what would seem to be his first letter to Söderblom, Lehmann had allowed himself a little outburst of enthusiasm over the joy of being involved in the study of Iranian religion: "Is it not a magnificent study we have become involved in? What spiritual power and refinement there is in this apparently so dry doctrine! And how delightful it is to belong to precisely this generation of Iranists, who can gather the fruit of the labors of our predecessors!"[26]

Such enthusiasm, however, could be generated in more than one way, and it is necessary that we remind ourselves once more that for the generation to which Söderblom and Lehmann belonged, the study of Iranian religion was motivated in the last resort by one major consideration: to determine the extent of Iranian influence on the thought world of the Old Testament, and hence indirectly on early Christianity. In the sources there were both resemblances and differences, and it was very much a matter of presupposition which of them each individual scholar gave precedence over the other. In

Söderblom's case, there was never any real doubt on this score. Inspired by James Hope Moulton, he was convinced that the fundamental differences were of much greater weight than surface resemblances.[27] This was to be the burden of his doctoral dissertation, but during the five years before its presentation he published several brief preliminary studies.

The first of these was a short essay contributed in 1896 to a *Festschrift* for de Harlez in Louvain, entitled *Du Génie du Mazdéisme*. Already he was emphasizing that which is *not* to be found in the Iranian sources, primarily eternal punishment of the wicked, but also the apocalyptic sentiment generally. Nor is there, he claimed, in the Iranian material any trace of bodily mortification—fasting, celibacy, the rejection of "the world," and the like. He concluded that Zoroastrianism is not really dualistic at all, if by "dualism" is meant belief in an essential difference between soul and body, spirit and matter. Most important, however, was the absence from Zoroastrianism of the apocalyptic violence so characteristic of at least part of late Judaism and early Christianity.[28]

Not for another three years did Söderblom publish anything further of any substance on matters concerning Iranian religion. Although he was undoubtedly working away at his Iranian sources in whatever time he was able to spare from his many other activities, from 1896 to 1898 for the most part he had other concerns on his mind. Of these, unquestionably the most important was his deepening involvement with Christian Socialism (otherwise, and perhaps preferably, Social Christianity).[29]

Ever since the publication in "the year of revolutions," 1848, of the Marx-Engels *Communist Manifesto*, the subject of class conflict had been forcing itself on Europe's attention. The Communists of course had identified religion, along with monopoly capitalism and the military establishment, as the chief enemies of the working proletariat; all were instruments in the hands of the upper classes for keeping the workers under subjection. The churches for their part often did little enough to free themselves from the stereotype. However, during the second half of the nineteenth century small groups of concerned Christian leaders in all the Western industrial countries attempted to the best of their ability to bring their people around to a sense of their responsibility toward the poor and underprivileged. The earliest impulses in this direction came from Britain, where the Chartist movement had collapsed in 1848, with the writings of such men as F. D. Maurice, Thomas Carlyle, Charles Kingsley, and George MacDonald. From Britain the wave spread to continental Europe and America, where by the turn of the century it had reached the peak of its influence as "the Social Gospel" and its fullest expression in the books of Walter Rauschenbusch. Social Christianity differed from secular socialism chiefly in the belief that the churches *could* be aroused to a sense of social responsibility, and that in Jesus' teachings on the subject of the Kingdom of God Christianity actually possessed the key to the "social" question. Secular socialists and Communists for their part were equally convinced that the dead weight of ecclesiastical vested interests would always prevent the churches from acting in the true interests of the working classes, and that nothing short of a revolutionary restructuring of the foundations of society would meet society's needs.

To this may be added that each extreme wing of what in the 1890s was already an impassioned and occasionally violent debate was so suspicious of the other's motives that rapprochement was practically impossible. This was particularly the case in the distrust shown by the conservative wing of Christian opinion of the persons and pronouncements of the "social Christians." That these social Christians were generally also liberal in most other respects made things that much worse. It seemed to most conservatives (and in this they were not altogether mistaken) that the espousing of liberal values in one direction meant that other liberal values would follow in their wake. Jettison traditional authority, and who could tell to what excesses the process might lead? David Friedrich Strauss in 1835 had made of his critical *Life of Jesus* an antiestablishment political manifesto.[30] The biblical researches of Julius Wellhausen had helped inspire the antichurch outbursts of Friedrich Nietzsche's *Antichrist* in the 1880s.[31] And in biblical scholarship at this same time, the "Kingdom of God movement" was seen by the conservative wing as the most serious threat to traditional hierarchical authority in the state as well as in the church. This danger was felt more acutely by Lutherans than by Calvinists, the Lutheran social pattern being hierarchical as the Calvinist was not. And within the Lutheran world, the most extreme positions emerged out of the Germany of Bismarck and Kaiser Wilhelm II.

Between about 1895 and 1900 Nathan Söderblom was involving himself more and more deeply in the Christian social movement of France and especially Germany. Writing to N. J. Göransson in January 1895, he admitted that

> What you once wrote about the need for Christianity to demonstrate its power amid social suffering has given me a great deal to think about. I am aware that this is a largely untreated ferment in my own religious interests. Theories threaten to make one esoteric in the sense that one's thoughts become concentrated entirely within the academic world of the present, while the masses, among whom we move around without knowing them, retreat into the background where the faith of the future is concerned; they are so hard to get to know and to reach. My own limited contact with the working classes has been strange. I encounter there a vast, unknown world, and the glimpses I have of it frighten me.[32]

Before 1894, his own country background notwithstanding, he had of course moved about chiefly among the well-heeled young men of Uppsala. What he had never thought to do was to relate what he knew of the Swedish country people to what he was learning on the intellectual level. In Paris and Calais he had been thrown among the urban and seafaring working classes, and entrusted with their care. But what were the implications of this duty in relation to the larger world of religion?

It was the Christian social movement in Germany that helped Söderblom to resolve this question. In Germany the movement had only a short history, the *Evangelisch-Sozialer Kongress* having been founded (by Adolf Harnack, among others) only in 1890, on the pattern of the Anglicans' Christian Social Union. Its two leading figures were Adolf Stöcker, politically and religiously conservative and, it is said, not without a streak of anti-semitism in him, and the more liberal Friedrich Naumann, who in later years distanced himself more and more from the church.[33] The movement's main journal at first was *Die Christliche Welt*, edited by Martin Rade and begun in 1887. However, in 1895 Naumann started his own journal, *Die Hilfe*. This fell into Söderblom's hands, and by May he was writing to Fries that "I like Naumann and *Die Hilfe* very much."[34] The next Protestant Social Congress was held in Erfurt in November the following year, 1896, and this Söderblom attended as part of a longer tour in Germany, taking in the universities of Giessen and Marburg and a visit to the Luther sanctuaries Eisenach and Wartburg. Writing from Erfurt on November 23 he enthusiastically declared, "What I have found here is Christianity as I should wish it to be, purposeful but not methodistic, manly without being ostentatious, deep without being pious. Naumann is a powerful person. I believe that he will achieve great things."[35]

Söderblom was in these years writing regular reports on the religious life of Europe for a Swedish newspaper, the *Nya Dagligt Allehanda*, and of course wrote describing the congress. But Söderblom would not have been Söderblom had not his impressions of the meeting centered on one man. This had been the case five years earlier at Northfield, when Dwight Moody filled his field of vision; so too on this occasion. Naumann's power, he wrote, "is remarkable, though it would be better to say not at all remarkable when one has learned to know him. World-famous scholars and uneducated workers sit side by side, equally captivated by his calm, simple and yet at the same time impressive eloquence. . . . The clear logic in everything he says is never a matter of cold intellectualism. One feels the beat of a sincere and loving heart. That is why he is convincing, and not merely logically consistent."[36] But, he went on, the church badly needs to listen to the socialist movement within her ranks: "That Christianity that has so forgotten its relationship to the friend of the suffering and the poor that it helps the heartless and selfish rich to keep their riches, and self-righteously distributes alms instead of being a power for righteousness and mercy in social life—that Christianity cannot hope to keep its place as the guardian of the highest social ideals."[37]

The same article also contained reflections on the situation elsewhere in Germany, where approval and disapproval of the social Christians seemed to depend on the whims of the Kaiser, recently on record as calling Christian Socialism *Unsinn* (madness) and the phenomenon of "politically" involved pastors *ein Unding* (a monstrosity).[38] Indeed, one Prussian pastor had been threatened with dismissal if he dared to attend the Erfurt conference.[39] Passions were not running so high in Sweden. Nevertheless Söderblom's articles were subjected to a certain censorship: much to his disgust, passages in which he spoke of the aspirations of the workers were cut out by the editors.

In the 1890s Christian Socialism seemed to many traditional Lutherans to be a combination of irreconcilables—a view which claimed to be Christian, while furthering the interests of a lower social class over a higher, and confusing the fundamental Lutheran distinction between church and state. Where Germany was concerned, socialism was a product of her two traditional enemies, France to the west and Russia to the east, as well as having been stated most provocatively and dogmatically by a Jew, Karl Marx. Theologically, to speak (as some of the Christian Socialists were in the habit of doing) of man's responsibility to "bring in" the Kingdom of God by social means was a further bone of contention, at least in the eyes of confessional Lutherans. From the horizons of Berlin, therefore, *any* kind of socialism was dangerous and deplorable, and a threat to the stability of the state. If it appeared under the banner of Christianity, then that to the conservatives was merely proof that socialist propaganda had won over the weak-minded, compelling them to adopt a position which was in no one's best interests. Of course the "proletariat" was numerically large, when compared with the *Junker* rulers of the Prussian state. But let them be attracted to these godless, violent, disrespectful principles, and the very fabric of the state would be in danger. Out-and-out socialism at least made its principles and its priorities very clear, and did not try to disguise its dislike of the establishment. *Christian* Socialists, on the other hand, were doubly suspect. Politically, they were playing into the hands of a dangerous enemy. Religiously, they were reading quite different things out of (or into) the pages of the Bible than that to which the establishment was accustomed. The Lutheran establishment had always read Jesus through Paul, and Paul through Luther. The socially minded liberals had learned to go to the sources, in this case to Jesus himself. This did not mean that they set less value on Paul or Luther, but at least they had learned not to allow Paul and Luther to obliterate Jesus in the interests of a socially convenient orthodoxy.

That, following Erfurt 1896, Söderblom stood out as a deeply committed social Christian is beyond any question. The clearest possible evidence of this was that during 1897 and 1898, his continued Iranian studies notwithstanding, he printed practically nothing classifiable as comparative religion. His major work in these years was a socioethical study of the Sermon on the Mount. But still more surprising was the fact that when the Stockholm Congress of the Science of Religion was held in 1897, again he lectured at considerable length on a socioethical subject, namely, "Religion and Social Development." This was not a temporary aberration on Söderblom's part. He was still a working pastor, and still unsure of his academic future. Professorial openings in Sweden's two theological faculties were very few and far between. There was only one chair (in Uppsala) into which comparative religion could possibly fit, and still in 1897 that was securely occupied. There was therefore no real reason for Söderblom to push ahead with his Iranian dissertation, for which he might have very little use, professionally speaking. It was in the short term far more important for him to clarify his theological position.

In 1897 the king of Sweden, Oscar II, celebrated his silver jubilee as king, having come to the throne in 1872, and it was thought appropriate to mark the jubilee, among other things, by a series of congresses linked with a General Exhibition of Arts and Industry.[40] The plans for these congresses had been announced a couple of years previously, at which time a Swedenborgian pastor in Stockholm, Albert Björck, had launched the idea of a congress or parliament of religions to take place in Stockholm in 1897 on the pattern of the World's Parliament of Religions which had met in Chicago in 1893. But the necessary support was not forthcoming. Later in 1896 a revised proposal was put forward, this time by a triumvirate consisting of Björck, the rabbi of the Stockholm synagogue, Dr. G. Klein, and Söderblom's closest friend, Samuel Fries. This was for a congress, not of religions, but of the *science* of religion. No doubt the proposal came in somewhat late, for which reason it was placed twenty-first in the Stockholm congress series of the jubilee year.

Stockholm 1897 might, then, have been a smaller repeat of Chicago 1893. That it was not was due very largely to Fries. To explain why it was not will require a glance four years backward in time, to Chicago 1893. The World's Parliament of Religions, held in Chicago in connection with the Columbian Exposition of 1893, is chiefly remembered today as the platform from which Swami Vivekananda first announced to the West a form of Hinduism the West could appreciate and even in some measure accept. It is not widely known that the parliament was first conceived as a practical demonstration of the principles of the Swedish visionary Emanuel

Swedenborg and of the "Church of the New Jerusalem" which his disciples had founded in his name. The parliament had been initially the brainchild of a Swedenborgian, Charles Carroll Bonney, an avowed "receiver of the heavenly doctrines of the New Jerusalem."[41] As early as 1889 Bonney had proposed a conference at which the religions of the world could take a step toward the goal envisaged by the New Church. "I had become convinced," he wrote, "that this Church would finally prove the reconciliation and crown of all the religions of the world."[42] Another Swedenborgian, Lewis P. Mercer, was also deeply involved in the organization of the parliament. Mercer, wrote Bonney, "procured for the New Church such a hearing before the whole religious world as was never before attained or hoped for by its apostles."[43] During the course of the parliament, a number of lectures were held on Swedenborgian subjects, including one by Mercer on "Swedenborg and the Harmony of Religions."[44] After the delegates had returned to their various countries—some enthusiastic, others bewildered, a few hostile, practically none aware of the Swedenborgian involvement—Swedenborgians in America and elsewhere were able to reflect with pride on a "second Pentecost, the birthday of a new Christianity," which had been "called together and presided over by a New Churchman."[45]

Reactions to Chicago among Western Christians varied greatly, from enthusiastic acceptance of the "Chicago principle" on the one hand to outright condemnation on the other—one British missionary journal calling it "this menagerie of religions . . . the most profane and the most unpardonable outrage upon Christianity that the world has known."[46] Doubtless most Swedish Christians leaned toward the second of these views, this being one of the reasons why the Stockholm conference was poorly supported; it was feared that Christianity was to be exhibited as merely one religion among many.

In Stockholm, Samuel Fries had been deeply interested in the Chicago phenomenon, and thought that gatherings of this kind could be of value, provided that they could be given a much more "scientific" character than had been evident at Chicago. Chicago had proved that religious leaders could be brought together under one roof. If, having been brought together, they could be set to discuss and think instead of merely delivering propaganda speeches, then much might be achieved. At the better sort of congresses of religion, wrote Fries, "which must necessarily have a strictly scientific character, the scholars and thinkers of the East and the West would be able to meet and present the treasures of their learning, in order to allow these to have their effect *solely* through their own power and through their free, scientific presentation."[47] It was the "strictly scientific character" of the proposed Stockholm conference which Fries wished to safeguard, believing that good science was bound to be in the church's interests. But Albert Björck was a fellow-organizer, and it was equally obvious that he too believed that the interests of *his* church would be furthered by the scientific approach (for had not Swedenborg himself been a famous scientist?). As we shall see, however, notions of precisely what constitutes "science" do not always coincide.

Reading the records of the Stockholm *Religionsvetenskapliga kongressen* of 1897, especially in the light of all that has transpired in the world of scholarship since that time, can be a slightly confusing experience. There is one reason above all others for this impression, namely the very close relationship in which the congress evidently stood to the church. Unlike Chicago 1893, in which religion was affirmed (officially at least) only in terms of a general theism, Stockholm 1897 was surrounded by the formalities of Christianity. It began and ended with sermons, and was punctuated by prayers. Aside from one Jewish rabbi, all those present were Christians. Affirmations of the Christian faith were frequent, and went unquestioned. The chairman was a bishop of the Church of Sweden. Professors, pastors, and active laymen and laywomen made up the bulk of the assembly.

We should be entirely mistaken, however, to dismiss the congress for that reason as (whatever it might claim) unscientific, or as a propaganda exercise on the part of a dominant Christian orthodoxy. That it certainly was not. A propaganda—or at least a publicity—exercise it may in some measure have been, though not for a dominant orthodoxy but rather for a small and so far little recognized or appreciated circle of liberals located somewhere within the church. These included the Uppsala student liberals of the late 1880s and early 1890s—Fries, Söderblom, Göransson—all of whom were by now occupying junior positions in the church's ministry. Their self-imposed task was in no way that of undermining their church, but of winning a measure of public recognition for their intellectual position. In their view scientifically, historically established truth could never be other than in Christianity's best interests, and therefore the scientific approach to all matters having to do with religion was to be cultivated and followed in whatever direction it might lead, though at the same time being consistently applied to what concerned them most, namely, the life of the Christian church.

Among the organizers there were, however, two who did not quite fit into this pattern. One was Rabbi Klein. The other was the Swedenborgian pastor Albert Björck. Björck's case was rather special, since he had most strongly advocated a congress on the lines of Chicago 1893, and clearly believed that the interests of *his* church would be served by this means. In the event, Björck made a bold attempt during the congress to advocate the allegorical methods of scriptural interpretation once taught by Emanuel Swedenborg, and even to call them "scientific". Fries was certainly scandalized at this.[48] So too in all probability was Söderblom, while Rabbi Klein dismissed Björck's attempt as tendentious. But this was an isolated occurrence.

The matters taken up in the course of the congress were all to a greater or lesser extent questions of liberal Christian concern, and questions on which the dominant orthodoxy might be expected to have quite different opinions: Old and New Testament criticism, culture, universal religion, prophecy, revelation, and in Söderblom's case, Social Christianity. Significantly, of the professorial members of the Uppsala faculty of theology, only Waldemar Rudin was on the list of delegates and took any part in the discussions. The remainder (all of whom had been invited as a matter of course) chose not to attend. But in compensation there were a number of overseas participants belonging to the circle of Fries's and Söderblom's acquaintances. Max Müller was invited and agreed to be present (the correspondence was cared for by Björck), but in the end was forced to decline for reasons of health. In his absence, the doyen of the conference was perhaps Auguste Sabatier from Paris. Other international scholars included P. D. Chantepie de la Saussaye from Holland and W. Brede Kristensen from Norway; Bertrand, Bonet-Maury, and Lods from France; and one solitary German, Arnold Meyer from Bonn. All in all, there were 318 delegates, 243 "active" and 75 "passive," 250 Swedish and 68 non-Swedish.

Söderblom's paper cannot possibly have been presented to the congress in the form in which it appeared in the volume of proceedings. In the proceedings it takes up almost seventy printed pages, and if read out in full could hardly have been completed in under three hours. There follow in the proceedings fifty more pages of "discussion," which if really took place as reported would have meant an evening of Wagnerian proportions.[49] Undoubtedly some of what was said was reported, and what was reported was in part what was said. One cannot be more precise, and Söderblom's paper must be taken as what he would have liked to have said, had he had the time.

Actually it is a very remarkable document, showing close acquaintance not only with the writings of Christian Socialists, but equally with secular socialists. Karl Marx is quoted frequently, not always with disapproval. There is discussion of social justice, wages, working conditions, rights, strikes, class warfare, solidarity, and much else which would hardly be out of place in a late twentieth-century theology of liberation. But Söderblom did not on this occasion appear in the guise of a Christian revolutionary, bent on lending the support of religion to whatever measures the socialist left might advocate for its own reasons. On the contrary, he insisted that religion (and throughout his paper he spoke very explicitly of "religion" as in the main Protestant Christianity) was an independent entity, operating on its own principles and not capable of being subordinated to any other without distortion. But that did not mean turning back the clock to any type of preindustrial society, and he criticized the tendency among French Catholics to appear to be trying to do just that by undoing the Revolution, obliterating the memory of Voltaire, and resurrecting the spirit of Joan of Arc. Protestantism's danger was a different one, that of becoming subservient to the spirit of the middle classes and the civil service, and entangled in public values appropriate to only a part of society. Nevertheless, thanks to the heritage of Luther and Calvin, Protestantism had the better chance of being able to return to the ultimate sources, and in the work and witness of Carlyle, Maurice, and Kingsley in Britain and Wichern, Stöcker, and Naumann in Germany was well on the way toward doing precisely that.

Jesus, on the other hand, though he was the friend of the poor and the despised, was not a revolutionary: "And I have often thought that in the modern world he might consider that the rich (*besittande*) and the well-off classes, with their advantages, their stocks and shares, could probably get along without him, and that it would be those who bear the burden and heat of the day . . . who would have rather more right to count on his sympathy and help."[50]

The followers of Jesus for their part ought to be capable of creating fellowship and understanding, even in the midst of manifest inequality, and of working toward a better and more equitable future. Of course the socialist mind would have none of that, even in Söderblom's day. Given the inequality, understanding and reconciliation must be forever impossible, and the only option open to the lower classes was and is out-and-out war. In the socialist position, however, Söderblom saw some serious faults. First was its stubborn belief in the perfectibility of human nature, given education and persuasion. That Söderblom as a Christian could not accept. What, he asked, of sin and guilt? Can human beings always be relied upon to lay aside their own selfish interests in the interests of the class or the race? Clearly not. This has never happened, and it can never happen. In this regard, the socialist left is without respect for the human reality, and makes human beings into something which they are not and can never be while separate from the grace of God: morally perfect (though perchance ignorant) beings. Further, even the socialists do not necessarily practice what they preach, and Söderblom quoted the anonymous epigram: "les socialists donnent à leurs partisans, le curé donne à tous" (socialists give to other socialists, the priest gives to everybody).[51]

Although the Christian congregation provides a basis for human mutuality and concern, and a prototype of a truly classless society, Söderblom was realistic enough to acknowledge that even this has not always worked in the past, quoting the horror story of the British and Foreign Bible Society failing to pay a living wage to girls in their bindery, forcing them into prostitution as a result. (Incidentally, Söderblom actually spoke of prostitution, avoiding all the customary circumlocutions of the 1890s.)

Concerning trades unions, Söderblom again appeared in the light of the cautious advocate of their rights, while being realistic enough to be unimpressed by the character and aspirations of some of those who had begun to emerge as trades-union bosses. He did not suggest that the church ought to align itself with any specific trades-union movement, but rather that its role ought wherever possible to be that of the peacemaker. Religion seeks to change society from within, slowly and indirectly, without tearing down that which it has no hope of rebuilding. In this connection it may be worth observing that in the 1890s the church was still in a position of considerable power in society, and that had the church so chosen, an honest attempt might have been made in this direction. Almost a century later, the church in the Protestant countries no longer occupies such a position. The secularization process has proceeded so far (and nowhere farther than in Söderblom's Sweden) that Christians wishing to change society are virtually reduced to the method of demonstrations outside parliament, rather than legislation within parliament, while the politicians are impervious to any form of persuasion other than that which threatens to lose them votes at the next election.

Nothing is so great that the kingdom of Christ is not greater. Söderblom's concern for the poor and the downtrodden of Western industrial society, whether in Paris or in Stockholm, was deep and instinctive. In this paper he was not, however, in a mood of compromise, or of submission either to the forces of the religious establishment to the right or to the agitating of the socialists on the left. Always he saw things in strictly personal terms: What does this or that situation mean to those individuals most closely involved in it? Who are those people? Have we ever tried to know and understand them? And if not, why not? The church possesses vast reserves of power and energy, of which it has grown practically unaware, and certainly blasé, while the people of the new industrial age were "voting with their feet" and staying away from the church in droves. The issues in 1897 were those of the right to work, the right to receive adequate wages, the right to rest and recreation, and the need for a fulfilling family life—all of these adding up to a sense of human dignity. To hate and dismiss the church, as so many of the German socialists were doing in the wake of Karl Marx, was to hate and dismiss the most effective cure for the ills of society at large. The church for her part seemed scarcely to recognize that a problem existed, save that of falling church attendances. All in all, it was time for a manifesto, for a declaration that these matters could be analyzed "scientifically" and aired in a congress devoted to the scientific study of religion.

Aside from his doctoral dissertation, the most important production of Söderblom's Paris years was an exegetical and theological study, *Jesu bärgspredikan och vår tid* (Jesus' Sermon on the Mount and our time), published in Stockholm late in 1898 but clearly completed before the "science of religion congress" of the previous year. It had begun life as a lecture delivered before the Paris Protestant theological society in May 1895, and had been inspired in part by his reading of Tolstoy, though also by the prominent place which was beginning to be taken by the Sermon on the Mount in the theological and particularly the "Kingdom of God" discussions of the time. A number of separate positions were being canvassed: that the Sermon is so idealistic and impractical that it cannot possibly be applied by anyone; that it *can* be taken at face value, though only at the price of complete separation from any "normal" social order; that it cannot possibly mean what it says, and needs to be reduced to what can be understood and applied; and that it has to be understood "eschatologically," that is, with regard to the early church's expectation of an early end to human history.

A little less than two hundred pages in length, Söderblom's book covers a great deal of ground, in an exuberant fashion and sometimes with a slight air of breathlessness. The doctoral candidate and the pastor in Söderblom take turns to occupy the center of the stage—though it is the doctoral candidate who generally speaking has the upper hand, or rather, who is offering the church the right hand of fellowship, in the hope of dispelling suspicion and (it must be added) of teaching the church a sounder method of scriptural interpretation. The actual exposition of the Sermon on the Mount occupies only a little over twenty pages in this study, the bulk being taken up by its relationship to Christian thought in various periods of the church's history, to "revolution," to the Roman Catholic church, and to Luther, among others. The last five chapters treat "special" subjects—marriage, the taking of oaths, war and resistance to evil, Christianity and culture (under the heading of "take no thought for the morrow"), and finally prayer and miracle. Illustrative material is taken from other religious traditions; the leading authorities of the period are quoted, but always with a view to discovering that which is *specifically* religious in the Christian, Protestant, and Lutheran traditions.

Even were it possible, there would be little point in attempting to summarize the whole of Söderblom's book. No part is without interest, and almost any part might be taken as illustrative of his theological and scholarly concerns. This being so, we are free to select.

This was, let us remember, Söderblom's first published book, written in Swedish and directed toward a home readership. In its pages he did not go out of his way to criticize Swedish conservative theologians but, although he did not name names, the gist of his argument and the direction of his criticism is very clear. For instance, the argument that (a) whatever Jesus said "in the Bible" must be true; (b) to take literally the injunctions in the Sermon on the Mount is unrealistic; therefore (c) Jesus' teaching must have meant something else, simpler and more practical, was common enough, then as later. Söderblom had met it in 1895 when he first presented his argument to the Paris theological society, and he knew that it was omnipresent in workaday Swedish Christianity. Literalist conservatism is one thing in theory, another in practice. In theory it affirms the whole of the Bible to be equally inspired, to the point of infallibility; in practice it selects and interprets. "Many who espouse the crassest form of the doctrine of inspiration—in theory, for in practice they all deny it—find no difficulty in freely reinterpreting Jesus' words in the Sermon on the Mount, or putting them on the shelf. In fact it turns out to be easier to incorporate a few more strange and irrational clauses into the church's Credo and claim them as a truth—which costs nothing—than to take the Master's uncomfortable words in the Sermon on the Mount completely seriously."[52]

The question then is not what Jesus ought to have said or might have said, but what he really said—a principle of "scientific" inquiry that the turn of the century was growing used to applying to non-Christian sources under the banner of "comparative religion," while still being nervous when those same methods were applied to the Christian sources. But the movement had begun. One of its most important focal points was the notion of "the Kingdom of God" in the teaching of Jesus.

From Kant, Schleiermacher, and Ritschl the "liberals" of the period had learned that the Kingdom of God was an embryonic ideal society on earth. Away in North America by the 1890s the advocates of the "social gospel" had already begun to inflate the kingdom idea into the be-all and end-all of Christian belief and Christian action in the world. The individualistic view advocated by Pietists and Evangelicals alike—that the kingdom's citizens are recruited one at a time through repentance and conversion—was in the process of being challenged by various forms of "social Christianity," of which the "social gospel" was only one variant. But this view in its turn had begun to come under attack, not on account of its dualism, but due to its methods of biblical interpretation. In 1892 Johannes Weiss had begun the assault with a book, *Die Predigt Jesu vom Reiche Gottes* (oddly enough, in view of its importance, not translated into English until 1971, as *Jesus' Proclamation of the Kingdom of God*). In it he had asserted with great force that Jesus had *not* taught that the Kingdom of God had anything to do with programs of social action, but that on the contrary, the kingdom in Jesus' teaching would be realized only at the end of the present world-order. In other words, it was and is an "eschatological" kingdom, that is, related to "the last things" (in Greek, *ta eschata*). For Weiss, the notion of bringing in the kingdom through the medium of determined social action was simply bad exegesis, a deposit of post-Enlightenment optimism for which justification was being sought in the wrong place.

In 1898, Weiss's reinterpretation of the Kingdom of God teachings of Jesus had won very little following, mainly because it was so obviously out of step with the theological Zeitgeist. Söderblom, on the other hand, had read his book, and was prepared to take it very seriously indeed. We must remember that Söderblom was in the midst of writing a doctoral dissertation on the subject of "the life to come," and that the question of eschatology was therefore close to the center of his concerns. But so too was the social application of the Christian message, and we have already seen what he had to say on that subject at the 1897 Stockholm conference. But Söderblom was still far too much of a Lutheran to be able simply to equate the two, in the manner of a Blumhardt or a Rauschenbusch.

Söderblom took up the Kingdom of God question in his *Sermon on the Mount* study, hailing the new eschatological emphasis as a valuable contribution to a more "realistic" interpretation of the Sermon:

> The words of the Sermon on the Mount were not spoken in order that they might serve as a law for a society secure in its cultural life, or in order to be incorporated into the dogmatic

schemes of churches which have found a permanent place in the world. Their object was to stress the absolute moral and religious conditions for membership in the Kingdom of God and thus to save souls, in that they are confronted by the final settling of accounts, which will not be long postponed. It is a vast and as yet a far from completed task to grasp Jesus' Kingdom of God teaching in all its richness and uniqueness.[53]

His old master Ritschl he praised for having taught Protestant theologians to take the Kingdom of God idea seriously, but then he went on to note (as Weiss had also done) that Ritschl had also been a consummate reader-in of his own interpretations and ideas into the biblical record.[54] For absolute eschatology Söderblom clearly had little real feeling. What then was his view of the eschatological question?

In brief, we might say that Söderblom took a mediating position. Of the eschatological emphasis in the teaching of Jesus there can be no doubt, but eschatology is "neither the only nor the most important element in Jesus' teaching on the Kingdom of God."[55] The most important element is the assurance to every person that the last judgment is coming, and that "opportunistic and social calculations" are of no importance in the face of this "unconditional imperative."[56] Had Jesus proclaimed *only* that the kingdom was imminent, then he would have been *only* a prophet. But he did more. That he performed "miracles" bore witness to the kingdom's presence and the kingdom's power: the blind were made to see and the lame to walk, the deaf had their hearing restored and lepers were cleansed. *These* had been the "signs of the kingdom" and the "proofs" of Jesus' Messiahship. And they were signs performed in the actual world, in a "here and now." But between this "here and now" and the kingdom still to come there remained a tension, an element of paradox.

Söderblom concluded that what was most original and most creative in Jesus' teaching was *not* its "eschatological" content—an element which was common enough in some Jewish circles in his day—but *his uncompromising individualism*.[57] Jesus had in effect removed the individual from the protection of the group and placed the individual face to face with God. "The infinite value of the individual human soul is the dominant idea in the Sermon on the

Mount and the whole of the teaching of Jesus"[58]—and here Söderblom refers approvingly to a sermon by the Swedish Pietist Anders Nohrborg. Thus, individualism is that which is best and most characteristic in Christianity, and the "hierarchical ideal" which would deny this is a product of a "romanization and latinization of the Gospel of Christ," an ideal more appropriate to Islam—the most theocratic and anti-individualistic of all religions—and is not to be countenanced in the world of the Gospel. Again and again Söderblom expresses himself in the language of Pietism, and beyond Pietism in that of Luther: the individual's calling is a matter of the faithful performance of religious and moral duty, and there are no shortcuts. But what paradox there is exists between the individual's calling in this life and the expectation of the life to come: salvation is an individual matter appropriated here, but with consequences hereafter. "For the Christian, the new age has begun in and through the knowledge of Christ and his work, but it has not been completed."[59]

Söderblom concluded this section of his book by stating that religion was never intended merely to be an idealistic superimposition upon culture (which we ought rather to spell *Kultur*, since the Swedish idea was strictly that of nineteenth-century Germany). Religion must be different. It must be independent. The Sermon on the Mount is there in order to prevent the world from sinking into self-satisfied slumber: "Without it the world would decay in the midst of its glorious culture and its social evolution."[60] The Sermon is a spur—certainly uncomfortable, but nonetheless necessary—but a spur urging on individuals as they are, and not societies as the theorists would have them be.

I have spent rather a long time on this part of Söderblom's *Sermon on the Mount* book, mainly to show that on the absolutely central matter of the Kingdom of God he was still at this stage thinking in centrally Lutheran and Pietist categories. His "liberalism" still consisted more in the steps by which he arrived at conclusions, rather than in the conclusions themselves: in the range of evidence he used, rather than in the goal to which it led him. One who was becoming more and more involved in the "social Christian" movement might have been expected to have used the idea of the Kingdom of God in a more "social" sense. He did not, mainly because he was unable to manipulate the New Testament in that way. Nor was he prepared to go to the opposite extreme and characterize the teachings of Jesus as "eschatological" through and through—had this been the case, they would have been prophetic, but they would not have been original. No. At this point he was still in all essentials an intellectual Lutheran Pietist. It was appropriate that this book should have been dedicated to his parents, "with respect and gratitude."

In 1898 the professor of theological propaedeutics and theological encyclopedia in Uppsala, Johan August Ekman, was appointed bishop of Västerås. The news came as somewhat of a surprise to Söderblom, who had more or less reconciled himself to staying in Paris until Ekman's retirement, and this was not due until 1910.[61] But now there was an opportunity to apply for an Uppsala chair more than a decade earlier than anticipated, an opportunity that he could not but take. This would also involve sending in "specimens" of scholarly literature for the assessors to consider, and of these Söderblom at the time had too few, nor had he completed his Paris doctorate. But the decision was hardly in doubt; in June 1898 he wrote to his father that he considered it his "sacred duty" to send in his documents. Jonas Söderblom might have become an Uppsala professor, had he so chosen, and in a sense Söderblom felt himself to be following in his father's footsteps in applying.[62]

To N. J. Göransson he wrote in more detail three months later, saying that he had little hope of success: "Certainly Ekman's chair is giving us much to think about. But I can hope for no other result than that I might get a couple of works finished. My respect for the position of professor itself makes me feel that the idea of my applying is a piece of pointless bravado."[63] Concerning his "specimens," Söderblom had only his book on the Sermon on the Mount (not yet in print) and an essay on *Les Fravashis* (the French of which was much in need of revision). His *major* specimen, however, would be "what my Persian and other eschatological studies have brought me to: a *morphology of eschatology,* based on the most complete eschatology we possess, the Zoroastrian [*mazdeistiska*]. The chronological uncertainty that attends many Avestan texts will *not* influence the scientific value of this investigation."[64] And he concluded: "Am I now going to be able to achieve something? I have made up my mind to apply. This is the direction in which all my studies have been pointing for years. And I have had more opportunity to study comparative religion than has Eklund [his most serious competitor]. But I don't know. And in any case some consider my theology—or lack of theology, whichever it might be—as an absolute hindrance in the way of my usefulness in Uppsala."[65]

This same feeling of inadequacy was to surface in other letters of the time: "What have I to give? Please cut your expectations down to what you can expect of a kind of missionary in the dispersion, who has grown less and not more academic over the years. When I write, I think just as much about people as about scholarship. And in the last reckoning it seemed fairly clear to me that I am made to be a minister, Sam to be a bishop and you to be a scholar."[66]

Chiefly, it would seem, Söderblom's nervousness was due to his not being able to allow himself to believe that anyone belonging to the Fehr school could or would be assessed on his merits by the conservative wing of the Uppsala faculty. Samuel Fries had just failed such an application, and was pessimistic about Söderblom's chances, writing that he had no real trust in academic justice: "I have experienced it and know that the gentlemen in Uppsala are capable of every kind of 'scientific' villainy."[67] Fries's pessimism was to continue, and as the appointment procedure went on, he was to supply Söderblom with a string of reports and rumors concerning his prospects: that one opponent had said that "heathenism" in Söderblom's person must be kept out of the faculty at all costs; that it was being said that Söderblom had already failed his Paris doctorate; and more in the same nervous style.[68]

Out of five applicants, in the end there was a short list of only two. Söderblom was one, the other was Johan Alfred Eklund, three years Söderblom's senior, who had the added advantage of having been Ekman's assistant since 1896 and acting professor since 1899. Undeniably he was better known locally than was Söderblom; also, he was trusted by the conservative wing of the faculty. Eklund had annoyed Söderblom by writing a scornful review of Sabatier's *Esquisse* in 1898, making clearer the real issue of the professorial election as a contest not so much between two individuals as between two theological schools, of which the conservative was in Swedish terms by far the more powerful.[69]

The issue was not finally decided—in Söderblom's favor—until the late spring of 1901. In the meantime, however, Söderblom had moved far out of the reach of Eklund in terms of international recognition, and of this even a somewhat suspicious faculty of theology in Uppsala could not remain unaware.

The monograph which won Söderblom the title of *Élève diplômé de l'École Pratique des Hautes Études, Section des Sciences Religieuses*, in 1899 was entitled, in full, *Les Fravashis: Étude sur les traces dans le Mazdéisme d'une ancienne conception sur la survivance des morts*. Published first in *Revue de l'Histoire des Religions*, volume 39, this seventy-seven-page essay also appeared separately, with a dedication to his three Uppsala friends, N. J. Göransson, S. A. Fries, and Samuel Freidenfelt. Almost alone of Söderblom's Iranian-based publications, this essay has been treated with a certain respect by at least some later specialists in the area—though that is of little consequence.

The *Fravashis* in the Old Persian texts were, to quote a more modern authority, "the pre-existent eternal souls of all good men and women."[70] Söderblom's interest, however, was less in their preexistence than in what became of them after death, and how they fitted into the pattern of early Zoroastrian belief and especially worship. His study he divided into three parts: first, concerning the rituals attending death and the dead in ancient Iran; secondly, the reasons behind those rituals; and thirdly, the objects of the rituals, the *Fravashis* themselves. Although based on a close study of the relevant texts, he made much use of comparative material from other religions and cultures to illustrate the steps by which the *Fravashis* came to occupy their place in ancient Iranian religion.

His contention was that they represented a popular survival of an earlier, undocumented stage of culture in which they were simply ghosts, and as such were both revered and feared. To look upon the dead in this way—to lament for them, to sacrifice to them, to welcome them to the counsels of the family or tribe—was in no way uniquely Iranian, being altogether characteristic of primal agricultural communities generally. But in later Iranian belief, as in Catholic Christianity, ways were found to lessen "la domination tyrannique que le culte des morts a exercée," by incorporating the *Fravashis* into a larger doctrinal system.[71] In the Avesta, the primitive excesses of the cult of the dead have been suppressed: there, the dead are still important, "mais leur tyrannie est finie."[72] Nevertheless there are still connections between the souls of the dead and the home, water, and plants; they still offer protection against enemies and relate in various ways to the heavenly bodies.

The problem of the *Fravashis* is, however, more than just a problem for Iranists. It is a problem for the history of religion, containing as it does an apparent contradiction between the less than desirable state of the dead on the one hand, dependent on the living for sustenance, and their superhuman power on the other. There is also a tension between the proximity and the remoteness of the dead. Which came first, Söderblom asks, the worship of the dead or the belief in the survival of the soul after death? Posed in this way, the question hardly admits of an answer, though Söderblom opts for a somewhat euhemeristic explanation, that the worship of the dead represents a continuation of reverence paid to living human beings, being "primarily a hypothesis to explain the authority exercised by the deceased ancestor over the feelings of his descendants."[73] But although they are powerful, the ancestors are not gods, which leaves this theory far short of Herbert Spencer's "manism."

Les Fravashis was of course a preliminary study for one side of Söderblom's dissertation on comparative eschatology, covering part of the theme of *personal* eschatology; cosmic eschatology he left aside on this occasion. The greater part of his argument was solidly based on Iranian texts. The interpretation, on the other hand, came rather from the anthropological wing of comparative religion and its theory of "primitive survivals" in even the greatest of the world's religious traditions. (Doubtless it was this element that has lessened its value in the eyes of the pure philologists.)

The Iranist Sven Hartman has written of this monograph: "In the whole of Söderblom's production, this is the essay which I appreciate most. In it we find an excellent combination of cultic and textual analysis on the subject of the Fravashis, which usually represent the spirits of the departed. A great deal of material is concentrated in its 77 pages. Nyberg praised this monograph in 1943, writing that it was 'of its kind still not outdated.' In my opinion the same might still be said in 1982."[74]

As well as submitting specimen publications, Söderblom had to go through one other formality in applying for the Uppsala chair. Since he had not completed his dissertation as originally planned in

1894, neither had he had the opportunity to deliver the trial lecture which would have placed his foot on the lowest rung of the Swedish academic ladder. So it was that in November 1899 he returned briefly to Uppsala to deliver the necessary lecture. It was held on November 11, and was on the subject of "The Significance of Schleiermacher's *Reden über die Religion*: A Centenary Tribute."

Why this subject, rather than something from the Iranian field or from comparative religion? There were two reasons. First, in *Les Fravashis* he already had one specialist work in the Iranian field, and in *La Vie future* he soon would have a large-scale comparative work. But secondly, the chair for which he was applying was a theological chair in which apologetics was an important component. Therefore he needed to demonstrate his ability to deal with a theological and apologetical subject. What greater modern apologete had there been than Friedrich Schleiermacher, whose 1799 lectures to religion's "cultured despisers" had just been reissued in a centenary edition by Rudolf Otto?

Fortunately, Söderblom printed and distributed his thirty-two-page lecture. It was wise that he did so, since in many ways it provides the best and most concise statement we have of the spirit in which he approached the Uppsala chair, and of his intentions, should he be appointed. Actually it would seem from the first sentence of the lecture that Söderblom had been faced with choosing from among a list of subjects specified by the faculty of theology, this being the one that appealed to him most. Even so, it suited his intentions perfectly.

The appearance of Schleiermacher's *Reden* in 1799 had, Söderblom observed, marked an epoch in Protestant theology. Before him was the Age of Reason, celebrated by Tom Paine at the eleventh hour before it was overtaken by romanticism; after him came an understanding of religion dominated by feelings and by history.[75] Before him there was a belief in the power of rationality to dispose of everything; after him, a recognition of deeper and more pervasive forces. The essence of religion, Schleiermacher had claimed, was to be found not in thought and action but in *Anschauung* (attitude) and emotion. The pursuit of metaphysics has its justification; ethics and morals are equally necessary; but religion cannot be encapsulated in either. "Praxis is art, speculation is science, religion is a sense of and a taste for the infinite."[76]

Perhaps Schleiermacher's understanding of religion was only

marginally Christian. Still, it could be interpreted in Christian terms to mean that "religion is not anything we do, nor is it anything we might think about God, but what God does with us; also that we can know God only to the extent that he reveals himself to us."[77] The heart of religion therefore lies not in theories nor in moral attitudes, but in revelation, as apprehended by the individual. This Söderblom calls a "psychological" observation. To this he adds a second, "historical" observation:

> Religion must be observed in actual religions; natural religion [as arrived at by the Age of Reason] is a nonentity. Real, genuine religion always appears in the form of a positive, historical religion. In other words: religion not only has a psychological justification, aside from metaphysics and morals; it also has a historical justification, independent of the washed-out pictures the human reason constructs for itself and calls religion.[78]

From Schleiermacher the student of religion may learn something of the utmost importance for the comparative study of religion: "that no paradigms or generalizations must prevent the reality of religion in history from coming to full expression."[79] So-called natural religion was never either natural or religion. Real religion is individual, eccentric, haphazard; natural religion "hates every form of originality and individuality."[80] Above all it could never come to grips with spontaneity, and therefore with the ecstatic and irrational side of religion. In its desire to establish religion-in-general, natural religion was ready to despise religions-in-particular; in its quest for artificial universals, it overlooked real particulars.

Söderblom went on from this point (to which he was to return in a fuller form over a decade later)[81] to urge that the days in which a "naive unity" between religion, speculation, and morals, or between theology, philosophy, and ethics, could be proclaimed were past. "Religion has its own province in human life alongside, or if you prefer, behind speculation and morals. Theology has its own sovereign territory, despite having had to abandon the claims of the schoolmen to control the whole of human knowledge."[82] But when it came to describing that "province," Schleiermacher had been less clear. Nor does Söderblom on this occasion say precisely what this might mean, though soon the two questions of revelation and mysticism were to be brought in by him in an attempt to do so.

Söderblom ended his lecture by comparing Schleiermacher with

Ritschl, not altogether to the latter's advantage. Ritschl had been of the utmost importance to Söderblom a few years earlier; now, however, it was time for him to turn to an authority more spontaneous, less scholastic, less contemptuous of mysticism, more prepared to give a place to the spontaneous element of religion. If Schleiermacher had been right in allocating to religion a very special place in the human response to the world, however, did this not have far-reaching consequences for the *study* of religion in a modern university? Here Söderblom anticipated the theme of his inaugural lecture of two years later. The scientific study of religion is not necessarily antichurch in principle. There is no need to urge, as Stöcker had been doing in Germany, for the faculties of theology to be abolished and replaced by faculties of *Religionswissenschaft*. We must not attempt to avoid the dualism of faith and science "by bending, with the best will in the world, the straight line of scientific method, and establishing a quasi-science on the Catholic pattern in the service of the church."[83]

The epoch-making importance of Schleiermacher's *Reden* lay in their religious, and not in their theological, character. Schleiermacher was not a prophet to be compared with Paul, Augustine, Francis, and Luther, or a theologian to be compared with Origen, Thomas Aquinas, or Melanchthon. What he did was to introduce a new method of accounting into Christian theology. Luther gave him the capital, and he did not add to it. And Söderblom concluded: "Our immediate task is to see to it that the capital of religion does not come from elsewhere than from revelation and faith, and to make sure that amid all the proposals for a better accounting, the treasures of Protestant faith are not in any part shut out or dispersed."[84]

There is much of importance in the substance of this lecture. Notably there is the insistence that experiential religion is something sui generis and irreducible to the categories of either morality or metaphysics; there is the dismissal of natural theology, and with it, the facile assumption of the "common denominator" approach to the study of religion; there is the emphasis on "real," historical religions as the only sources of evidence concerning the nature of religion itself; above all, perhaps, there is the question of what in actual fact lies at the heart of religion to distinguish it from metaphysics and morals. Significantly, for Söderblom and for Schleiermacher's editor Rudolf Otto, that question was answered with reference to a religious experience—the experience of the holy, or sacred. Also there is the profound conviction that the scientific study of religion, if carried out professionally and conscientiously, *must* in the last analysis serve the cause of true religion. Lastly there is the equal conviction that true religion is that proclaimed most fully along a chain of tradition extending from Jesus to Paul to Augustine, Francis of Assisi, Luther and Pascal, to Kierkegaard and Schleiermacher himself—also to Ritschl and from Ritschl to Fehr. The perspective is wide—so wide as to be almost beyond the reach of one person to grasp, especially when filled out by all the material of the world's *other* religious traditions, all the prophets, all the lawmakers, all the visionaries, and all the footsoldiers of the great religions. Yet this was what Söderblom was setting himself to accomplish. Perhaps those who listened to his trial lecture understood all this; more likely most did not.

Söderblom's doctoral dissertation took final form during a period of some eighteen months, in 1899 and 1900. Söderblom's enormous Swedish manuscript, some of it barely legible (his handwriting, then as later, requiring special skills for successful decipherment), was translated into French by the daughter of the first Roman Catholic family the Söderbloms had come to know well in Paris, Barbe de Quirielle (who otherwise wrote under the name of Jacques de Coussanges). On Söderblom's return to Paris from a visit to Sweden in December 1899 the two worked together for two or three hours every morning. Some parts of the text the translator had been unable to decipher; some sections she had rewritten (not without certain misunderstandings, as she afterward admitted). But in their working sessions, discussion ranged far and wide, though always it proved to be the case that "Sweden occupied the forefront of his thoughts and interests."[85]

Very early in 1901 the work appeared, under the imprint of Ernest Leroux, as the ninth volume of the Annales du Musée Guimet. Its full title was *La Vie future d'après le Mazdéisme à la lumière des croyances parallèles dans les autres religions: étude d'eschatologie comparée*.

La Vie future defies summary. It is, however, important to remember that it was conceived and written not as a specialist study in Iranian eschatology, though the Iranian material supplies the hub around which all else turns, but as an extended essay in *comparative* eschatology. Its broad outline takes up in turn the various issues subsumed under the term "eschatology"—originally "the science of the last things"—not yet dissolved into general speculation concerning the meaning and end of human history.[86] The dissertation consists of five chapters: "Belief in the continuation of life"; "The doctrine of retribution"; "The end and physical renewal of the world"; "Eschatologies: the end and the new life of the world and of humanity, from the religious and moral point of view"; and "Eternal life obtained here and now through communion with God."

The proportion of the Iranian to the non-Iranian material in *La Vie future* is also interesting. A rough calculation shows that the Iranian sources account for no more than, at most, 39 percent of the book. The remaining 61 percent is "comparative," and here Söderblom ranges far and wide through all the interconnected mansions of comparative religion, from the "primitives" through the Ancient Near East and India, Judaism and Islam, to Greece and pre-Christian Scandinavia. The last forty-five pages are devoted to the subject of "Eternal life in Christianity." Sundkler has written that "the whole volume is, from one point of view, only a preparation for the final section of the book."[87] This may be a little overstated. It is, on the other hand, abundantly clear that Söderblom was here summing up all that he had so far learned from the comparative study of religion, and that in his view, the study possessed a teleology of its own. Dispassionate, "value-free" recording of the evidence without any attempt to draw conclusions from it was totally foreign to Söderblom. Those conclusions, however, might be of more than one kind.

First there was the historical question that had impelled Söderblom into the comparative field in the first place: had Judaism (and hence Christianity) borrowed extensively from Iranian sources in shaping its own beliefs concerning the end of the world and the resurrection of the dead? Söderblom never believed that such a large-scale borrowing had ever taken place. *La Vie future* therefore is in part an attempted vindication of this conviction. Space does not permit a summary of his arguments. We may, on the other hand, cite his conclusion: "In sum, Jewish eschatology owes to Zoroastrianism [*mazdéisme*] only a few insignificant details; it was certainly not inspired by it. There is only one important point on which

Judaism might have been subject to a certain influence due to its contact with Zoroastrianism, and that is in its idea of resurrection. But even this idea has a Jewish origin and developed along independent lines; it may have exercised influence, but at least it was not borrowed."[88] Söderblom pointed out, on the other hand, that Avestan and biblical eschatology provided the material for one of the most striking of *Islamic* doctrines, namely, the belief in the coming of the Mahdi—which belief draws on both the Iranian doctrine of the Saosyant and the Jewish doctrine of the Messiah.

A second historical question had to do with the relative impact of the Jewish and Hellenistic components in the formation of early Christianity. Here the whole of Söderblom's argument tends in a Hebraic direction, at least to the extent to which he returns his argument again and again to the person of Jesus himself. The stress Jesus placed on his own person in respect of final salvation is in no way comparable with the roles of, say, the Buddha or Socrates in their traditions: it is "a fact unique in the history of religion."[89] This of course brought up the difficulty of basing eschatological faith on a single group of historical events and one single historical personality, once critical historical science had entered the scene. Söderblom at this point is content to accept the paradox of the infinite in history in Kierkegaardian terms, and declines to discuss it further.[90] History has brought scholarship back to the person of Jesus; what subsequently happened to Christianity in the Hellenistic world was another matter, and this Söderblom does not tackle. A later age would not be prepared to stop at that point—which is perhaps another way of saying that historians taught by Harnack to read the evidence in their way would ultimately have the upper hand of theologians taught by Ritschl to read it in another.

Is it too crude to characterize the members of the *Religionsgeschichtliche Schule* as HISTORIANS of religion, and the post-Ritschlians (among them Söderblom) as historians of RELIGION? The former were pulled away from the church, while the latter were drawn closer to it. Neither group was necessarily better or worse informed than the other where the factual material was concerned. But whereas the former group made use of historical evidence to relativize the transcendent and encapsulate it in the categories of a given time and place, the latter used the identical evidence to transcendentalize the historical process itself. In Söderblom's case, the publication and successful defense of *La Vie future*, while bringing to an end his academic apprenticeship, also marked him out as a comparative religionist significantly different from those gaining ground in Germany at the time. We should be unwise to read it in isolation from his work on the Sermon on the Mount, or without reference to his position as a social Christian. As Tor Andrae has said, Söderblom's relationship to science was "not impersonal." He had not set off in an Iranian direction "merely in order to be able to report the way things once were."[91] He had entered the field in order to make a theological point—as his own statements bear out. Only in his study of *Les Fravashis* did he become so far mastered by the Iranian material as to produce a monograph acceptable in style and approach to later Iranists, among them Widengren and Hartman.[92] *La Vie future* was least of all a piece of dispassionate historical reporting; rather it marked his point of departure for a career in the theology of comparative religion.

Söderblom's disciple and biographer Tor Andrae was not himself an Iranist, having taken up the study of Arabic and opened up the byways of early Islamic tradition, while having a second string to his bow in the field of the psychology of religion. He gives no real account of *La Vie future*. Later scholarship has had little to say about it, finding it hard to locate in any accepted professional field. Van Veen notes only that his dissertation *"maakt hem spoedig bekend"* ("quickly make him known").[93] R. C. Zaehner disliked it, perhaps because Söderblom's theology was of the wrong kind.[94] Sven Hartman is noncommittal, though he does draw attention to a passage from the original Swedish manuscript which did not find its way into the final French version, and which read: "Seven years ago I began these studies in the eschatology of Mazdeism with the purpose of discovering its influence on Judaism."[95] Of more recent scholars known to me, only S. G. F. Brandon would seem to have made much use of *La Vie future* in the context of his own investigations into the problem of eschatology.[96]

It is, however, striking that, once *La Vie future* had been printed, Söderblom never again returned to the serious study of Iranian religion. Iran to him had been an exercise in the theological implications of the comparative study of religion. His philological capacities in this area probably always were somewhat limited, though doubtless adequate for the purpose for which they were needed.

Out of the issues raised in its pages, however, there were to emerge many further publications.

Söderblom's public examination (in Swedish parlance, disputation) took place in Paris on January 24, 1901. Presided over by Sabatier in one of his last public appearances, the disputation lasted for four hours. The three examiners (only one of whom was an Iranist) were Albert Réville, Alfred Lods, and Léon Marillier. Söderblom's *apothéose triomphale* was complete when he was awarded the highest mark attainable, making him the one and only doctor of theology ever to be created by the Protestant faculty of the Sorbonne. The disputation over, Söderblom promptly went back to his seamen in Calais![97]

The first year of the twentieth century was also the year in which Söderblom won international scholarly recognition. From being an overworked pastor of a church practically without parish boundaries, following his other, academic calling in whatever time he could find amid all his other duties, in a few short months he became a scholar with an international reputation.

But it was as though the Determiner of Destiny wanted him to be under no illusions that he was, in fact, crossing a frontier in more than one sense. In 1895 one transition—from Uppsala to Paris—had been marked by the death of Fehr. In 1914 another—from professor to archbishop—was to be marked by the death of Fries. In 1901, between his academic disputation and the final confirmation of his Uppsala appointment, death intervened twice to remove the two men he respected most highly and loved most deeply. In April 1901 Auguste Sabatier died, and in June Jonas Söderblom followed. These were Nathan Söderblom's living links with his two identities, the "elder brethren" to whom he gave his devotion, representing the nineteenth century in scholarship and religion respectively. It was as though Söderblom's new century was to be one in which he would have to find his own way.

Sabatier was already very ill in January 1901, but accepted a dinner invitation, even though on a milk diet. He had received his copy of *La Vie future*, and was reading it with pleasure: "I feel myself [he wrote] in deep intellectual sympathy with the overall conception and with the conclusion of your masterly study."[98] Mme. Sabatier had been wondering whether her husband's *Esquisse* might perhaps be nominated for a Nobel Prize, and Sabatier passed on the message, while confessing himself "assez détaché de tout cela."

Soon *La Vie future* was being read by comparative religionists everywhere in Europe and welcomed as a bold and innovative work. Edvard Lehmann pronounced himself amazed by its breadth and scope.[99] The Nestor of the discipline, C. P. Tiele, apostrophized it as "this new proof of your erudition and wisdom," adding that although he did not always agree on points of detail, nevertheless he admired the book as "a serious and profound study of the subject and above all as a comparative study."[100] Paul Sabatier, St. Francis of Assisi's Protestant biographer (no relation to Auguste), confessed that on reading Söderblom's "admirable book," "I felt overcome by the wish to leave Assisi and the thirteenth century to plumb with you the curious states of mind of these strange peoples," adding that at a time when Catholicism seemed more and more to be slipping into "materialism, politics and superstition," it was good to see that Protestantism was on a path of renewal.[101] Samuel Fries shed a tear over the book, confessing (before having read it!) that the very sight of it made him feel like "a pygmy in scholarship."[102]

What all these people had in common was the conviction that comparative study, if carried out scientifically, would show that New Testament Christianity was *not* merely an untidy and incomplete synthesis of other religions and superstitions of the time, but unique and distinctive in everything of religious importance. This was what Söderblom had learned from Moulton, and this was what divided his position from that of the *Religionsgeschichtliche Schule*. The question now was what the members of that *Schule* would have to say about *La Vie future*.

The answer came soon enough. In May Söderblom's book was reviewed at some length in *Theologische Literaturzeitung* by none other than Bousset himself.[103] The tone of the review was entirely positive; the book was called "most important" (*hochbedeutsam*), and its author welcomed as a new recruit to the professional guild of Iranists, qualified initially by *Les Fravashis* and now by *La Vie future*. However, Bousset was compelled to disagree fairly substantially on some points: he felt, for instance, that Söderblom was arguing a priori in stressing the difference between the Iranian material on the one hand and the Judeo-Christian on the other; also, he considered that a good deal of Söderblom's material was irrelevant to his main argument. Bousset's view was that the resemblances far outweighed the differences. If the differences actually had been as far-reaching as Söderblom was claiming, then later Judaism would have had to be far more creative than Bousset was prepared to allow. On that point, Bousset's mind was already made up—that the eschatological literature of Judaism was the product of a tradition in decline, a fringe manifestation scarcely measuring up to the prophetic tradition. Nevertheless, Bousset concluded, "we theologians" are grateful to Söderblom for opening up an obscure field *mit grosser Gründlichkeit*—with great attention to detail.[104]

As winter passed into spring, it was becoming more and more likely that Söderblom, his earlier misgivings notwithstanding, would be appointed to the Uppsala chair. Although the final decision was not due to be made before July, already in February Söderblom felt confident enough to tell the desperately ill Sabatier of the likely outcome. Sabatier was too weak to answer Söderblom's letter, but told his wife, "Si quelque chose pouvait me faire du bien . . . c'est cette bonne nouvelle."[105]

Writing from Sweden, Fries was unable to muster up a like confidence, though he felt that with a monumental work like *La Vie future* before them, even a partly hostile faculty of theology in Uppsala would find it hard to reject Söderblom. Fries himself was applying for a chair in Lund, and still in February writing that it would be hard for them to turn him down.[106] Hard or not, they did so—though since this is not Fries's story, we have to leave the related intrigues on one side.

On March 21, 1901, the faculty of theology made its decision. To the last, Fries had feared that the conservatives might win out: "It is always possible that things might go wrong."[107] Ten days later he was able to write that his fears had been unfounded: "In a month and a half you will be a professor."[108] And that, strictly speaking, was what mattered. Out in the Swedish parishes, the news of Söderblom's preferment had not been taken kindly. One especially wild rumor, as reported by Fries, was that if Söderblom were to be appointed to Uppsala, the archbishopric would have to be moved to Lund![109] Another—this time emanating from Rabbi Klein—was that Waldemar Rudin had been to see the queen and had petitioned her to see to it that Eklund was appointed. Klein had wondered whether it might not be worth his while to deliver a counterpetition to the king on Söderblom's behalf. Fortunately for the Swedish royal family, Fries had managed to persuade Klein not to! By this time, Fries was seeing conspiracies everywhere. As we have said, he was in the process of suffering yet another disappointment on the academic front. Later in the year, he was writing to Söderblom as his "comrade in arms" (*vapenbroder*), by now home and dry in Uppsala, of his sense of loneliness and of the "feeling of the compact injustice they have been trying to do to me."[110] But while Fries was working in a field on which every theologian had the firmest and most deeply entrenched of opinions, that of the interpretation of the Bible, Söderblom had in a manner of speaking moved beyond the range of criticism by taking up Iranian eschatology—a subject on which only one member of the Uppsala faculty had any opinion at all, and of which practically no other minister of the Church of Sweden at the time had ever heard.

On March 21, 1901, Söderblom's appointment was ratified by the Uppsala faculty of theology, by a vote of four to two, the two negative votes being those of Danell and Quensel. But the good news was turned to bitterness shortly afterward. Auguste Sabatier died (of cancer of the stomach, it would seem) on April 12. At their last meeting, he had taken Söderblom's hands and said: "Vous ne savez pas, quel bon et cher ami vous êtes devenu pour moi." In his diary, Söderblom wrote:

> Sabatier, Sabatier, is the glorious time in Paris to come to such a bitter end? On Friday April 12, 1901, Auguste Sabatier died at 12:30 midday. We saw him, like himself, no paler than at my disputation. Rest and peace after his terrible sufferings. Once he said to my wife, when they gave him morphine: "Je me demande ce que Saint-Paul aurait pensé de la morphine, lui qui savait si bien apprécier la souffrance." The end came quietly. He was conscious to the last. During the night he said: "Je remets mon âme entre tes mains." The last thing he said before the last half-hour, when he could no longer speak, was with an effort and only audible in part: "Notre père qui est aux cieux." The memorial service will be in l'Oratoire du Louvre, but his remains will be laid in Vallon, his home village, where his peasant forefathers fought for their faith. He also did battle,

with the same sacrificial spirit, the same tenacity, under the conditions of another period, for the evangelical faith, for its success and victory. He understood, something which those whose vision is limited by the horizons of the church could not understand, and for which they (who see in a constant reformation a constant threat to their sickly power base) could never forgive him: that the evangelical faith can emerge victorious only if it is faithful to its origins, and therefore only if it satisfies itself with nothing less than to be and possess the best in our culture.

Enter into the joy of thy Lord, enter in, thou good and faithful servant.[111]

Söderblom had met C. P. Tiele in Leiden for the first time a couple of years earlier. Tiele was the old master, one of the "founding fathers" of comparative religion in Europe, Söderblom still essentially the apprentice. Tiele, however, was impressed by Söderblom's qualities and by what he had so far published in the pages of *Revue de l'Histoire des Religions*, and, as we have seen, had proposed to his publisher that Söderblom should be approached with a view to editing a new German edition of his *Kompendium der Religionsgeschichte*. Söderblom had actually agreed to do this in the previous year, happy for the recognition it implied while being a little apprehensive at the amount of time it would take. But better was to follow.

On April 19, 1901, only four days after Sabatier's funeral, Söderblom happened to be breakfasting with the Swedish minister in Paris. One of the other guests, a Professor Lieblein, broke the news that Tiele's successor in the chair at Leiden was to be a Norwegian, W. Brede Kristensen, and that the runner-up was a Dane, Edvard Lehmann. In third place there was a Swede. But what was his name? "Sö . . . Söder . . ." Lieblein could not remember. "I felt myself blushing," Söderblom wrote in his diary, "as the minister explained that I was the one. I had *never* expected anything like that. Three Scandinavians!"[112]

Söderblom had not in any way applied for the Leiden chair, and indeed was already practically certain of returning to Uppsala. But this gesture of recognition was important to him at this juncture. Otherwise it is remarkable that in its search for a successor to Tiele, the Leiden authorities should have considered only this trio, a Norwegian, a Dane, and a Swede. But they were a formidable trio. Kristensen was preferred mainly because he had studied under Tiele, and spoke Dutch. But he was of a more retiring disposition than either Söderblom or Lehmann, and in the end exercised far less influence internationally than did his two friends and colleagues. The two Dutch-produced German-language textbooks, Tiele's *Kompendium* and Chantepie de la Saussaye's *Handbuch*, were turned over to Söderblom and Lehmann respectively.[113] A decade later, the two were to be found occupying the only chairs of comparative religion that then existed in Germany, in Leipzig and Berlin. In the late 1890s the chances of such a spectacular development would have seemed practically nonexistent.

On May 14, 1901, Tiele wrote to Söderblom, saying that he must not think that "we put the list together out of mere politeness; we would have been happy to have had any of you."[114] Lehmann, however, assured Söderblom that he would not have dared to accept the Leiden chair, even had it been offered to him.[115] Nor, in all likelihood, would Söderblom, even had he been unsuccessful in Uppsala. As it was, he was expecting the final confirmation of his appointment in late June or early July. In the meantime, however, he was to suffer another personal blow.

On June 23 a telegram arrived, saying that at home in Norrala, Sweden, Jonas Söderblom was dying. Nathan rushed home (it took him three days), pausing only to write to Göransson, then in Marburg, telling him not to come to Paris, and adding, "O that the dear, dear old man could live to experience my appointment!"[116] It was not to be, however. Jonas Söderblom died on June 28, though not before father and son had been permitted a long conversation on the life of the spirit. For many years the conservative Jonas Söderblom had been deeply suspicious of his son's theology. But while Nathan Söderblom was a liberal intellectually, still in questions of faith he was very close to his father's position. Such conversations had been rare in the past. In his diary Söderblom recorded much of what was said. One passage read:

> "Imagine that a poor lad like you should get such a high position. You know that I don't agree with you about some things, but that doesn't matter. Be very careful about what you say. But you know where the foundation is, in Christ, and you will

have to win over your opponents by working for that foundation and through your life. They call me a pietist [*läsarpräst*], but that isn't true. I have been a godfearing man, and so must you be. I have never wanted to belong to a party, only to save souls." "Yes, father, you have never spared yourself, you are my model in the way you gave yourself for the Church." "Yes, my conscience is clear on that matter."[117]

Apparently, too, at the end Söderblom's book on the Sermon on the Mount had won his father's approval.

Interestingly enough, the diary in which the death of his father is recorded passes on immediately to an (undated) draft of what was to be Söderblom's inaugural lecture. This may have been fortuitous. Many of Söderblom's diaries were odd notebooks, written irregularly and unsystematically, but the link is intriguing for all that. Söderblom did not return to Uppsala in 1901 merely as an academic. He did so far more as a servant of the church, and there can be little doubt that the precept and example of his father was constantly in his mind. It may be laboring the point, but much in Söderblom's scholarship will be clearer if it be remembered that in *theological* terms, he was not really a "liberal" at all, despite his total acceptance of the principles of historical and critical scholarship. He never relaxed his hold on the fundamentals of the theological tradition to which he belonged, though like others of his generation, he had discovered new approaches to them and new ways of arguing about them. In all *religious* essentials, he and his father had always been of one mind. Writing to Rabbi Klein in Stockholm after his return to Uppsala in the summer of 1901, he recalled what had happened a few weeks earlier: "It was a precious and inestimable gift of God that I was allowed to hear my dying father's last message. *I know myself to be eternally united with him* [my italics]. God grant us all the grace to reach a peaceful end after a fruitful day's work."[118]

Söderblom arrived back in Paris on the morning of July 5, 1901. Later on the same day a telegram arrived, informing him that he had been appointed to the Uppsala chair. A month later, he was back again in Uppsala, wondering whether he had ever been away. His seven-year apprenticeship was over, and the real business of academic life could get under way.

5

Professor in Uppsala, 1901–1912

So many things have happened to me. The last few weeks have been calm, but I have been exhausted. Am I really in Uppsala again? Have I ever been anywhere else? Up to now I have had no time to measure my feelings. I have a feeling that it will be hard here.[1]

Personal upheavals aside, Söderblom was under no illusion as to the difficulties he would have to face on his return to Uppsala. Partly this was the thought of being among colleagues some of whom disapproved of him and his friends very strongly indeed. But there were also his professional duties. He had known for some months that he would have a heavy teaching program, on top of which he would have a church to care for (Holy Trinity, alongside the cathedral). As prebendary of Holy Trinity he would live some way out of town, at Staby vicarage; a more complete contrast to a Paris city apartment was hardly imaginable. Public speaking as such was by now second nature to him, but he had never previously had to sustain a program of regular university lectures and seminars—three or four public lectures a week, and seminars once every two weeks for specially enrolled students. On the other hand, the duties of Söderblom's chair were not defined with much precision, and therefore he would have considerable freedom to choose his lecture and seminar subjects.

Bengt Sundkler has compiled a complete list of the subjects on which Söderblom lectured throughout his Uppsala professorial career.[2] His lectures, attended by between forty and seventy listeners (not all of whom were students) began in 1901 with the general history of religion, and proceeded year by year through most of the main historical areas, ancient and modern. After 1910 he went on to phenomenological studies: prayer, gods, myths, legends, eschatology, and the like. Much of this lecture material found its way into print in one or another form, sometimes after a lapse of many years.[3] The seminar series generally had fewer student participants (as few as five in 1911). He began with "the philosophy of religion," and authors studied in detail were the Dane Harald Höffding, the Scotsman Andrew Martin Fairbairn, and the far more celebrated (or at least better remembered) Germans Eucken and Troeltsch. From there he went on to the study of the psychology of religion and mysticism, by way of Sufism, Madame Guyon, and Augustine. The fall of 1905 he devoted to Socrates, with a larger-than-normal student enrollment. Thereafter he and his students were to range far and wide through the interconnected mansions of religion, from Francis of Assisi to Teresa, from Buddhism to Bergson, and from Egyptian mystery cults to popular piety in Sweden.

Söderblom never felt himself to be a philosopher. Although the philosophy of religion was reckoned among the "preliminary studies" of his chair's title, he was less than happy about having to tackle what had never been his field. Writing to Göransson only a couple of months after his return to Uppsala, he spoke of his misgivings:

> In particular I have a strong sense that I am deficient in speculative gifts, and I feel the inadequacy of my philosophical substructure. I have missed out on too much to be able to fulfill this obligation. In the last analysis, I suppose that I shall never be anything other than a student, trying to the best of my ability to guide fellow-students. May the students not expect too much from me! There is only one thing in which I can be sure they will not be disappointed: that is in my enthusiasm and my good intentions.[4]

Among every new professor's first duties in Uppsala is the delivery of an inaugural lecture in the Great Hall of the University. Söderblom was free to choose a date, and of course a subject. As his subject he took *Den allmänna religionshistorien och den kyrkliga teologien* (The general history of religion and the theology of the church); the date, September 24, 1901, was his wife's thirty-fourth birthday.

In a sense the question of the relationship between the history of religion (or comparative religion) and theology was precisely that with which Söderblom had been wrestling for seven or eight years already, and it was therefore natural for him to have taken it up as his personal statement of intention. But another lecture delivered in Berlin a few weeks previously gave Söderblom's words added point. On August 3 one of Söderblom's mentors, Adolf Harnack, had addressed the question of *Die Aufgabe der theologischen Fakultäten und die allgemeine Religionsgeschichte* (The task of the faculties of theology and the general history of religion).[5] Whether or not Söderblom had Harnack chiefly in mind as he mounted the podium in the university Aula is unclear. However, a brief look at Harnack's position—in many ways diametrically opposed to Söderblom's—will be useful at this point.

Harnack's lecture argued *against* the admission of comparative religion into faculties of theology, on the grounds that the study of religion, if it was to rise clear of mere dabbling, must be based on the highest level of historical and linguistic competence in *every* area. Without such competence, the history of religions would be condemned to a hopeless dilettantism.[6] It is the business of faculties of theology, he argued, to study the Judeo-Christian tradition, and for this they are amply qualified; they are not so qualified in respect of other religious traditions. Buddhism, Islam, and the rest may be studied—indeed must be studied—but only under conditions of the utmost scientific stringency, which faculties of theology cannot guarantee. In any case, he added, Christianity is not one religion alongside others: it is *the* religion, the absolute religion, just as Jesus is not a master, but *the* Master, and must be the midpoint of theological investigation. Thus there is absolutely no need, as some were urging, for faculties of theology to be dissolved into faculties of *allgemeine Religionsgeschichte*—characterized by Harnack as "this unsurveyable science" (*diese unübersehbare Wissenschaft*). Let comparative religion be taught by all means, but in faculties of arts, not in faculties of theology.[7]

In a postscript to his lecture as subsequently published, Harnack was more specific still. Of comparative religion textbooks he was scornful. The tomes of Tiele and Chantepie de la Saussaye—the only surveys then available, Tiele's having just been turned over to Söderblom for revision—he dismissed as useless and unreadable: "Anyone who is able to read through Chantepie de la Saussaye has my warm admiration."[8] And even were chairs of comparative religion to be set up, where could professors be found to fill them?[9] The historical background to the Old and New Testaments should be studied: it should be taught by subject specialists for the sake of the light that can be thrown on the background and origins of Christianity. But beyond that, faculties of theology have no direct responsibility, except perhaps marginally, in the training of future missionaries.

Söderblom knew of Harnack's lecture (though at that stage he might not actually have read it in its entirety), and in his inaugural lecture mentioned one of its main arguments—that the scholar possesses everything needed for the study of religion within the Judeo-Christian tradition—in passing.[10] The situation in Germany he was not, however, prepared to accept as normative. Certainly Germany had "scientific" theologians in profusion, from whom he had learned much. Where they were unsafe guides was in respect of the relationship between theology and the church. Part of the trouble, Söderblom felt, was that in Germany there were far too many university theologians having no experience of the practical work of the Christian ministry, and in the absence of that experience they had to some extent contributed to the level of suspicion that often existed in Germany between university theology and the church. But, insisted Söderblom, such suspicion was by no means a necessary consequence of the acceptance of a "scientific" theology.[11] It was, on the other hand, a consequence of what had been happening in Germany, cumulatively over many years in respect of biblical criticism, and intensively in the 1890s in respect of *Religionsgeschichte*—a subject to which we shall return shortly. Söderblom, newly returned from France and with valuable contacts in Holland, felt on this occasion that he had far better models to call upon than those provided by Germany.

What he was setting out to show in his lecture was that there could be a "scientific" study of religion that was church-related without being confessionally dominated. He began by surveying what had already been done in Europe and America to establish the new approach to the study of religion, taking his examples from Switzerland, Holland, Belgium, the United States, and of course the France he had left only a few weeks earlier. The wide-angle study of religion, he insisted, could not be excluded from the universities without descending into "barbaric ignorance," but neither could it be shunted off into faculties of arts or subsumed under some more general concept, such as "culture-history": its subject matter was too distinctive to permit that particular shortcut. And although at the heart of religion there lay an unanalyzable and enigmatic experience of God, the churches should not expect to have the study of religion entirely under their control: "The science of religion must preserve its independence without having any ecclesiastical character and without a deliberate practical end in view."[12]

Söderblom dismissed out of hand the notion that only the totally uncommitted were the right and proper persons to study religion. One might as well, he stated, claim that the tone-deaf were those best fitted to study music. No, acquaintance with the innermost content of religion was a sine qua non for its understanding. This might seem to give theologians a built-in advantage in the study of religion, except that this was not the way in which things had worked out. The church was fearful of comparative religion and comparative religion was scornful of the church, neither understanding the other. In the light of this misunderstanding, simply to shut theology up in one academic compartment, comparative religion in another, would do no more than exacerbate the situation. In Germany even academic theology had almost parted company with the church—and in Söderblom's view, scholarship in the university setting (including the comparative study of religion) had its justification only to the extent to which it actually served the church. The goals of the two were, in the light of scientific inquiry, not two goals, but one: "Every piece of scientific research into religion, provided always that it is carried out with competence and has to do with important matters, must serve the cause of religion, with or without the researcher's will, whether he is conscious of it or not."[13]

As to the subject matter, though Harnack had drawn a clear line of demarcation between the Judeo-Christian and other traditions, to Söderblom all was subsumed under the category of "religion." The whole must be sought and grasped, and though this may be a long and difficult task, it must not be shunned: "Do not be premature! Dare to expect distant results! Dare to work for distant goals! In our individual lives, as in history, many times we have had the experience of finding that events that once had terrified us . . . long afterward were seen to be blessings."[14]

The church cannot afford to neglect comparative religion. Nor can it, on the other hand, acquiesce in a tame acceptance of total religious relativity. "All comparative religion must in the nature of things lead to an evaluation of the various religions."[15] That involves knowing what religion is, and within religion, knowing what Christianity is. For in Söderblom's view, comparative study would inevitably demonstrate what was new and unique in Christianity, and not merely that in which it bore resemblances to other traditions. There are such resemblances, demonstrations of God's "general revelation" to the world. But over and above that there is the "special revelation" of God in Christ, the content of which it is absolutely essential that the theological enterprise should attempt to fathom. One must compare the teachings and the person of Christ with those of other prophets, saints, and revealers (among whom Söderblom was already prepared to give pride of place to the Buddha on the one hand, and to Zoroaster on the other). Only when this is done can one *demonstrate* the claims of Christianity to be the absolute and final religion, as opposed to the bare *assertion* that it is so.

What was remarkable about this statement was not, strictly speaking, anything it contained. Practically every word could be paralleled from elsewhere in the liberal Protestant tradition of the time. As an illustration we may perhaps take the words of James Hope Moulton (remembering that it was Moulton who first inspired Söderblom to begin the study of Iranian religion), published a dozen years later but expressing identical sentiments:

> We may claim that Christianity has proved its claim overwhelmingly. Our study of Comparative Religion has made us thankful for the truth understood by those who have not yet received the Gospel, and has removed the reproach which narrower views of God brought upon religion. He has not left Himself without witness anywhere, nor allowed a small proportion of His children to monopolize the life-giving knowledge of Himself. But the more carefully and sympathetically we study other religions, the more clearly does it appear that Christ completes and crowns them all.[16]

These, however, were tones unfamiliar to Sweden, where "narrower views of God" were still largely in force. Still newer was the spirit in which, at the close of his lecture, Söderblom addressed the students of theology who made up a considerable part of his audience.

Already the students of theology were in the main Söderblom's supporters. In his personal address to them (the full text of which is reproduced in Appendix I below), he made them his admirers; some of them he made his slaves. You will find many who pity you, he told them, for being students of theology and the servants of an outmoded church: I congratulate you! I congratulate you on the excitement of the theological enterprise, and on being privileged to keep company with Amos, Hosea, Isaiah, Jeremiah, Paul, Augustine, Francis, Luther, Pascal, Kierkegaard—and with Jesus. Certainly there is a crisis in the study of theology, but this is due not to theology itself, but to narrowness and foolishness on both sides. Therefore, he went on, "I can say to you with confidence, out of my own experience: not less science, but more science, a deeper sense of reality, more serious research: for with it will come new clarity, new humility, and new strength."[17] Alongside this remember your role as pastors, especially in troubled times: "You are natural peace-makers in the class war," so avoid taking sides, avoid identifying yourselves with one or another social class: simply be human.

These words reflected an optimism the like of which had not been heard in a Swedish theological faculty for many a year. Ever since Söderblom's own undergraduate days in the 1880s, to be a theological student had been tantamount, in the eyes of the radicals, to being a naive obscurantist. Not knowing how to meet the radical challenge, theology itself had retreated behind high confessional walls. Now, perhaps, it was time for something new to happen. One of the students in the audience was Gustaf Aulén. Almost forty years later he was to record that Söderblom's words had the sound of "a brilliant fanfare," and went on: "Those of us who heard the address were not used to hearing tones like these. Refreshing and encouraging, they reached us as heralds of a new era. They aroused hope, and hope was not disappointed. It was not long before we were able to claim categorically that a change had come about in the climate of theological opinion."[18]

Söderblom made his mark on academic life in Uppsala remarkably quickly, partly through his lecturing, partly through his preaching, but to no small extent through the force of his personality and the breadth of his interests. Years later the Norwegian scholar Lyder Brun reminisced:

> In the course of a visit to Uppsala late in 1903 I gained a vivid impression of how much he had come to mean, so soon after his return from Paris, to the study of theology and student life in his own university town; and at the same time of how wide his circle of acquaintances was. . . . One day when he invited me to dinner out in his home together with a group of academics, the people I met were almost all non-theologians. He told me that he saw enough of ministers and theologians at other times; now he wanted me to meet men and women from another milieu.[19]

That even after a couple of years in Uppsala Söderblom found a certain sense of relief in distancing himself physically from at least some of his professorial colleagues is obvious enough. To most of them, and to one or two in particular, he simply belonged to a different totem. As Sundkler has observed, "His colleagues in the faculty may have had reason to think that they did not know where he stood theologically; Söderblom, on the other hand, realized that he knew *their* positions only too well."[20]

We do not propose to pursue the domestic controversies of Söderblom's first few years in Uppsala, except to say that they came along with dismal regularity. Those who had not wanted him as an Uppsala professor in the first place missed few opportunities of showing it, in ways sometimes subtle, sometimes clumsy, and often petty. His sense of belonging and yet not belonging to the faculty of theology wounded him more deeply than most realized. It is small wonder, then, that he sought his friends elsewhere. Fortunately there was Anna at home to confide in. In Stockholm there was Samuel Fries, making one hopeless attempt after another to break into an academic establishment that had long since made up its mind to have nothing to do with him. The sensible Göransson could still be reached by post. So too could that kindred spirit Edvard Lehmann in Denmark.

In Uppsala, his friends came mainly from among the historians and philologists of the faculty of arts. Chief among the historians was the great Harald Hjärne: Söderblom had admired him as a student, and now they became firm friends. Heinrich Schück, professor of literature, was another. Among the philologists there were Almkvist and Zetterstéen in Semitics, Noreen in Nordic languages, Danielsson in Greek, Persson in Latin, and Johansson in Sanskrit: "it was easy for them to find their way to Söderblom's house."[21] A few years later, when the time came for Söderblom to put together his modest Swedish counterpart to the mighty Max Müller's *Sacred Books of the East*, these were the men who did the hard work of reducing the languages of the history of religions into careful Swedish.

Unlike the theologians and churchmen, these men supported him fully. But otherwise Söderblom had to maintain his professional position chiefly through the written word, in a voluminous correspondence with colleagues elsewhere in Europe, and in a series of Swedish-language books and essays. Of course what he most wanted to do was to establish the "scientific" study of religion in Sweden, but this was least of all what some of his theological colleagues wanted. Partly this was because, although they had very little knowledge of what was happening in this area in most parts of the world (other than what Söderblom had told them in his inaugural lecture), they did have some acquaintance with the waves of controversy that had washed around the subject of *Religionsgeschichte* in Germany over the past decade or so. Söderblom had touched on this matter in his inaugural, and we must take a moment to examine the controversy a little more closely.

In 1913, describing the origins of the *Religionsgeschichtliche Schule*, Hermann Gunkel wrote:

> From the beginning we understood by *Religionsgeschichte* not the history of religions, but the *history of religion*. . . . Our work was permeated by the idea that the ultimate objective of the study of the Bible should be so to look into the heart of the believers of the time as to enter into their innermost experiences and give them adequate description. We desired not so much to think about the books of the Bible and their criticism as to attempt rather to discern in them living religion.[22]

In view of its importance to the history of twentieth-century religious and theological ideas, it is curious that there would seem to be no full account in English of the personalities, history, methods, and approaches of this group of scholars, and few even in German.[23] In English we hardly know even what to call it, though most writers have opted either for "the history of religions school" (which is wrong) or "the religiohistorical school" (which is imprecise). It is far too easy to miss the point made by Gunkel, that in its label—apparently coined by Wilhelm Bousset in 1903—the word "religion" is in the singular, and not in the plural. (In English we have the same semantic carelessness in respect of "comparative religions" versus "comparative religion" as shorthand for "the comparative study of religion" in the singular.) Certainly the members of the school began with the Judeo-Christian tradition, moving outward from there into the hinterland of the Ancient Near East on the one hand and Hellenism on the other. Their intention, however, was more ambitious: in illuminating a historical problem, that of the interplay of traditions in the ancient world, they sought to penetrate to the heart of religion itself.

In 1901 none of the eight most prominent members of the school—Albert Eichhorn, William Wrede, Hermann Gunkel, Johannes Weiss, Wilhelm Bousset (generally acknowledged as primus inter pares), Ernst Troeltsch (the chief ideologist of the group), Wilhelm Heitmüller, and Hugo Gressmann—was more than forty-five years old, and most were in their thirties. Thus it was a young men's movement. Its background, theologically and historically speaking, had been largely identical to that of Söderblom and his circle: proceeding from Wellhausen and Baur, through various intermediate stages, to the theology of Ritschl and the historical investigations of Harnack, thence out into the Umwelt of the Bible. In many ways the school was a Ritschlian movement, or a deviationist subdepartment of Ritschlian theology. As Verheule has written, it was "in the first instance an intra-theological movement." But although taking their point of departure from Ritschl, these theologians were moving away from him in important respects; their key signature was not so much that written in by Ritschl as that superimposed by Schleiermacher—notably less systematic and more spontaneous, by no means limited as Ritschl had been by a dislike of the irrational and the "mystical."[24]

The three principles of the movement, as it emerged in the 1890s, were all to some extent contra-Ritschlian. First, the members of the school concentrated on religion, rather than on theology; secondly, they had a notable interest in popular, or mass, religion, and not only in high-level doctrinal statements *about* religion; and thirdly, they insisted that the origins of Christianity are to be understood only if adequate attention be paid to its contemporary background in the Hellenistic world.

The first notable book produced along these lines was, perhaps, Gunkel's *Die Wirkungen des heiligen Geistes nach den populären Anschauungen der apostolischen Zeit und der Lehre des Apostels Paulus* (The fruits of the Holy Spirit according to the popular views of the Apostolic age and in the teachings of the Apostle Paul, 1888). In 1892 there followed Weiss's book on Jesus' message of the Kingdom of God and Bousset's study of Jesus' teachings in contrast to those of Judaism, and in 1895, Gunkel's *Schöpfung und Chaos* (Creation and chaos) and Bousset's *Der Antichrist*. From this point on, the floodgates were down: books, monographs, essays, and reviews poured forth, and these like-minded scholars coalesced into a school.

In point of subject matter, the first great discovery was that the space between the Old and New Testaments was far from having been religiously empty. In between there was "later Judaism" (*Spätjudentum*), the world of Apocrypha, Pseudepigrapha, and Apocalyptic, and it was out of this, rather than out of the Old Testament, that the New Testament and the early church had emerged. The second was that once Paul took Christianity out of the Jewish world, opened "a door of faith to the gentiles" and set it free in the Hellenistic world, there was a vast new background area to be taken into consideration—the world of the mysteries and the initiations, Greek, Egyptian, Anatolian, Persian, and perhaps even Indian. This discovery, however, was only just beginning to be made when Söderblom returned to Uppsala in 1901. Richard Reitzenstein's *Poimandres* (1904) was to set this second trend, and the same author's *Die Hellenistischen Mysterienreligionen* (The Hellenistic mystery religions, 1910) was to be a definitive statement. As yet, though, that lay some way in the future.

It will be evident that the theological progression from confessional orthodoxy to Ritschl and from Ritschl to Schleiermacher, with Harnack holding the historical middle ground, was precisely the path which Söderblom had followed. Can Söderblom, then, be classified as at this stage a "corresponding member" of the *Religionsgeschichtliche Schule*?

In some ways, perhaps he can. Nevertheless, in one important respect he was of a different disposition. The school by and large was coolly disposed to the Christian church as it existed in Germany at the time. As Söderblom had hinted in his inaugural lecture, the trouble with many German radical theologians was often that they had had no pastoral experience, and were little concerned to relate their academic findings to the needs of congregations. Söderblom was finding conservative churchmen hard to shift in a scientific direction; in Germany his colleagues were hardly disposed even to try. True, they were prepared to spend time and effort to popularize their findings among the educated laity. But there were significant reasons why they were finding it difficult. For one thing, they were laying a great deal of emphasis on the Jewish element in early Christianity, and this German nationalism found distasteful. For another, their populist interpretation of the early church suggested a form of retrospective socialism, and this too was problematical. Above all, their implicit suggestion that the Christian message was less the product of a sublime revelation than a haphazard conglomeration of fragments from what I once heard described as "the *religionsgeschichtliche* menagerie" was starkly unacceptable to the orthodox. The school spoke much of religion, but seldom of the church—and therein lay the point at which Söderblom parted company with it.

Söderblom was not German, and therefore was not caught up in the intricacies of the German religious and political situation. More importantly, he did not stand in relation to his church in the position the Germans occupied in relation to theirs. But that having been said, two qualifications may be added. Intellectually, his position and that of the school were greatly similar; he had read, it is safe to say, all that they had read and written, and one side of his mind was certainly that of the *Schule*, many of whose members and associates were his personal friends. The other qualification must, however, be that whatever his intentions, those in Sweden who suspected him of being less than orthodox were all too ready to classify him with the German historians of religion as an enemy of the church as they understood it. To Söderblom there could be no question of the history of religion being anything other than in the church's best interests. "I cannot," he had said in the course of his inaugural lecture, "understand my church in such a way as to suppose that her cause should stand in opposition to the cause of religion, [or] that she might perchance exclude the religious needs of the modern educated classes. To suppose that would be to misunderstand her interests."[25] And the "cause of religion" implied the cause of the study of religion, its historical and critical study according to the best methods then available. A decade later, significantly, it was Söderblom's churchmanship that, in combination with his international scholarly reputation, was to secure him an appointment in Leipzig.

It would have been remarkable indeed had Söderblom been able to produce any large-scale scholarly work so soon after *La Vie future*, and amid the pressures of readjustment to Uppsala. However, within the next couple of years he was able to begin the work of consolidating comparative religion in Sweden. Work on Tiele's *Kompendium* he found tedious and time-consuming: "It would be more fun, and easier, to write something of my own."[26] Being a professor of theology had forced him to consider his own theological position, and this he was finding difficult. He was neither the first nor the last comparative religionist to be pulled in two directions, in one direction by his personal faith and in another by science. In January 1902 he confided to Göransson:

> In theology I suppose that I shall never be other than a seeker after truth, since I don't seem able to state my own position clearly. But I have a position, at least to the extent that it is clear to me that the revelation in Christ is supramundane [*öfvervärldslig*], different from everything else in the history of religion, an incarnation in flesh and blood. My own religious experience convinces me strongly that that is a revelation of God himself and of his saving power, so that I—paradoxical and unphilosophical as it may seem—can rest my religious assurance on Jesus alone, as that which all the rest of what the world contains could not sustain. But how can I formulate my theological position, in terms of which philosophy, and how can I reconcile it with the idea of evolution? That is the problem.[27]

There were echoes here of Sabatier, and also of Ritschl (Söderblom was by no means the only post-Ritschlian to speak in these terms); but there were also older echoes, of Pietism and the Evangelical

Awakening, though without their particular form of biblical support. The root problem, however, concerned the nature of revelation, in Christ and beyond Christ, or as the terminology of the time had it, "special" and "general."

One can barely deal with questions of this magnitude in textbooks, which are designed to present merely an elementary factual basis for tyros. Söderblom was, however, able to publish occasional articles on the subject. Two call for special mention. They were provoked by his reading of two entirely different authors, the mercurial Scottish anthropologist, folklorist, historian, and poet Andrew Lang, and the German Assyriologist Friedrich Delitzsch.

It is greatly to be regretted that Söderblom would seem never to have corresponded with Andrew Lang, since the two certainly had interests in common (while being vastly different in most other respects). Lang was originally a classical scholar, but was attracted to anthropology through his reading of E. B. Tylor. In the 1880s he had championed Tylor's evolutionary theory of myth over against that of Friedrich Max Müller, but in the 1890s he had broken away from Tylor over the subject of "high gods" (Lang's term for primal creator-gods who, so he believed, could not possibly have "evolved" out of ghosts or lower denizens of the spirit world). Lang had written on the subject in two books, *Cock Lane and Common Sense* (1895) and *The Making of Religion* (1898).[28] These Söderblom had read, along with Lang's other anthropological works, *Custom and Myth* (1884) and *Myth, Ritual and Religion* (2d ed., 1899). He was impressed both by Lang's versatility and by the strain of common sense running through his books, even when dealing with matters curious and irrational enough in themselves—for Lang was also something of a specialist in hauntings, extrasensory perception and the like.

In 1902, Söderblom's first scholarly article as professor had the clumsy title of "Andrew Lang's Theory of the Oldest Form of Religion Accessible to Us," and was devoted very largely to a summary of Lang's arguments *for* taking seriously the presence of "high gods" at an early stage of cultural development, and *against* the all-sufficiency of Tylor's animistic hypothesis.[29]

Söderblom's Lang article is basically a summary of the latter's arguments, as found in the second edition of *Myth, Ritual and Religion*. These are by now well known, and we have no need to summarize Söderblom's summary. The main point Lang was making was that the moral conception of deity does not necessarily belong only to a late stage in human evolution, but rather that it was there from the beginning—or would seem to have been, from the evidence we have. This of course contradicted the normal evolutionary pattern, as represented by Tylor, Frazer, and the other Victorian anthropologists. Wrote Söderblom: "Andrew Lang's suggestion is one of the most remarkable that is presently to be found in the comparative science of religion. It opens up unexpected and wide perspectives. Probably it will take many years before his hypothesis can be gratefully laid aside as having been made use of, accepted in its main outlines or reduced to its true value."[30] This was not to say that he accepted everything in Lang's construction. No one ever has. "But [he went on] I am bound to add that in his main point—a high creator god among the lowest races—Lang builds on information and combinations that cannot be challenged."[31] With all necessary reservations, he concluded, it is impossible to dismiss Lang's main result, "or absolve [oneself] from the duty of absorbing his work. The science of religion shares with every other science the fate of being forced constantly to revise itself. It is not improbable that Lang's discoveries will bring about a considerable upheaval in certain branches of the history of religion."[32]

Söderblom never took Lang's theories to the extremes they were taken a few years later by Father Wilhelm Schmidt, who pressed them into the service of Catholic apologetics as in essentials bearing out the truth of the biblical record. Söderblom might have been expected to have done so, except that his sights were set at a different level, even in the matter of apologetics. In his book on the origin of religion, *Gudstrons uppkomst* (1914), Söderblom was to make further use of Lang's arguments; there, however, Lang's "high god" has become Söderblom's "Producer" (in Swedish, *frambringare*), and part—but only part—of the early religious panorama. "Söderblom would not accept . . . Lang's ambition to derive the belief in God solely from such gods."[33]

While scholarship for the most part proceeds calmly and deliberately in accordance with its own internal laws and conventions, from time to time there are little explosions of activity precipitated by a theory, a publication, a discovery, a lecture, a personality, or all of these in combination. One such catalyst of opinion was introduced into the debate on January 13, 1902, when the German Assyriologist Friedrich Delitzsch delivered in Berlin the first of three lectures on "Babylon and the Bible" (*Babel und Bibel*). A month later this lecture was repeated by imperial command in the presence of Kaiser Wilhelm II. A second lecture, also attended by the Kaiser, was given in January 1903, prompting a furious rejoinder from the Kaiser, who did not like what he heard. A third and final lecture followed three years later, in 1905, by which time a considerable war of words had been fought out around the *Babel und Bibel* theme.

What was at issue in all this was the accuracy and the uniqueness of the Old Testament record. The first archaeological discoveries in Mesopotamia in the earlier part of the nineteenth century had generally been greeted calmly and even enthusiastically by Christians, who were sure that whatever emerged was bound to support the truth of the biblical record. This phase, however, did not last, particularly not after the decipherment of the cuneiform script. Now the Mesopotamian records could be read, and proved to contain many curious and uncomfortable parallels to parts of the Old Testament, notably to the flood story in Genesis. Then in 1887 there were discovered in Egypt the Tell el-Amarna tablets in the ruins of what had once been the capital of the pharaoh Akhenaton. By the mid-1890s much of this material had been published, and provisional conclusions could be drawn.

One was historical, the other theological. On the historical front, it was argued that practically the whole of the eastern end of the Mediterranean was for centuries under Babylonian cultural influence, to which the use of cuneiform testified.[34] Thus it was at least conceivable that Mesopotamian thought had formed part of the atmosphere that Israel had breathed. That was a question that only the specialist historian could attempt to answer, and during the *Babel und Bibel* debate many admitted that Assyriology was still in its infancy, and that it would not do to be too dogmatic on such complex issues.

What Kaiser Wilhelm had most of all objected to while listening to Delitzsch was his leaving the ground of the strict historian and Assyriologist he was employed to be, and venturing into the territory of religion and theology. "*Er erkennt die Gottheit Christi nicht an*"—he does not acknowledge the divinity of Christ.[35] This was what a shocked emperor wrote to the president of the German Oriental Society, Admiral Hollmann. In fact Delitzsch "harbored a deep antipathy to the religion of the Old Testament."[36] *Babel* came before *Bibel* in every sense: ethically and religiously as well as historically. Whatever of religious worth the Old Testament might perchance contain, thought Delitzsch, had been derived from Babylon: not only creation and flood narratives, but equally the Sabbath, the notion of sin, eschatological beliefs, the angels, and much more. The intelligent Babylonian, according to Delitzsch, had not been a polytheist, but had seen the images of the various gods and goddesses (almost in the manner of a modern Hindu) as symbols of one ultimate reality. Least of all, therefore, was there any unique divine revelation in the Old Testament. And of course, as Otto Weber pointed out, this "is not a historical question about originality and borrowing, but a religious question about revelation."[37]

One thing the larger theological community could not do was to answer Delitzsch on his own terms. It was simply unequipped for that task. This did not prevent many theologians and churchmen from trying. But it was left to a very few scholars who possessed both theological and Assyriological training—chief among them Alfred Jeremias—to draw attention to Delitzsch's extravagances on the one hand, and on the other to suggest that the question of revelation had little or nothing to do with the kind of question he had raised.[38] But in the same year that Jeremias published *Im Kampfe um Babel und Bibel* (The Babylon and Bible struggle), 1903, Söderblom took Delitzsch's lectures as the starting point for a statement of his own on the problem of revelation.

Söderblom's fifty-five-page essay *Uppenbarelsereligion* (The religion of revelation, 1903), subtitled "Some points of view provoked by the Babel-Bible debate," began life as a *Festschrift* article. Söderblom of course was no Assyriologist, and he made no attempt to do other than draw attention to the *religious* issues embedded in the debate thus far.

First, he pointed out what he had learned from Schleiermacher, that religion and morals are not identical: "A lofty and strict and sensitive moral order without religion is a stately and admirable poverty, alongside which religion without morals is a shameful pretension."[39] Thus to argue about the primacy of Babylonian and Israelite ethical systems misses the mark altogether.

Secondly, he drew a distinction between two modes of religion. On the one side there is the "religion of revelation" of his title, on the other the "religion of culture" (*kulturreligion*). "There is a revelation of God wherever there is real religion."[40] It does not have to be a perfect revelation; provided that there is an intuitive sense of God there, it is real. And in this sense no religion is purely a product of culture; all religion rests on revelation. Culture and religion walk side by side, though seldom in step. But let the culture insist that religion must always serve the interests of the community or the state, and it will not be long before that which is centrally religious is lost sight of. At that point there enters the prophet, the revealer of the holy will of God, and there begins the "religion of revelation." Even then, however, it may be difficult to draw a line between the former and the latter, between what is culturally produced and what is revealed and re-revealed. For the prophet in the last resort moves on a level other than that of culture (whose more typical representative might well be the priest). He is the "genius" in the world of the spirit.[41] He receives a *special* revelation of the holiness and will of God, and passes that revelation on to the people.

What we have here is Söderblom's own adaptation of what in 1903 was still a relatively new distinction between "general revelation" and "special revelation," and of the fulfillment of the former in the latter. Over the next two or three decades this was to become virtually a dogma of the liberal wing of Protestant theology, that the genuine but partial insights of the world's religious traditions are "fulfilled," brought to completion, by Jesus Christ as the greatest of the prophets and revealers.[42]

Söderblom's 1903 essay contained a further distinction, between contrasting types of religious experience. On the one hand there is that which proceeds out of religion when religion is most closely linked with the natural or cultural process, and when the individual human personality is of less consequence. On the other there is that which emerges out of prophetic religion, in which the personality comes into contact with the living God. Ritschl had classified the former as "mysticism" and put it aside, concentrating instead on the ethical imperative of the latter. This Söderblom could no longer accept: neither the implicit devaluation of mysticism as an inferior form of religious experience, nor the one-sided moralism of Ritschl's version of Christianity.

What he did was to classify *both* as types of mysticism. He compared the most extreme representatives of the two kinds of religion he had in mind (leaving Babylon far behind in the process), the Buddha and Jesus Christ. Previously the Buddha had been the mystic, Jesus the prophet. To Söderblom, both were mystics: "But the two types do not stop there, but are always to be found also among the many who are religious at second-, third- or fourth-hand and refer back to the great ones, and, since the mysterious, indivisible and impenetrable is to be found in both, I propose to use the word 'mysticism' to describe both, and distinguish them from each other as the mysticism of personality [*personlighetsmystik*] and nature-mysticism, or perhaps better, the mysticism of infinity [*oändlighetsmystik*]."[43]

In the remainder of his essay Söderblom further described some of the differences between these two forms of religion, when regarded as ideal types. The mysticism of infinity is not without an ethical sense, but allocates to ethics only a purificatory role at a lower level than that of the experience for which it strives. Implicitly it is elitist, accessible only to the few; it is *blanda, tranquilla, devota, et religiosa*, and ultimately places reality *jenseits von Gut und Böse*, beyond good and evil.

The mysticism of personality is not without its visions and ecstasies, but does not make these central to its case. It allocates to personal authority, and especially to that of the prophet, a very special role. Its ultimate reality is not bland and tranquil, but a consuming fire, against which the believer can experience only *terrores conscientiae*, "fear and trembling." The line of such mystics proceeds from Jeremiah, by way of Paul, Augustine, and Luther, to Kierkegaard. It is not beyond good and evil; rather it is caught up in that very struggle, which it tackles head-on. It seeks not the elimination, but the purification of personality. And it is called forth by divine revelation.

Arguing along these lines, Söderblom had proceeded some way beyond the *Babel-Bibel* debate with which he had started. His intention, however, was to show that the kind of historical evidence cited by Delitzsch could not affect the revelation question one way or the other. We may quote from the last paragraph of his essay.

> The Christian church cannot base its assurance of having the revelation of God, the word of God through the prophets and in Christ, on any historical or psychological investigation. She cannot wait in uncertainty while that takes place, but she bases her assurance on the experience to which every reborn soul bears witness. . . . *But it is important that the claims that come of such assurance should be investigated in the light of the whole of the historical reality of religion in the world* [my italics]. Surprisingly, then, it proves to be the case that the assurance of revelation in Christianity is not merely analogous to the assurance that every religion possesses in regard to its object, but relates to a deep and clearly marked difference in history and spirituality within the world of religion. For the most part the comparative science of religion is still so blinded by the kaleidoscopic richness of its field, and so happy at having escaped—to its own as well as the church's comfort and true benefit—from the restrictions of the church's confessions, that it has not yet looked closely at this remarkable line of demarcation in the history of religion.[44]

In *Uppenbarelsereligion* there came together a number of strands in Söderblom's own personal intellectual development. There was the Pietist strand, learned in his youth and reinforced by his contacts with men as different as Moody and Sabatier. There was the historical strand absorbed from Hjärne in Sweden and Harnack in Germany. There was the comparative religion strand, to the study of which a good deal of the previous decade had been devoted. But over and above all this there was the factor of "mysticism," derived obliquely from his reading of Schleiermacher. A slight digression will be necessary at this point.

Why the years around the turn of the century should have witnessed such an upsurge of interest in, and proliferation of writings about, mysticism (especially among Protestants) is a subject much in need of thorough investigation. In one sense it was a matter of a generation reacting against an earlier overemphasis on the rational and moral side of religion. In another it was a genuine rediscovery of lost treasures. But in a third sense one is forced to conclude that the *words* "mystic," "mystical," and "mysticism" in these years became vogue-words, quite apart from the human phenomena to which they were taken to refer. Those phenomena—visions, auditions, out-of-the-body experiences of all kinds, the quest of oneness with the divine—could be given either a theological or a psychological explanation, and the rising star of the psychology of religion contributed notably to the manner in which the subject was tackled. But what in the end was at issue was the immediate, personal, spontaneous side of religion versus the rational, ethical, and communal—the ecstatic versus the controlled.[45]

During most of the nineteenth century, Protestants looked upon *Mystik* as a by-product of the Catholic temper, and upon *Mystizismus* as undesirable on every count, chiefly because whatever the word might be taken to mean, it implied the intrusion of irrationality into the sphere of the divine reason. In the Catholic Middle Ages, mysticism had flourished partly because of the unhealthy atmosphere generated in the monasteries and among the compulsorily celibate. Institutionalized opposition to mysticism among Protestants came to a head in the writings of Ritschl, who considered *Mystik* no more than a derivative of Neoplatonism.[46] Hence it was fundamentally sub-Christian (*an sich unterchristlich*), in many ways the opposite of the religion of the Reformation. To Ritschl, mysticism—and for that matter Pietism—was antisocial and incapable of contributing in any way to human progress.

Söderblom had of course learned much from Ritschl, chiefly about the importance of history. But he had not learned everything from him, and as his studies had proceeded in the 1890s he had seen how impossible it was to subsume the spontaneous, unstructured aspect of religion under the Ritschlian categories: "What I miss in him [Ritschl] is the enthusiastic, the spontaneous, the early Christian, the individually religious in its spontaneous, often strange, but nonetheless captivating expressions. Everything [in Ritschl] is so well organized. [I miss] . . . the wild, untamed, unpremeditated religious instinct. It was there in Pietism. Without it I am sure that the church, in spite of all its regular and normal piety, will have to live on a starvation diet."[47]

A couple of years later, the tide had turned. Rudolf Otto had reissued Schleiermacher's *Reden*, to which, as we have seen, Söderblom had devoted his 1899 trial lecture. In the same year in England W. R. Inge had published his book on *Christian Mysticism*—thoroughly Neoplatonic and at the same time highly rationalistic, but coming at precisely the right moment. This too Söderblom had read. Not for a few more years, on the other hand, was he to read R. R. Marett's *The Threshold of Religion*, but it had also been in 1899 that Marett had first spoken in public about "preanimistic religion," suggesting that religion had originated less with morals and primitive philosophies than with a sense of the uncanny in face of the humanly inexplicable. Taken together, Schleiermacher, Otto, Inge, and Marett, when added to the populism of the *Religionsgeschichtliche Schule* and the early findings of the psychology of religion, helped to create an atmosphere in which religious immediacy could be rediscovered.

That this should have been labeled "mysticism" would seem to have been no more than a consequence of the currency of the word at that particular time. Then, as later, mysticism remained highly resistant to precise definition, for how can one define the ineffable? Söderblom therefore was wholly within his rights in pointing out that there is more than one kind of spontaneous religion, and that spontaneous religion (i.e., mysticism) is by no means all of a piece. In the years to come, Söderblom was to widen out and seek fresh examples of his two categories, and to propose extensions of the process of revelation. But the fundamental contrast he established in this 1903 essay was to remain in force throughout the remainder of his life.

So too were the profound convictions on his part that the study of religion should first and last be concerned with "reality" (*verklighet*), that is, with what is actually *there* in the world of religion, and not what might be there or ought to be there, and that only on such a basis can any claim that Christianity might make to embody a normative revelation of God be substantiated. Whatever claims Christianity might make "should be investigated in the light of the whole of the historical reality of religion in the world." Without such an investigation, claims and assertions would remain at best hollow, at worst the merest special pleading.

Kaiser Wilhelm's infuriated response to Delitzsch's seeming lack of interest in true religion had had one positive consequence, in that it brought the question of the meaning and place of *Religionsgeschichte* before a much wider German public than might otherwise have been the case. To an educated minority, *Religionsgeschichte* appeared in the light of a discrediting of the church and its traditional claims to exclusive revelation, and this the members of the "school" did little to dispel. Most were notably interested in religion; few had any very high level of commitment to the church as it then was. But popular interest called for a more popular response than that which normally emerged from the literature of biblical scholarship. Before 1904 that interest had been met chiefly through the lecture circuit, and to some extent through the liberal church press.

The series of "popular pamphlets in the history of religion" (*Religionsgeschichtliche Volksbücher*), which was to do the most to weld the history of religion school into something like a unit, began in the summer of 1904 on the initiative of Wilhelm Bousset.[48] The plan was ambitious. There were to be five subseries, devoted to the New Testament, the Old Testament, comparative religion, church history, and the philosophy of religion respectively, all in all some ninety volumes. Some of the pamphlets achieved remarkable sales, for instance Bousset's *Jesus*, which by 1907 had sold twenty thousand copies. Whether the series achieved what it set out to do is impossible to judge, except in one particular: intentionally or not, it conveyed the impression of a scientific approach to religion standing in isolation from the ongoing life of the church. Those who wrote the *Volksbücher* were certainly the best scholars available, but they belonged to the universities rather than to the churches. So instead of awakening the larger Christian community to a sense of the importance of the scientific approach, they helped further the process of secularization by widening the gulf that already existed between the sanctuary and the academy. One result was a species of *Kulturprotestantismus*, elitist, intelligent, well-informed, and yet cool, if not actually hostile, to the simpler aspirations of the Christian majority.

In a sense, what this series set out to do was at least comparable with Söderblom's intentions with regard to the history of religion in Sweden, that is, to present the best scholarship of the day in assimilable form. Beyond that, however, the ways parted. Söderblom's scholarship was never other than work done in the service of the church, however culturally and geographically remote it might be. This was to have one important long-term consequence. When in 1912 Söderblom was called to Leipzig, it was chiefly because he was *not* a member of the *Religionsgeschichtliche Schule*, and did not share the school's generally negative attitude to the church.[49]

Mention has previously been made of Söderblom's friendship with his Danish colleague Edvard Lehmann. Valuable as they of course were, his friends in *Samfundet fritt ur hjärtat* were too much embroiled in the Swedish scene to give Söderblom that sense of distance and perspective that he so much needed at this stage in his career. This Lehmann provided—or rather, this Lehmann and Söderblom gave one another. Writing to Söderblom in December 1902, Lehmann had confessed that "my scientific soul cannot live without being conscious that there are colleagues who are working for the same cause, and that we are following one another's work."[50]

Among Lehmann's (and to some extent also Söderblom's) colleagues in Holland were Chantepie de la Saussaye and Kristensen, Tiele having died, full of years and honors, in 1902. Lehmann thought Kristensen "the best placed of the three of us," since he could devote himself entirely to scholarship. At the same time there was that in Kristensen's nature which, Lehmann felt, might prevent him from making a lasting contribution to scholarship—the Björnson side of his nature, better for poets than for scholars.[51] As to Chantepie, Lehmann had been engaged to do for his *Lehrbuch* what Söderblom was doing for Tiele: to bring it up to date, and actually to rewrite it (in German), though not on his own.

Of his oldest friends, it was to Göransson that Söderblom opened up most notably in his letters. Writing in August 1902 after a visit to his old home in Hälsingland, he confessed how touched he was to find his father's memory still fresh in Bjuråker, and how in his former home he had found a friendliness "strongly reminiscent of Paris, but hardly of Uppsala."[52] In May 1903 he spoke freely of his innermost convictions:

> I believe there to be a point at which the historian must cease to be merely a historian, and the psychologist to be merely a psychologist, and that is close to Jesus. The more one sees of

the history of religion, the more completely one is cured of the evolutionist tendency to make Jesus one of many.

But I believe that the dogmatic way of presenting Christ in our day is hardly bringing a single modern person a step closer to him, rather the opposite. For they are starting at the wrong end. They begin from above, "true God," instead of from below: with a change of heart. We cannot be convinced of and know anything about the supernatural without living in it.[53]

Over the next couple of months Söderblom's letters to Göransson returned to this theme on numerous occasions. Ought one to seek the psychologists' help in studying Jesus? Perhaps, in a sense, though even then it must be remembered that Jesus was part of the prophetic line from Moses, and "has a quite different relationship to God" than even the religious genius. The philosophy of history "must give him an entirely unique place."[54] "It is a circular argument to prove revelation by means of its content. But that is not quite what I am doing. I am simply presupposing revelation in the sense of God and his work. What I want to show is that in religion there appears a certain series of manifestations in such a way, psychologically, historically, and with regard to content, such that—irrespective of their value—the series impresses one as revelation in a special sense. It is a matter of degree."[55]

In the summer of 1904 it was once more time for a history of religion congress, this time in Basel, Switzerland, the second in the modern sequence after Paris 1900 and the third after Stockholm 1897. Although not published until a decade after his death, Söderblom's personal account is full of personalities and issues, and gives a fascinating picture of the state of the discipline at the time.

The congress was chaired by Professor Conrad von Orelli of the University of Basel, a guarantee, thought Söderblom, to the aristocratic burghers of Basel that "nothing harmful to religion and revelation should mark the congress."[56] Religion, however, was presented in many different ways. Some delegates preached, "despite the program": one such was the celebrated Paul Deussen of Kiel, who urged that since the human makeup consists of reason, emotion, and will, Brahmanism, Buddhism, and Christianity must be brought together, each having an appeal to one aspect of human experience. "It is that simple for the Kiel philosopher. But in reality it is more difficult and more complicated than that!"[57] Nor was Söderblom greatly impressed by Leopold von Schröder of Vienna, whose lecture on Aryan high gods he thought "strange" and whose approach he felt more romantic than scholarly. Moderate pan-Babylonism was represented by Alfred Jeremias. "There was much interest in his two lectures, delivered with resonance and sweeping gestures, as though they were about matters of importance for the highest life of humanity."[58] Although not aimed particularly at Jeremias, Söderblom allowed himself to observe that the extreme pan-Babylonians had fallen for the old illusion that "one key will open up all the locks of religion and mythology."[59] But without a sense of history, its reality and life, monotonous insistence on the primacy of Babylon is empty talk.

Other papers delivered at the congress and reported by Söderblom included one by Samuel Fries on "the prince of this world" in the Gospel of John, identified not as the devil, but as the Talmudic *Metatron*—which theory Söderblom loyally called "worth considering."[60] Also the school of Usener was well and worthily represented in the section on Greco-Roman religion, with the master himself present, and with Dieterich of Heidelberg as his most competent disciple. With approval Söderblom noted that Dieterich was now editing *Archiv für Religionswissenschaft*, and that "German scholarship now at last had a history of religion journal which might in time be comparable with the French *Revue de l'Histoire des Religions*."[61] And he concluded: "Among the delegates on this occasion there were very, very few of the sort of people who take the opportunity, in a more well-meaning than pleasing way, to be conspicuously religious. On the other hand among the 260 delegates there were numerous priests and ministers."[62]

Söderblom was in Basel together with one of his Paris teachers, Professor Eugène Ménégoz, who had for years spent his summers in the Swiss Alpine village of Mürren. There a young woman had died tragically of tuberculosis, only a month after giving birth to her first child. The two professors attended the funeral, conducted by the local organist, after a two-hour solemn procession in the pouring rain up hill and down dale. Söderblom had experienced worse in Sweden. But that same morning the baby had also been brought down to the church in Lauterbrunnen to be baptized, and that the organist could not do. Had Professor Ménégoz not mentioned that Söderblom was a minister of the church? A Swiss-style black gown was produced to cover his soaked outdoor clothes. The family gathered in the unoccupied manse, and from there, with Söderblom very properly in the lead, the family went to the church, where Magdalena Paulina Feutz was baptized by the visiting scholar. One recalls how that same scholar, not much more than three years earlier, had left his academic disputation at the Sorbonne to return to his seamen in Calais.[63]

During the eighteen months or so after the Basel congress, Söderblom published little of any consequence. This is not to say that he was inactive. On the contrary: one has the impression of days and nights of frantic work on several fronts simultaneously. But his bibliography for 1905 and 1906 is notably lacking in longer entries. Three published papers from 1906 were, on the other hand, later incorporated into the collection *Ur religionens historia* (From the history of religion, 1915), one on Christian missions and the question of culture, the second on the origins of secret rituals, and the third—a pioneering work, to which we shall return in a moment—on the place of intoxicants in the history of religion.

Most important of all was the editing of a Swedish sourcebook in the sacred literature of the world, which Söderblom was both organizing and supplying with material. This involved the writing of the whole of an introductory volume surveying as much of the field as was then considered necessary, and the translating into Swedish of a hundred pages or so of Iranian material as well as smaller sections devoted to Japanese and pre-Columbian American sources (naturally not from the original languages). Also there were shorter comparative religion textbooks in preparation, generally on the lines of the Tiele *Kompendium*, which since Tiele's death was now Söderblom's exclusive property. Viewed internationally, little of this work was breaking new ground. Most, on the other hand, was entirely new to Sweden—indeed, to the whole of Scandinavia.

Söderblom's lecture *Rusdryckerna i religionens historia* (Intoxicating drinks in the history of religion), subsequently published as *Rus och religion* (Intoxication and religion) was more novel.[64] Delivered on February 14, 1906, to a student temperance society in Uppsala, there was something slightly mischievous about the subject (Söderblom's sense of humor was well developed, as was that of Edvard Lehmann, and he was not averse on an occasion to *épater les bourgeois*). So on this occasion. The solemn young total abstainers heard first of all a quotation from Lord Byron (in English): "The best of life is intoxication," after which they were treated to an enthusiastic tour around a province of religion to which few, it is safe to say, had ever previously given a thought. The various "drinks of the gods" were reviewed in turn: mead, *soma*, *haoma*, wine, *eau de vie*. The intoxicated language of mysticism was dealt with, especially that of the Sufis. From there Söderblom went to the opposite corner of the ring and took up the religious history of prohibition, first in Buddhism and then in Islam and Zoroastrianism. Lastly he considered, briefly, the place of intoxicants in Christian history. And he ended by suggesting that there are two attitudes to life, calculating sobriety and being intoxicated by life itself. "I suppose that I consider being intoxicated by life good and necessary," he concluded, "but it must be drawn out of deeper and purer sources than any that the grape can provide."[65]

Only a few days after delivering this lecture Söderblom was taken seriously ill. He was still only forty years old. Basically the trouble was intestinal, though his heart might also have been affected. Anna Söderblom wrote to Göransson that "we have been at the edge, and I have been desperately worried. . . . He is so terribly weak, and I dare not hope for much."[66] He was given morphine and placed on a strict diet; in his diary he wrote pages of reflections which, I think, it would be improper to quote, except for one phrase: "the inner guest in the soul"—the God within who gave him strength and comfort in his physical and mental extremity.

There can be no doubt that one of the causes of this breakdown was the pressure of fighting for an unpopular cause amid the most compact and uncomprehending opposition. Another would seem to have been the great difficulty he found in ever relaxing. On the first count, there were individuals close at hand from whom Söderblom would much rather have separated himself altogether. Of one he wrote bitterly, during his convalescence: "From special love for us and care for our eternal destiny, he treats his misguided friends with super-abundant pastoral concern, in a manner which normal human morals calls—swinish."[67] In any case convalescence was a relative thing. Söderblom recovered his mobility quite quickly, and soon was in the thick of things again, beavering away at the introduction to his book of texts and writing long articles for Hastings's *Encyclopaedia*. He did what he had to do, but it was not surprising that he did not fully recoup his health during the next couple of years.

No professor in any subject—and least of all in a new and beleaguered subject—can avoid the responsibility of that subject's academic succession through the training of young men and women to carry on the work in later years. Söderblom's teaching was partly public, in the form of the lectures we have already mentioned. From these lectures were to emerge his most important books, and we shall have more to say about some of these later. But beyond that there was the guidance of young and aspiring scholars. Over the years there were a number of these in both Uppsala and Leipzig. Relatively few were to become internationally known. One who did, however, was the great Islamist Tor Andrae (1885–1947), who studied under Söderblom from 1909 to 1912, later occupied his chair in Uppsala, and in 1931 became his first biographer.

Having just graduated in theology, on a certain day Andrae was summoned to Söderblom's room and asked, to his astonishment, whether he wanted to become a lecturer in comparative religion. He stammered something about not being qualified, only to be interrupted by the impatient words: "That was not what I asked. I am asking you whether you *want* to!" In his Söderblom biography of 1931 Andrae characterized Söderblom as a supervisor:

> As an academic supervisor Söderblom was inspiring as few others could be. What was most notable was his generosity and his freedom from the nervous need always to be defending his own position. He had no trace of defensiveness in respect of his professorial authority and was big enough to be always able to acknowledge merit and ability, even that of the impatient, difficult and youthfully contrary student. This did not mean that he could not be a severe critic or that he could not, in a friendly but firm way, trim the young flame when he found it necessary. Here I can speak from my own experience. In my licentiate dissertation I had criticized, with the hopeful courage

of the beginner, current opinion on the Prophet Muhammad—
opinion which I knew the Professor shared—and had put forward my own views. It was met with quite devastating criticism. I still have it, with the Professor's comments, irritated exclamation marks and questions. To be sure, I have not felt it necessary to abandon all the opinions I expressed on that occasion, but I have never been more grateful to my teacher than for that thorough criticism.

To this reminiscence Andrae added some more general comments on Söderblom's style as a supervisor:

> Napoleon claimed that he never gave his generals detailed orders. He only ordered them to win battles. To be given too detailed instructions paralyzes inventiveness and the ability to use one's own initiative. This applies also to scholarly supervision. In scholarship as in life it is equally true that the teacher's first duty is to make himself superfluous. Söderblom gave his students great liberty. His supervision was limited to what was most necessary: to give the student a subject that in his view was scientifically important and feasible, and then to enthuse the student about precisely that subject. He gave me the subject of my dissertation [the understanding of the person of Muhammad as held by the earliest Muslim communities], chosen through a happy intuition. He put me in contact with Ignaz Goldziher in Budapest for initial guidance with the literature. After that, scientifically speaking, I was on my own. But without his continued personal encouragement and support my work would never have been completed. I relate this case only because it is so typical.[68]

In 1907 there appeared in France the first edition of a work which might be regarded as the last piece of French scholarship to feed into Söderblom's own interpretation of religion. This was Bergson's *L'Évolution créatrice* (1907; English translation, *Creative Evolution*, 1911). Henri Bergson (1859–1941) was of Jewish extraction, and became professor of philosophy at the Collège de France in 1900. His originality as a thinker lay in his dynamic conception of the time process. Being itself is least of all static; rather it is in constant movement and subject to constant change. Time brings forth constantly new forms of life, expression, and understanding. Further, it was a pillar of Bergson's thought that the true nature of things cannot be grasped by the human reason; it can only be intuited. However, the paths of life are neither causally nor finally determined: what will happen can never be predicted, simply because life itself is a free and above all spontaneous creative process.

From the first Söderblom saw in Bergson's work an affinity with the prophetic, eschatological consciousness. Certainly it was expressed philosophically rather than in religiohistorical or theological terms. But, he was later to ask: "Is it a coincidence that Bergson belongs to that people among whom the prophetic view of life, history, and God saw the light of day?"[69] Years later, in 1928, Söderblom was to be instrumental in securing for Bergson the Nobel Prize for Literature, as a late acknowledgment of a debt of gratitude.[70] Söderblom was hardly a full-fledged Bergsonian, but much of the final part of his later book *Religionsproblemet* (to which we shall return) will be better understood if Bergson's creative evolution be kept in mind.

Another French philosopher of the period whose work was also influencing Söderblom in the same direction was Émile Boutroux (1845–1921). He had heard Boutroux lecture at the Sorbonne in 1896–97, and was reminded of Pascal. However, it was Boutroux's book *Science et Religion dans la philosophie contemporaine* (1908) which impressed him most deeply at this time. Boutroux was close to Bergson in emphasizing that a truth that does not stand in close touch with life is without value, while a life ungoverned by truth is not worth the living. Truth and life must go hand in hand, and when they do, then we have the genius. "Truth [Boutroux had written in another context] is not ready-made, is not simply there like material objects, but it comes into being; and what really exists is not chance, but reason."[71]

Between 1908 and 1912 Söderblom was busy preparing in Swedish a series of textbooks in the study of religion, the first of their kind in the language. Their proportions tell one a great deal about Söderblom's priorities. First came a four-volume collection of texts from all the great religious traditions of the world (three volumes of texts, with a long introduction by Söderblom himself), amounting to more than fifteen hundred pages in all. Under the title of *Främmande religionsurkunder* (literally "Foreign sources in religion"), their publication was completed in 1908. Still it represents a quite remarkable achievement of Swedish scholarship at the time. Tiny in comparison was the textbook *Studiet av religionen* (The study of religion), which also appeared in 1908. Little over one hundred pages in length, it had something in common with the German series of *Religionsgeschichtliche Volksbücher* in being aimed at a general reading public, rather than at university students. It is noteworthy that here the general history of religion (i.e., comparative religion) is included as only one approach among many, and takes up less than twenty pages. Equally worthy of note is that the book's last section considers the relationship between comparative religion and theology.[72] The third volume in the textbook sequence, *Översikt av allmänna religionshistorien* (Survey of the general history of religion), appeared first in 1912, and again was a "popular" survey for a more general readership. Corresponding generally in outline to the Tiele *Kompendium*, it followed a country-by-country, tradition-by-tradition line from the "primitives," by way of the Ancient Near East, Greece, Rome, Islam, Germanic religion, India, China and Japan, to Buddhism. It concluded with a twenty-page section on "the basic concepts of religion" (*Religionens grundbegrepp*), under three headings, "Holiness," "Belief in God," and "Worship of God."

Söderblom's celebrated "Holiness" article in Hastings's *Encyclopaedia of Religion and Ethics* was to appear in the following year, 1913, and is a subject important enough to call for separate discussion in Chapter 7 below. First, however, a few words on Söderblom and Islam—bearing in mind Tor Andrae's testimony just quoted.

Söderblom was generally attracted (aside from Christianity, of course) only to Buddhism, among the world's *living* religions. His attitude to Islam was much less receptive, and this may strike the present-day reader as a curious omission from his all-around competence. In *Främmande religionsurkunder* he was careful to include a translation of most of the Koran and a sixteen-page summary of some of its teachings. Certainly Muhammad himself could be regarded as a prophetic genius, but in his followers (those whom he had urged Andrae to investigate, which he did brilliantly) what in Söderblom's view had begun as prophecy had shifted into the realm of politics, while Islam itself had developed a hard shell of dogma not altogether dissimilar to that of Lutheran orthodoxy. Söderblom's interest in Islam therefore began and ended with Muhammad himself.[73] He treated its later history very summarily, hinting that it might well appeal more to the simple people of the world than to the more developed nations. And in his 1912 book he ended, somewhat abruptly: "Islam appears to provide a certain discipline and cohesion, but at the same time is resistant to the possibility of higher development."[74] It was not until 1917 that Tor Andrae was to publish his masterly book *Die person Muhammeds i lehre und glauben seiner gemeinde* (the Swedish editor of the series in which it appeared did not believe in German capitals), and Andrae's study of Muhammad did not appear until 1930. And yet in the latter especially, the influence of Söderblom is very much evident—not in respect of the later religiopolitical history of Islam, but in the acknowledgment of Muhammad as a religious genius. Later still came Andrae's book *I myrtenträdgården* (1947; English translation, *In the Garden of Myrtles*, 1987), which again follows a theme—that of early Muslim mysticism—of which Söderblom would have greatly approved. For although Söderblom's own studies in mysticism concentrated on Buddhism on the one hand and Evangelical Christianity on the other, each representing a "type" of mystical piety and devotion, his apparent lack of interest in its Muslim forms was no more than a reflection of a climate of opinion and the unavailability of sources. At least he was prepared to point his best student in the direction of Islamic studies—and for this later scholarship has had occasion to be grateful.

In the first decade of the twentieth century, Sweden could hardly be said to have held a prominent position in the world of religious—or other—scholarship. It was a poor country, greatly uncomfortable for two-thirds of each year, difficult to reach at any time and hampered in international communications by having a language which very few foreigners ever took the trouble to learn. These were the most obvious hindrances in the way of open communications between Sweden and the rest of the world—or rather of two-way communications, since those few Swedes who could afford to travel in the pursuit of scholarship had long done so. Contacts with the outside scholarly world were, however, uneven.

In the area of religion, Sweden's natural contacts since the Reformation had been mainly in the direction of Germany. Contacts with France and Britain were at best sporadic, while the factor of distance and expense had placed America very largely out of reach. Missionaries were working in areas as far afield as China, India, and South Africa and sending their letters and reports back to Sweden and the other Scandinavian countries; this, however, was a fairly special case, often productive of good and reliable information but not often furthering the scholarly debate.

Before about 1900, even Söderblom's contacts with the world outside Sweden had been somewhat fortuitous. His first visit to Germany, France, and the United States had come about quite unexpectedly, as the result of an invitation to attend a conference. His pastorate in Paris might equally well not have happened, though it was to shape the direction and course of his later life in scholarship as no other factor could possibly have done. But Söderblom had been, in a manner of speaking, fortunate, and he knew well enough that for Swedish scholarship in either theology or comparative religion to win acknowledgment internationally, something more permanent would have to be found than reliance on the workings of divine providence. Precisely the same applied to contacts between Christians in Sweden and other countries.

In 1907 an important development took place, which was to help in two directions—in sending Swedish theologians for periods of study abroad, and in bringing overseas scholars to lecture and acquaint themselves with conditions in Sweden. On October 23, 1907, Söderblom met for the first time in Uppsala a Mrs. Anna Lindblad, who told him that her family had had something of a windfall as a result of the sale of a factory, and that she wished to make a sum of money available to provide grants for (for instance) young ministers to study abroad. The sum of 100,000 Swedish kronor was mentioned—a very considerable sum at that time. At this stage, Söderblom's ecclesiastical sights were set mainly on England, believing as he did that Sweden—Lutheran and Episcopal—could serve as a mediating influence between two of Europe's three superpowers. And it was to this end that the Lindblad donation was first applied. The first travel grant was allocated later in the same year, 1907, to a young minister from Dalarna, Samuel Gabrielsson.[75]

The sending out of young theologians to study abroad was, however, only part of what Söderblom had in mind. Mrs. Lindblad wrote on November 5, 1907: "In Uppsala you mentioned a lectureship or something of the kind in Scotland, which had been a great source of blessing. I should be pleased if you had something about it that I could read, either in Swedish or English. I know very little about Scotland and England, only Robertson and Drummond."[76]

The Scottish foundation in question was the Gifford Lectureship, set up on the death of Lord Gifford in 1887 as a lectureship in "Natural Theology," with a series of lectures held in the four Scottish universities of Edinburgh, Glasgow, Aberdeen, and St. Andrews. The first series had been held by Friedrich Max Müller in 1888, and subsequent lecturers had included C. P. Tiele, Edward Caird, E. B. Tylor, A. M. Fairbairn, and Andrew Lang. Söderblom had mentioned the Gifford Lectureship in his inaugural lecture of 1901 as an important landmark in the establishing of comparative religion as an independent and respectable academic discipline.

It was while Söderblom was in the hospital in 1908 that the news reached him that the legalities in connection with Anna Lindblad's donation had been virtually completed. His wife was quite convinced that this news contributed materially to his recovery. Mrs. Lindblad came to visit him once more, and during their discussions the Gifford Lectures were again mentioned as the prototype of what Söderblom had in mind for the new Uppsala lectureship. In his private correspondence with the donor, Söderblom was in the habit of referring to "the Anna Foundation" (*Annastiftelsen*) as the name of the new lectureship. In the end, however, it came to be called "the Olaus Petri Foundation" after the great Swedish Reformer. Mrs. Lindblad, incidentally, insisted that she should remain anonymous, and that her name should not be associated in any way with the foundation. Her name does not appear to have been made public before 1956, when an account of her involvement in the foundation was published by Anna Söderblom.[77]

The inaugural lecture delivered under the auspices of the new foundation—or rather with its money, since the statutes had not yet been finalized—was a single lecture (not a series) by Edvard Lehmann on the subject of Thomas Carlyle! On April 29, 1908, Söderblom had written to Mrs. Lindblad, who apparently had heard Lehmann lecture in Stockholm: "I was very happy to hear that you had heard my dear friend Lehmann, who has been spending a few days with us in Uppsala. . . . From the very first I had him in mind as one of the best possible lecturers for the 'Anna Foundation.' But we are such close friends that I did not want him to be the first."[78] A few days later, however, he wrote again: "You will be glad to hear that in spite of everything yesterday I began the Anna Foundation lectures cautiously—though without anyone being named personally—with an impressive lecture on Carlyle by Lehmann. The largest lecture room in the University was full. The lecture made a powerful impression."[79] The very first Olaus Petri lecture thus took place entirely anonymously on May 2, 1908. The name "Olaus Petri Foundation" was settled by consultation between Söderblom and Samuel Fries later in the same month. It became public on March 6, 1909, when the first lecture in the first series was delivered by Rudolf Eucken of Jena. Thereafter the Olaus Petri Foundation was to become increasingly influential in the academic world, its list of lecturers serving almost as a roll of honor among scholars of religion. In the Söderblom era such names as Deissmann, Hauck, Otto, G. Kittel, and Reichelt all lectured and published under its auspices. It is still very much active.

Congresses of the history of religion originally met at four-year intervals, and in 1908 it was the turn of Oxford to host the assembly. Early in 1908 Söderblom had been ill again, and had been forced to suspend his lectures in Uppsala. After some weeks in the hospital it was determined that he should "take a cure" at Karlsbad. The most one could claim for such "cures" was perhaps that the rest did the patient good, while the diet and the mineral waters did little harm. Söderblom was particularly in need of rest. In Karlsbad he lodged at the Villa Lord Byron, prompting Edvard Lehmann to send a postcard, written in rough-and-ready English: "Hail thee in the house of lord Byron—and make you a stomach of iron!"[80] He was by no means cured, but set off for Oxford nevertheless. He had two ends in view. One was of course to attend the congress and meet professional colleagues, among them R. R. Marett and the reclusive J. G. Frazer (upon whom he paid a courtesy call in Cambridge). The other had to do with the developing relationship between the Churches of Sweden and England. Although falling outside the scope of this study, it may be mentioned that while in England

Söderblom lunched with the archbishop of Canterbury (Randall Davidson), and met the bishop of Salisbury (John Wordsworth, soon to produce the first English-language history of the church in Sweden) and the bishop of Winchester (H. E. Ryle).[81] Intercommunion between the two churches was still some way in the future, but it was a matter in which Söderblom was deeply involved, and may have been the most important reason for his wanting to visit England at a time of much physical discomfort.

During the Oxford congress itself Söderblom stayed at St. John's College, amid academic customs and courtesies somewhat different from those of either Uppsala or Paris. He enjoyed having a personal servant, and appreciated the toast to "The Church and the King!"—which he felt placed things in their right sequence. He tested out his English on all and sundry, in preparation for the unaccustomed ordeal of having for the first time to deliver a paper in that language. The paper itself took up a theme he had first tackled five years previously, in a Swedish-language essay.[82] At Oxford it was reshaped into "The Place of the Christian Trinity and the Buddhist Triratna amongst Holy Triads."[83]

The years 1909–12 in Söderblom's career we must pass over somewhat summarily. His most important publication was the book *Religionsproblemet* (1910), to which we shall return later. Otherwise, his health being somewhat improved, he maintained his customary literary output on a wide range of subjects—seventeen items in 1909, thirteen in 1910, eighteen in 1911, and nineteen in 1912, according to the 1931 bibliography.

Most spectacular of the events of the time was his longest overseas journey since his venture to America in 1890, a visit to Constantinople as a delegate to the April 1911 Conference of the World's Student Christian Federation. As in 1890, the prime mover would seem to have been Karl Fries. Present at the conference were such international Christian leaders as John R. Mott, Robert P. Wilder, D. S. Cairns, J. N. Farquhar, and C. F. Andrews.

Söderblom wrote a little book about his experiences entitled *Tre heliga veckor* (Three holy weeks, 1911).[84] He traveled by way of Rome, where he disliked intensely the Palm Sunday Mass he attended at the Church of the Lateran. An audience with Pope Pius X depressed more than it inspired him; the pope appeared inhibited, tired, and only superficially friendly, and was accompanied by a *majordomo* who (Söderblom wrote) resembled nothing so much as a bad-tempered cat.[85] During a conversation with Monsignor Duchesne, the best of the Catholic church historians, there was a minor earthquake, which alarmed everyone. "Modernism" was a largely forbidden subject. In the Church of Santa Maria Maggiore things were more natural, and on Good Friday in the Church of Santa Croce in Gerusalemme there was something of what Söderblom could recognize as "true" religion: reverence for a mystery. On Easter Day he visited Nemi—the same Nemi immortalized by Frazer's fantasies—and reflected on "the Easter of natural religion."[86]

From Italy his journey continued by way of Corinth and Athens to Constantinople. There he was most of all struck by the contrast between the chaos of the city at large and the "Anglo-Saxon" comfort of Robert College, so reminiscent of New England twenty-one years earlier. Another contrast impressed him: that between the ancient and slow rhythms of the Orthodox church, encountered face to face for the first time, and the organizational energy of such as Mott. He was pleased with the amount of time the conference gave to questions of theological principle, and had a special word of praise for a lecture by David S. Cairns of Aberdeen (which did not appear in the proceedings). But most important, from his point of view, was to observe how "modern" the conference was: "Not a single voice was heard advocating sterile protests and apologetical ingenuity as an alternative to honest thought."[87] Clearly, he felt, the Anglo-Saxon world had moved further in a scientific direction than had either Sweden or Germany. "Through the Constantinople conference the free and respectful attitude to science has become a fact. If one asks, who created the new biblical scholarship and theology, the answer must be: chiefly the Germans. But if one asks, who has established the clear program of the student movement in respect of theological research, obviously the answer must be: the English, the Anglo-Saxons."[88] In comparison with such "Anglo-Saxons" as Cairns, Farquhar, and Tatlow, the Germans were still somewhat paranoid, even about their own great scholars. Still, some day they might learn to appreciate and recognize them, "and stop treating them as contraband."[89]

Söderblom's own paper bore the title "Does God Continue to Reveal Himself to Mankind?"[90] and carried forward a line of thought begun in *Uppenbarelsereligion* almost a decade earlier. It argued that God's continued revelation is to be found in human genius, in history, and in the regeneration of the individual. One wonders what the delegates made of it. Cairns was deeply impressed—but Cairns was a theologian who read widely. Others may have found it unfamiliar in its approach, and its English was sometimes convoluted as well. At times, though, the authentic Söderblom breaks through: "God reveals himself in genius. Genius proves that the real essence of existence is creation, eternal, incessant creation. . . . Great men of genius when serving God consciously and with all their hearts become saints. A saint is he who reveals God's might. . . . Eschatology does not mean a pause in God's workings and a hidden God that will once more appear. Eschatology means a living God and a working humanity."[91]

Otherwise Constantinople 1911 was important to Söderblom in that it gave him his first real insight into the living world of Eastern Orthodoxy. This was to be of the greatest significance for his coming ecumenical work. That, however, falls outside the bounds of this study to investigate further.

There remain two further events from 1911 to record briefly. In the summer there assembled in Uppsala a conference of Lutheran theologians, one of whom was the celebrated church historian Albert Hauck of the University of Leipzig; this visit was to have unexpected consequences, which we shall consider more fully in our next chapter. And in September 1911 Söderblom was once more in Britain, taking part in the five-hundredth anniversary of the University of St. Andrews, in connection with which he received the third of his fourteen honorary doctorates. In his travel diary he paid delighted attention to the fact that St. Andrews was most of all sacred to the name of Andrew Lang, a man for whom Söderblom had immense, though not uncritical, respect. Lang was also present at the celebrations, and it is impossible to suppose that the two did *not* meet and talk—though assuming that they did, no record was kept on either side. In his diary Söderblom described Lang as "St. Andrews's spoiled child . . . slim and elegant, wearing a monocle under black eyebrows and sparse, short, greying hair."[92] He also noted that after the jubilee banquet, Lang was one of the first to flee from the purgatory of the after-dinner speeches. Lang had less than a year to live, dying in July 1912, an enigma to the end. Of the history of religion establishment of his day, few had appreciated him as did Söderblom. On this one occasion, their paths crossed.

Amid all these travels, in the late summer of 1911 Söderblom was struggling with a new edition of the Tiele *Kompendium*, the last for which he was entirely responsible: "Not patched up—entirely new—but on the old pattern."[93] Away in Germany, his friend Edvard Lehmann had allowed himself to be persuaded to take up the first chair of *Religionsgeschichte* in the country, at the illustrious University of Berlin. He was not sure whether he liked it. He was finding his feet, but was already longing for some respite from the pressures of work, and already beginning to feel lonely and homesick. While Söderblom was negotiating with Leipzig, Lehmann was writing that now he had no time for study, adding maliciously that "This is because we Berlin professors are so prodigiously wise, that we have no need to learn more than the rubbish we already know."[94] A couple of months later, the news of Söderblom's Leipzig appointment having broken, Lehmann was rejoicing that if he did accept, the two would be only three hours apart on the train.

By June 1912 Söderblom was on his way to Germany and his last academic appointment, feeling—as he had felt on his first arrival in Paris—suddenly and strangely uprooted and disoriented.[95]

6
Leipzig, 1912–1914

Great internationalist though he undoubtedly was, during the last twenty or so years of his life—four of them under the bloody imprint of war and the remainder under the hardly less oppressive shadow of all that followed in the wake of war—Söderblom's allegiance belonged chiefly to Germany. In the context of the 1914–18 conflict he has been described as "a discreet Germanophile."[1] This was so, not because he did not appreciate and admire America, France, and Britain, but because he was a Lutheran, and because the Lutheran heartlands centered on Erfurt, Wittenburg, and not least Leipzig. In comparison, the Catholic and Calvinist lands had less of an appeal, as did the traditions they represented.

Germany and Scandinavia since the Reformation had been bound together by the strongest of ties. Where Calvin's reforms had taken root chiefly in Switzerland, the Netherlands, Britain, and America, the Lutheran tradition had taken firm hold in Scandinavia and the Baltic countries. The two great Swedish warrior kings, Gustavus Adolphus and Charles XII, had defended the principles of the Reformation far beyond Sweden's natural frontiers. After the age of the wars came the age of trade and the age of science, and in the nineteenth century a united Germany had excelled in every field of the intellect. In religious and theological study and speculation, where Germany led, Sweden followed—not too closely at first, since speculation could lead into dangerous waters, but in the same general direction. The Swedish student was expected to be proficient in German and, especially in theology, to accept German methods and German approaches. In comparison, the average Swedish student of the late nineteenth and early twentieth centuries would make little use of either English or French. In all essentials, to study theology in nineteenth-century Sweden had been to be in almost complete and willing bondage to a cumulative Lutheran tradition expressed in German (or if not German, at least Germanic) terms. If and when the tradition was called in question, by a Schleiermacher, a Strauss, a Baur, or a Ritschl, that impulse, too, was fed into Sweden from the south.

German Protestantism, however, was least of all simple and monolithic. On the contrary, it was bewildering in its variety. *Religionswissenschaft*, as cultivated during the second half of the nineteenth century, insisted on subjecting religion to scientific examination: all well and good. But finding the churches suspicious of the scientific principle, advanced academic theology in Germany had in many cases come to occupy a position separate from the Lutheran establishment. Each university tended to have a profile and a character of its own, as did the *Landeskirchen*; religious and political organizations overlapped and multiplied. And as we have seen, by 1910 no subject was more hotly disputed than the place of *Religionsgeschichte* in the study of theology. In 1901 Harnack had thrown his very considerable influence behind *not* admitting the general history of religion into the theological curriculum. Since the early 1890s the members of the Tübingen-based "history of religion school" had operated chiefly from a position to one side of the faculties of theology in Germany. Whatever their intentions, the members of this "school" were not regarded kindly by the more orthodox theologians of the Lutheran establishment. They were anticonfessional in a church that set great store by its confessions; populist in a hierarchical society; and apparently relativist in a world of religious absolutes. They could not, on the other hand, be ignored. They had the ear of the educated laity, and of a growing number of future ministers in the universities.

At this time one of the most solidly confessional of the faculties of theology in Germany was that at the University of Leipzig, in Saxony (where Luther himself had been a student from 1501 to 1505).[2] On the Leipzig faculty there were some outstanding scholars, the dogmatician Ludwig Ihmels, the church historian Albert Hauck, and the biblical scholar Rudolf Kittel among them. Leipzig opposition to the methods and approaches of the "history of religion school" was compact. And yet there was also a growing feeling that mere polemics would serve no useful purpose. Perhaps the Tübingen scholars were painting on too limited a canvas, and rushing to conclusions on the basis of too few facts; certainly, so the Leipzig theologians thought, they were harming the church. In the circumstances it would have been quite possible to have ignored the subject altogether. This clearly would not have made the problem of *Religionsgeschichte* go away, however. The alternative was to arrange for the subject to be taught by someone who was not a dilettante, not a relativist, and not an enemy of (or contemptuous of) the church. So it was that the Leipzig theologians determined to establish a chair of *Allgemeine Religionsgeschichte*, believing that by this means they could best counteract "the mistakes and eccentricities of the *Religionsgeschichtliche Volksbücher*."[3]

But such a chair would be extremely difficult to fill. One could, it seemed, find and appoint *either* a historian of religion *or* a churchman, but not both at once. In Gerhard Kittel's words, "It was virtually unthinkable at that time in Germany that one could be a competent historian of religion . . . and at the same time a theologian conscious of his task, even church-minded: that one could find one's way through all the religions and myths of the world without losing one's way in a relativistic view of the history of religion."[4] However, within the University of Leipzig there were scholars who were by no means strangers to the history of religion field. Rudolf Kittel was working on the relationship between the religion of Israel and the pre-Israelite cults of Canaan. The celebrated psychologist Wilhelm Wundt, though of course not a theologian, had begun his lectures on *Völkerpsychologie* in the summer of 1911, showing how religion is interwoven with all other elements in the lives of nations and peoples. There was Karl Lamprecht and his *Institut für Kultur- und Universalgeschichte*, with its fine library. All in all, the climate of opinion was favorable. But it was determined not to make any positive move for the setting up of a chair before a suitable incumbent had been found.

It was at this juncture that Albert Hauck visited Uppsala in the summer of 1911. On his return to Leipzig, he went to see Rudolf Kittel, saying that now the faculty could apply to the government of Saxony for the setting up of a chair of *Allgemeine Religionsgeschichte*, since he had found the man to fill the post—Nathan Söderblom.[5] Söderblom was not approached officially until early in 1912.[6] Thereafter things moved quickly.

Söderblom had been a professor in Uppsala for eleven years, and he would seem not to have been contemplating anything other than a continued academic career. The Leipzig invitation came as something of a surprise, and as an honor. It was, however, not the first time he had been approached from Germany. In 1909 overtures had been made to him from Berlin, though on that occasion he had declined to move, both because Berlin would, he felt, have been a place of exile, and because his friend Edvard Lehmann was also in contention.[7] But Leipzig was a more attractive proposition than was Berlin: less central, less sensitive to the pressures of Prussian politics, and above all more Lutheran. Even so, Söderblom had no wish to leave Uppsala permanently. Therefore he accepted the Leipzig chair only for two years initially, and on condition that he was permitted to retain his Uppsala chair at the same time—which meant in practice returning to Uppsala during the Leipzig vacations to deliver a number of lectures. This arrangement lasted from the summer of 1912 to the summer of 1914 and his elevation to the archbishopric of Uppsala.

On Gerhard Kittel's later testimony, one of the Leipzig faculty's purposes in setting up a chair of *Allgemeine Religionsgeschichte* had been to counteract what they saw as the unhealthy influences of the members of the "history of religion school" and the superficialities of the *Religionsgeschichtliche Volksbücher*.[8] Ironically, perhaps, Söderblom had actually written one of those much-criticized "popular pamphlets," the third volume in the third series, on *Die Religionen der Erde* (The religions of the world). It had not, however, been written for the *Volksbücher* series originally, being in fact a translation of a fifty-page Swedish booklet, *Kristendomen och religionerna* (Christianity and the religions), which first appeared in 1904 and was later translated into Danish, Finnish, Italian, and French as well as German. Aimed at a general readership, it nevertheless compressed a good deal of material into a very few pages. From the Leipzig point of view it is perhaps also worth noting that unlike many of the booklets in the series, it had ended with an unequivocal confession of faith, couched in the words of Matthew 11:27: "no one knows the Father except the Son and any one to whom the Son chooses to reveal him."

In late June 1912 Söderblom was on his way to Germany, and on the Trelleborg-Sassnitz ferry wrote to Anna (who would join him, with their children, later) to describe what he had in mind—and to practice his German, since the greater part of the letter was in German.[9] Although he had been hired on a two-year contract, he already anticipated a third year, and proposed to divide up his teaching under three phenomenological headings: holiness, faith, and worship.[10] But as well as phenomenology, there was the history of religion to be taken into account, and this he proposed to label *der Gang der Religion zur Weltgeschichte* (Religion's way to world history). He sketched the subjects of his lecture courses and his seminars over the next two years. And approaching the German coast, he added (in Swedish): "Soon we shall be approaching our old possessions. Terrible how much patriotism one has in one's blood!"

The summer was uncomfortable in more ways than one. Fries in Stockholm had clearly not on this occasion been taken into Söderblom's confidence, and learned of the Leipzig fait accompli only from the newspapers: "Since now you have managed to arrange things as you wish, your friends can only wish you well. But whether we are to congratulate Uppsala University and the faculty of theology remains to be seen."[11] He sounded irritated—or at least disappointed. Söderblom himself had been ill again, with a fresh attack of gallstones, and in August had once more been packed off to Karlsbad, where he had at least learned that to be a Leipzig professor was "infinitely fine," adding: "Happily I am a professor in Uppsala."[12] But he was tired and nervous about whether his decision had been the right one. He was well enough, however, to begin his teaching in the fall.

One personal long-term collaboration to which he had looked forward failed to materialize. Edvard Lehmann had never been happy in Berlin, the atmosphere of which he found oppressive. Early in 1913 he was appointed to a newly established chair in Lund, just across the water from his native Denmark. In June 1913 he wrote to Söderblom: "Here one has no friends, only colleagues. I am not happy in this city and I would a hundred times rather have my children grow up Swedes than Germans. So I have sufficient cause to make this move."[13] On his arrival in Lund he felt that he had been set free from a Babylonian captivity.[14]

Söderblom's Leipzig years were fruitful in other ways, however. He had relatively few students, since his subject was not examinable, but the few were expected to work, to work hard, and to work in an unfamiliar way. Söderblom gave his students more latitude than was usual in Germany at the time. He was the youngest professor in the faculty, and this helped him to establish personal contacts with his students. But he made considerable demands of them: one he gave six weeks to acquire enough English to read a Buddhist text so far untranslated into German. Although in class he never engaged in any form of apologetical special pleading on behalf of Christianity, one of his students later recorded that: "Anyone who let himself be really influenced by Söderblom's lectures was permanently cured of the mistaken notion that the religio-historical method as such was the child of unbelief and doubt."[15]

The only thing standing in the way of Söderblom's becoming a permanent force in German scholarship was the brevity of his time in Leipzig. In two years an atmosphere could be created and a few individual students could be pointed in the right direction, but an academic succession could not be established. Nor was this uppermost in his mind. "My bold plan," he wrote to Fries in May 1913, "is to have the history of religion recognized as a necessary part of theology."[16] This was partly an intellectual and partly an administrative matter. On the administrative side, by late in 1913 the faculty decided to include a course in the history of religion in the ministerial training curriculum—a first stage in making the subject compulsory: "Though as yet still only a very small step."[17] The intellectual arguments were another matter, but Söderblom was making a beginning with a lecture-based monograph on the subject of *Natürliche Theologie und allgemeine Religionsgeschichte* (Natural theology and the general history of religion, 1913). This was the most important of Söderblom's shorter publications of his Leipzig period, and is worth a closer examination.

The roots of the *Natürliche Theologie* study can without difficulty be traced back to Söderblom's reading of Schleiermacher in the late 1890s, while still in Paris. Lecturing in Meissen early in 1913 he had taken Schleiermacher's critique of "natural theology" a step further. Natural theology (or natural religion) is dead, but it has left a gap. This gap can be filled by the history of religion, though in a much modified sense, since what we now know of "natural" religion is that it is neither natural nor rational, but positive, irrational, individual, and (if one so wishes) revealed.

Just at this time, Fries in Stockholm was negotiating to start a new monograph series to help bring Swedish scholarship before an international readership, and was only too happy to have Söderblom's lecture as a first contribution. It appeared, accordingly, as the first in a projected series of *Beiträge zur Religionswissenschaft* (Contributions to the science of religion) under the joint imprint of Bonnier in Stockholm and Hinrichs in Leipzig. It was published in November 1913, though at too high a price to be accessible to students in Leipzig—which Söderblom found irritating. In the following year, 1914, there also appeared a slightly expanded version in Swedish, *Naturlig religion och religionshistoria: en historik och ett program*.[18]

The argument of this study relates to an age-old question: what precisely is it that religions have in common? Viewed from a traditional Christian angle, the tendency had been to dismiss other forms of belief and practice as either man-made or demonically inspired surrogates for the pure light of a religious truth made known once and for all in the revelation of God in Jesus Christ. But from time to time other voices had made themselves heard, voices coming from the Hellenic rather than from the Hebraic side of Christianity: that there is a core of truth in all human expressions of religion, a common foundation on which the various traditions have erected superstructures of their own devising. Remove the respective superstructures—myth, ritual, dogma, and theological speculation—and what remains will be the golden core of truth. This core is "natural" in that it is part of the normal and natural rational equipment of every thinking human being, and its premises—that there is a creator-god and that he had made laws for the ordering of human life, which laws must be obeyed—can be deduced from normal human experience without the aid of any supernaturally contrived act of revelation. Anticipated in various ways in the history of Western religion, this view of "natural religion" was stated initially in the writings of the so-called Deists, beginning in the seventeenth century and coming to its fullest expression in the eighteenth. At the end of the nineteenth century the view still persisted that what religions have in common cannot be other than a conception of the moral order of the universe, an attitude deeply rooted in the human mental and spiritual makeup. Human beings have no need to be taught this—so the argument went—though they certainly need to be taught the steps which have to be taken when the moral order is broken and the moral sense collapses.

Söderblom's study of the concept of natural theology was designed expressly to contradict this rationalist view of the nature of religion. He argued that there was in fact no evidence at all that the "natural religion" so beloved of the Deists had ever been anything but an intellectual construction, the product of the speculative schools rather than of the human religious impulse—which impulse expressed itself in other ways entirely. From this it followed that if common ground among religions is to be sought, rational deduction from the evidence of the senses is the wrong place to look. The study of religion does not lay bare a core of rationality in all religion; on the contrary, concentration on the "realities" of religion shows precisely the opposite: that what is common to religions is the *nonrational* point at which they begin. But "nonrational" is in this instance not the equivalent of "nonsensical"; rather, it is the only appropriate human response to a transcendental reality, which can be understood only in the categories of revelation.

Much of this short study is taken up with the history of the "natural religion" idea in Western religion. Beginning with faint traces in the New Testament, much time is taken discussing the *logos spermatikos* (the seminal Word) idea in the Fathers, and especially Justin. But while non-Christian religions were still a serious threat to the church, there was little chance that close attention would be paid to the possibility of extrabiblical revelation. The rediscovery of Aristotle and the vast systems of Aquinas, coupled with a greater degree of stability on the church's part in the post-Charlemagne years, provoked thinkers to draw distinctions between natural and supernatural knowledge, natural knowledge being inborn while supernatural knowledge (for instance, concerning the Trinity) had to be taught and received by faith. Parallel to this there had grown up a distinction between natural and revealed religion. Natural religion is the necessary precondition for the reception of divine revelation, since otherwise the message would fall on deaf ears: one cannot address an exhortation to a person in a totally unknown language. But natural religion is not *saving* religion. It lays necessary foundations, but never addresses itself to the question: what must I *do* to be saved?

In the eighteenth century, it had become an intellectual fashion to claim that all religion (all religion worthy of the name, that is) is natural religion, and the third part of Söderblom's book deals with this period, discussing authors from Locke to Leibniz, Rousseau, Kant, and Daniel Defoe. Revealed religion was held to be so encumbered with the irrational and the miraculous as to be worthless in the age of scientific discovery. Refuge was sought in the moral abstractions of the Age of Reason, which could be affirmed without taking up any position on the matter of direct supernatural intervention in the affairs of the world—which indeed was frequently denied. The Creator remained, evidenced by "the spacious firmament on high"; the Savior became the moral exemplar; humanity's task was the creation of a (moral) Kingdom of God on earth; humanity's burden was the weight of the moral law. All this, it was assumed, was natural and religious in equal measure, cool and rational, law-abiding and blessedly free from enthusiasm.

The first counterattack on "natural religion" had been mounted by the Scottish philosopher David Hume, in his *Natural History of Religion* (1757), followed by Friedrich Schleiermacher, in his celebrated *Reden* (1799). Hume stated that from all the available evidence, religion certainly had not originated in the way the Deists tended to suppose, that is, deductively from the contemplation of the orderly pageant of nature; rather it had begun in the most irrational of human instincts, that of fear. Schleiermacher had come to what appeared to be a different conclusion, that the primary human religious impulse was what he elsewhere called "the feeling of absolute dependence." Both impulses, though, were instinctive, rather than rationally deduced: fear on the one hand, dependence on the other; both related to an ineffable transcendence at the heart of the universe, and neither had anything to do with a pattern of rational deductions and conclusions. Following Hume and Schleiermacher, so Söderblom claimed, and taking into account all that had transpired in the world of scholarship since 1800, it was no longer possible to speak of "natural religion" in the old sense, or indeed in any sense: *Theologia naturalis nulla est*. It had been abolished once and for all, shown up for the intellectual construction it always was.

But the need that had produced the theory of natural religion in the seventeenth and eighteenth centuries remained in the twentieth. The plurality of religious traditions remained to try and tantalize the believer. Theology could not avoid taking note of religious plurality, and already the wide-awake study of religion had done more than centuries of dogmatic assertion to establish the place of Christianity in world history.[19] "The general history of religion" (*Allgemeine Religionsgeschichte*) had achieved one result above all: to show that religion, though multiform, actually is one interlocking entity, "an interconnected series of phenomena, of which Christianity is also a part."[20] This, stated Söderblom, is a simple matter of fact, having nothing to do with judgments of value.

At this point there is an interesting footnote. It reads: "It is perhaps not altogether unnecessary to add that I am in no way advocating a 'method' which, through all manner of comparisons, often with a vast contempt for time and place, would seek to bypass the only fruitful task—that of understanding a phenomenon [*företeelse*] on a basis of its own presuppositions."[21] Perhaps Söderblom was a phenomenologist before phenomenology. But he had no "phenomenological method." He had a point of view, certainly, but again and again he returned to the theme of the intractability of "reality" and the need *not* to squeeze that reality into predetermined molds. The common ground among religions is not to be established by random comparisons "with a vast contempt for time and place": he was too much of a historian to accept that common shortcut. What the history of religion *could* do, on the other hand, was to establish the essence of religion as lying in the incomprehensible encounter with the holy, a nonrational encounter far different from anything that the "natural theologians" could ever have contemplated. Thus, "The history of natural theology and the contents of the history of religion lead us to state this thesis: the general history of religion must now occupy the place given by an older dogmatics to natural theology."[22]

Söderblom agreed both with Max Müller, that he who knows one religion knows none, and with Harnack, that the student has all that is needful in the study of religion in the study of Christianity—especially in the light of the role of Christianity in Western culture. But he was not prepared to play off the one against the other. Rather he advocated a pattern in which that which is "general," human, and universal is complemented and completed by that which is "special," that is, unique to the Christian tradition. The latter cannot be understood at all unless the former is grasped in all its vast diversity. Therefore—and this was the position toward which his monograph was aiming—the study of the Christian tradition should not be undertaken apart from a wider consideration of the history of religion. If done properly, both would bear their witness to a truth of human history and human experience.

Söderblom at the end of his study insisted that on this occasion he was not arguing about revelation, and added: "To draw up laws in the name of divine righteousness and a priori logical probability, is very foreign to me. To defend God, ever since the Book of Job, seems to me to be irreligious. Here I am speaking simply and without pretensions, as a historian."[23] And he concluded: "If one accepts the testimony of the religions, their spirit and their development, he [the historian of religion] gains the impression that human beings have always been under the influence of a divine reality that is both inaccessible and at the same time inescapable."[24] This of course was his own testimony, his own witness.

One might add, as a footnote, that whoever reads German might well take *Natürliche Theologie und allgemeine Religionsgeschichte* as a point of departure for an approach to Söderblom the religiohistorical theologian. Elsewhere he expressed himself more fully—for instance in *Religionsproblemet*, published earlier but on this occasion considered later. This essay, however, gives an admirable summary. The concentration on the "reality" of religion is there; the indebtedness to the tradition of Hume and Schleiermacher is fully evident; history is balanced against experience, Max Müller against Harnack; the possibilities of the study of religion are laid out. Söderblom wrote many bigger books, but few that have stood the test of time better.

In a study of this kind one has little enough opportunity to record the kind of personal episode that the biographer normally seizes upon as a snapshot of his or her subject. There were, however, two such episodes toward the end of 1913 which I cannot resist including. Söderblom's instinctive patriotism has already been mentioned. In October and November 1913 the Söderbloms were visited by Barbe de Quirielle (translator of *La Vie future*) and her husband, and together they went to Lützen, where Gustavus Adolphus had fallen in battle in 1632; there Söderblom preached in Swedish in the chapel. On the following day, a Sunday, after church in Naumburg they went for coffee to a *Konditorei*, where there happened to be a piano. Söderblom sat down at the keyboard and played—and sang—*La Marseillaise*! What the Germans present thought was not recorded, though had it been Prussia rather than Saxony, a riot might well have ensued. But Söderblom's guests were from Paris![25]

In November, the Swedish community in Leipzig celebrated the memory of King Charles XII. Again after a service in Swedish in the castle chapel of Altranstädt, Germans and Swedes together went out and stood around a bonfire, and Söderblom, his longish fair hair blowing in the wind, gave an impromptu speech. According to a German present, "Just then he seemed more Viking than minister of the church, as he spoke about the king and his men, about Germanic joy in battle and sense of justice, and about the fellowship of faith between the Protestants of Germany and Sweden, for which Charles XII fought, as the great Gustavus Adolphus had done before him."[26]

By the end of 1913, with the clouds of war already beginning to pile up over Europe, Söderblom had practically made up his mind to extend his stay in Leipzig by a further year. Lehmann having left Germany for Lund, the university authorities in Berlin were attempting to persuade Söderblom to leave Leipzig for Berlin, and he was able to reflect with a certain satisfaction that it was good to be so much in demand.[27] He wanted to return to Sweden, but felt strongly obliged to offer Leipzig one more year, and with that end in view applied to Uppsala for an extension of his leave of absence. In academic terms he had achieved a great deal during his two years in Leipzig; he had a big book on the origins of religion in the press, and he had every right to suppose that his period of productivity would continue.

But then came the bombshell. The archbishop of Uppsala, Johan August Ekman, who had been Söderblom's first academic supervisor, died on the very day of the Altranstädt meeting, November 30, 1913, and pressure was put on Söderblom to become a candidate for the archbishopric. He and Anna decided in private that Samuel Fries was the man for the post, and he wrote to Fries to say so, while probably realizing that this was hardly a serious possibility.[28] For his own candidature, Söderblom had still less hope. After several months of behind-the-scenes lobbying (in which he took no personal part), he was still unprepared to think of himself as having any chance at all. Writing to Göransson in May 1914, he was still calling his involvement "platonic," and went on: "In the matter of the election, remarkable things are being said about what some see as the probability of my being appointed. But when I think about it, this seems to be utterly unreasonable. And I have come more and more to the feeling that such a position would be undesirable for me personally—to say nothing of the Church of Sweden. . . . For my own part I am inwardly completely free, and so busy that I am unable to give this important matter so much attention as perhaps I should."[29]

A lucid account of the extraordinary steps by which Söderblom came to be appointed has been given in Bengt Sundkler's biography, and it is unnecessary to recapitulate in detail.[30] The chief features, however, were these: in the normal way, after elections among the clergy of each diocese, the names of the three candidates with the most votes were submitted to the king, who (on the advice of the government of the day) selected one of them. Söderblom's name was hardly mentioned in many dioceses, where (not being a diocesan bishop) he was either unknown, or greatly suspect on account of his theological liberalism. Nevertheless, in the final reckoning the March 18 election placed Söderblom third, far behind the two front-runners, Hjalmar Danell and Johan Alfred Eklund.

That Söderblom was chosen was due entirely to the degree of support he enjoyed among influential persons in Stockholm, where a new Conservative government had come to power in February 1914. This was a little paradoxical, given Söderblom's earlier socialist leanings, but on the individual level it was there nonetheless. Chief among his supporters was the new minister for ecclesiastical affairs, K. G. Westman, like Söderblom "a member of the Hjärne school of history in Uppsala."[31] But it was not a one-man decision. The cabinet met on May 20 behind closed doors, and at the end of the meeting it was announced that Söderblom was the new archbishop of Uppsala.

Reactions in Sweden varied from disbelief to anger at the government's seeming irresponsibility, only a very few sensing that under Söderblom, the Swedish church would assume a far different position than it previously had occupied in the Christian world. Söderblom himself was overwhelmed by the news. He wrote to Samuel Fries that he would certainly have enjoyed a quieter and happier life had he been able to remain a professor, and expressed his wish to get out among the people as soon as possible "to take the edge off the understandable displeasure they must feel now that His Majesty has thrown me into such a position."[32] Fries had been taken ill, and before the year was out he was dead following a series of strokes—yet another of Söderblom's personal rites de passage to add to the deaths of Fehr, Sabatier, and his own father.

This was of course the summer that saw the beginning of the first world war. Archduke Francis Ferdinand was assassinated at Sarajevo on June 28. A month later, on July 29, Austria invaded Serbia, and the war had begun. Germany entered the lists as an ally of Austria, Russia as protector of Serbia, and in August, France and Britain in alliance with Russia. But international conflict aside, Söderblom had other problems.[33]

On July 6 Anna gave birth to their twelfth and last child, baptized Gustaf Göran Samuel Karl, and called by his father "Karl XII." It had been a difficult confinement, and Anna recovered only slowly. Originally it had been their intention that Nathan should return to Uppsala in August, and come back and fetch his family at the end of September. This was of course now impossible, and on August 8 the whole family left Leipzig together by way of Berlin and Sassnitz, under dreadful conditions on packed military trains, to return home.[34]

Then there was the problem of who would carry on Söderblom's teaching in Leipzig. After a great deal of negotiation, the choice fell on a Belgian, Franz Cumont, a Catholic and the greatest expert of the time on the subject of Roman Mithraism and the mystery religions generally. But even had there been no war (and it was of course Germany's invasion of Belgium that had brought Britain into the war), Cumont was not interested. On June 20 he wrote to Söderblom to congratulate him on his appointment to the archbishopric, and to explain that he had already turned down a similar offer from Berlin, but that in any case he had disliked teaching in Belgium so much that he had no wish to be a professor.[35] His German was not up to lecturing in Leipzig, and all he wanted to do was to retire to Rome and write three or four more books. The initiative was an interesting one, however, and a sign that there was that in *Religionsgeschichte* which was capable of transcending confessional frontiers.

Söderblom delivered his last lecture in Leipzig (on the subject of Buddhism and Christianity) on July 31.[36] On August 5 he dispatched a postcard to Göransson, written for safety's sake in German. At midnight Britain had declared war on Germany in consequence of the invasion of Belgium. "England's declaration of war was a dreadful blow. . . . Everything worse than the most pessimistic expectations. You cannot imagine how painful it is, not to be at home at this fateful hour."[37]

In German terms, the war had been forced upon Germany by the combined pressure of Russia in the east and France in the west, and the initial level of confidence in the outcome was high. Söderblom was pulled in two directions: by a profound detestation of war (especially among Christians) on the one hand, and by a great admiration for Germany on the other. Writing from Lund on August 12 to Fries, he rhapsodized slightly:

> The last week [in Leipzig] was overwhelming. A great people, united, willing to bear the heaviest sacrifice for the sake of their honor and the future of the nation. For the first time the world is seeing a genuine citizens' army. It is frightful that this glorious people should be bled in this way by a Europe whose peace had been kept by the German emperor. And we [in Sweden], we just look on. . . . I cannot understand how people here are so little affected by the roar of the riders of the Apocalypse, and by the danger to us that every weakening of Germany means.[38]

That in coming years Söderblom himself was to have a not inconsiderable role, first in attempting to resolve the conflict and later in repairing the wounds it inflicted on the Christian churches, no one could at this stage have foreseen. His Nobel Peace Prize lay sixteen years in the future.

Söderblom was consecrated archbishop of Uppsala Cathedral on November 8, 1914. It would have been his father's ninety-first birthday, had he lived. The Pastoral Letter which he wrote and published was dedicated in no small measure to the memory of Jonas Söderblom, and to a few words passed on by him on his deathbed: "Not as lords over the congregation, but as helpers of your joy."

Professor Söderblom had delivered his last professorial lecture. But that did not mean that Archbishop Söderblom ever lost the taste for scholarship or the ability to be a scholar, though the opportunities were naturally fewer. In a final chapter we shall look briefly at some of those opportunities. First, however, we must retrace our steps briefly, leave *personalia* on one side, and survey the most important publications of Söderblom's last few professorial years.

7
Toward a Phenomenology of Religion

At the beginning of this study we had occasion to cite Gerardus van der Leeuw's statement that the name of Söderblom stands as a symbol of "the current phenomenological viewpoint" in the study of religion.[1] We should not forget that that was written in the 1930s and not in the 1980s. Nevertheless, it is still not without interest—the more so in view of present uncertainty as to what "the phenomenological viewpoint" might be.[2]

In all essentials, Söderblom's approach to the study of religion was in place by the time he took up his Uppsala appointment in 1901, and had received its first definitive statement in his monograph *Uppenbarelsereligion* very soon thereafter.[3] However, between 1910 and 1920 he published four large books, numerous articles, and one important monograph from which it is possible to reconstruct his mature views practically in their entirety. In their Swedish editions, articles and monographs aside, the four books amount to a massive sixteen hundred pages or so, and only one of them has ever found a translator (into German). The fourth was not published until five years after he became archbishop, and therefore falls outside the time-scheme of this study. It may, however, be considered briefly in this connection.

The four books in question are: *Religionsproblemet inom katolicism och protestantism* (The problem of religion in Catholicism and Protestantism, 1910), *Gudstrons uppkomst* (The origins of theism, 1913), *Ur religionens historia* (From the history of religion, 1915), and *Humor och melankoli och andra Lutherstudier* (Humor and melancholy and other Luther studies, 1919). To these we may add Söderblom's two most important *Encyclopaedia of Religion and Ethics* articles, those on "Communion with Deity" (1910) and "Holiness" (1913), and *Natürliche Theologie und allgemeine Religionsgeschichte* (1913), which we have already discussed. In these seven works of the 1910s we have the necessary sources for an evaluation of Söderblom's "phenomenology."

Again we may emphasize that Söderblom did not use the *language* of phenomenology: the word itself was not part of his vocabulary. What we do have, on the other hand, is his insistence that it is the business of the student of religion to be concerned with *verklighet* (i.e., reality, though hardly in a metaphysical sense), that is, with what is actually *there* in the world of religion. Precisely the same point emerged from Edvard Lehmann's own Swedish-language textbook *Religionsvetenskapen* (The science of religion, 1914), which contained a section labeled *Den synliga religionen: religionens fenomenologi* (Visible religion: the phenomenology of religion). Lehmann's language differed from Söderblom's; their concerns were identical.

Further, let us recall again that in the scholarly vocabulary of the time, "religion" occurs almost always in the singular, in *Religionsgeschichte, religionshistoria*, "comparative religion," and the other more or less interchangeable terms. All religion is in the last resort one, however wide its range of variants. The Judeo-Christian tradition does not operate according to rules different from all the rest. The more one knows, the more clearly one can discern types and patterns, operative to a greater or lesser extent wherever one cares to concentrate one's investigations. The place of Christianity among the religions of the world cannot be seen in terms of a divinely protected enclave, immune from outside influence. It does not help in the slightest to pour scorn on "the opposition," while at the same time subjecting Christianity to an idealized and idealizing treatment in accordance with what later Christian generations would like Christianity to be. All religion is one, and all religious traditions in some degree represent a human response to divine revelation—for the Barthian insistence that "the word of God" is discontinuous with "religion," Söderblom and his generation had no time at all.

Söderblom was a Christian—deeply, devoutly Christian. That in itself is sufficient, in the eyes of a later generation of scholarly empiricists, to disqualify him from having a voice in the present-day debate. They are entitled to their opinions. Here let us only observe that Söderblom's Christian presuppositions were never for one moment concealed; on the contrary, they were always stated with complete clarity. It is another matter that latter-day critics do not share them, both scholarship and Christianity having moved some way beyond the positions both occupied in the pre-1914 years—whether for better or worse, others may decide. But this at least bears out one of Söderblom's deepest convictions, that religion is a species of life, and that life is not static.

The notion that the phenomenological enterprise holds up as an ideal the state of being free from presuppositions in matters having to do with religion and values generally, Söderblom would have found incomprehensible for two reasons. For one, those who have made such claims have not infrequently been engaged less in the quest of value-free scholarship than in the attempt to free themselves from the need to defer to values of which they happen not to approve. And for another, since the state of being value-free is evidently thought to be worth striving after, it can hardly be other than a value itself, resting to be sure on a different authority but no less an imperative. In Söderblom's case, the religious panorama of the world was to be viewed and interpreted in the light of the conviction that God *is*, and that humanity throughout history has responded; that the record is there, and can be read with the most scrupulous accuracy of which one is capable. What one reads is to be ordered, not according to the principles in force in only one corner of the world of religion, but according to whatever perspectives may emerge from all that is accessible of the human record as a whole. That record he was in the habit of calling "reality," often pointing out how diverse and indeed chaotic it may seem. Often it resists organization—the more so, the closer one approaches any part of it. Structures and patterns there are nonetheless, and it is the scholar's task to try and find them, interpret them, and subject them to his or her own best judgment. If that is phenomenology, then Söderblom was a phenomenologist.

Söderblom had his own way of writing books.[4] Often they grew out of lecture series and shorter articles, and they do not as a rule follow a single line of argument from beginning to end. Nor do they always keep to the same style. He could, and occasionally did, write Germanic academic prose, with long and intricate sentences and strings of subordinate clauses. More often he was an entirely untypical academic of the time, in preferring one-clause, short sentences, breaking up his narrative in a striking fashion. (This was even more marked in his letters.)[5] In his younger days he had experimented with short-lived Swedish spelling reforms, and even with artificial international languages.[6] His mature books present the aspect of assembled (though by no means disconnected) essays on separate subjects, in which a problem is approached from one angle and then another, much as one might view a three-dimensional sculpture. Occasionally he can change perspective quite abruptly, almost on impulse, in response to the shifting nature of his material. And he is never dull as some earnest academics can be dull.

The "early" Söderblom is known to the academic world at large (outside Scandinavia, that is) only through a few short articles in Hastings's *Encyclopaedia of Religion and Ethics* and the German translation of *Gudstrons uppkomst, Das Werden des Gottesglaubens*. The encyclopedia articles simply reproduce in highly compressed form what is better and more fully expressed elsewhere. His book on the origins of religion (to which we shall return in a moment), while original in its approach, contains no really new material. Meantime his best book has gone largely unnoticed, and indeed remains almost completely unknown, especially to the English-speaking world. This was *Religionsproblemet inom katolicism och protestantism* (The problem of religion in Catholicism and Protestantism), 518 pages long and published in 1910.

Always the best judge, Anna Söderblom thought *Religionsproblemet* to contain the best of her husband's writing:

> It gives insights into his intellectual workshop such as are hardly to be found elsewhere. But it is an enigmatic book. It is in no way a systematic presentation of what he himself thinks about the persons and events he describes. . . . Sometimes it seems to me as though he was consumed from beginning to end by a burning eagerness to tell about these remarkable personalities—I mean mainly Newman, [von] Hügel, Loisy and Tyrrell—and about the reaction they called forth. It was with the same eagerness that he wanted to communicate the riches of his own thinking.[7]

In the late 1960s, Friedrich Heiler called this same work "the best and most insightful book ever written about Catholic Modernism."[8]

And yet it is about Catholic Modernism—that intellectual movement in the Catholic church that tried to effect an accommodation with modern historical and critical scholarship, only to founder in 1907 on the rock of Vatican disapproval—only in part. The book's first 370 pages deal with modern scholarship and the churches, chiefly the Church of Rome. But thereafter Söderblom turns from personalities to principles, and it is this second part of the book that contains the best and most systematic account of Söderblom's thinking that he was ever to achieve. So as well as a fascinating—and contemporary—account of the leading figures in the Modernism movement in Europe and America, notably Newman, Loisy, Tyrrell, and Friedrich von Hügel, and of the conflicts and intrigues with which many of them were surrounded, this book provides the fullest statement of a systematic *Religionswissenschaft* to be found in the Söderblom literature.

On the first count, though Söderblom was well disposed to many Catholics individually, he was never greatly impressed by the Roman Catholic church as an institution. The Modernists' fate he clearly regarded as a great tragedy, and as a blow against true religion and true scholarship. But although Catholic Modernism had begun to move in the right direction, it had not moved far enough. Even at its best, in the work of Baron von Hügel, it had elevated the institution over the creative personalities, the geniuses of the world of religion—the Prophets, Jesus Christ, Paul, and especially Luther. The Bible was too little known, and even among the Modernists there was a distressing gap between scholarship and piety. It had been left to a Protestant, Paul Sabatier (no relation to Söderblom's mentor Auguste Sabatier) to write the first modern critical study of St. Francis of Assisi, rescuing him from the excesses of popular devotion and giving him his rightful place in history.[9] The path chosen by the liberal wing of Protestantism was dangerous, since once one had begun to subject religion to the searchlight of critical scholarship, the process could not be brought arbitrarily to a halt without denying its own principles. But at least Protestantism had levered the geniuses from beneath the weight of the institution, and on them could rest at least part of its case. Mostly, though, the first part of *Religionsproblemet* is less critical than narrative, the product of wide reading in the constructive and polemical literature of the 1890s and 1900s and "phenomenological" in the best sense of the term.

The second part, a hundred pages headed "The Breakthrough of Religion," paints on a much wider canvas. The problem of religion at the present time consists in the way in which old words and ideas have taken on new meaning under the impact of the revolution in thought brought about by modern science on the one hand, and by post-Kantian philosophy on the other. This is confusing, but it is inevitable: "Life means change. Therefore at different times the same rituals and words are used to clothe different ideas. . . . Words do not have a monopoly on stagnant or stereotyped content."[10] The language of religion is open to constant revision. Words like "sacrifice," "God," "devil," "guilt," and "atonement" do not mean what they meant to former ages, and after us they will continue to take on new meaning. The stars in their courses fight against all that is static and stagnant in life, in ideas—and in religion.

Always religion appears in two forms, and these are always to some extent in tension. There is the immediate, spontaneous, personal (figuratively speaking, the "soul" of religion), and there is the intellectual and institutional (the "body"). In Protestant history, Luther and Schleiermacher stand for the former, Calvin and Kant for the latter. Mostly it is the latter that has the upper hand. This, however, is not "true" religion: "True religion begins only when a person is forced in spirit, if not outwardly, to kneel by a sense of powerlessness and a sense of being a debtor and a recipient, without the possibility of paying the debt."[11] One recalls Söderblom's 1893 experience of the *holiness* (otherness, power) of God and its devastating physical, as well as spiritual, effect upon him. One recalls Kierkegaard's "fear and trembling," and even Isaiah's "Woe is me! For I am lost; for I am a man of unclean lips, and I dwell in the midst of a people of unclean lips; for my eyes have seen the King" (Isa. 6:5). Rudolf Otto's *Das Heilige*, incidentally, with its coining of the word "numinous" to label this experience, was not to appear for another seven years. But on page 388 of *Religionsproblemet* there appear the words "*From är den människa, som på allvar håller någonting för heligt.*" Let me translate literally: "Pious (or religious) is the person, who seriously holds something to be holy." And whatever else this experience may do, it forces one to recognize one's own insignificance.

A chapter on science and religion stresses, in a manner still familiar today, almost eighty years on, that science is a map, not an image of reality, and that the scientist "cannot grasp the whole of the purpose" he or she serves.[12] A chapter on "existence as life" anticipates some of the concerns of modern process theology. Life is movement, never static, always caught up in the struggle between life and death, light and darkness, and therefore profoundly dualistic.[13] In this struggle, new things are brought about, no matter whether we choose to speak of evolution, mutation, or liberty.[14] God therefore is not changeless, except "in purpose, in will, in love."[15]

Some pages previously, in discussing the religious vision of the future and religion's ways of coming to grips with the problem of time, Söderblom had spoken of the two "prophetic religions" (those of Israel and Iran) and their "terrible experience of the nearness and overwhelming power of the living God."[16] The phrase "the living God" (in Swedish, *den levande Guden*) was to occur again, as the title of his last book. On this occasion Söderblom does not shy away from the problems attached to such a view: the problem of retribution, approached in different ways in the Indian and Judeo-Christian traditions, but solved finally in neither; and the more general problem of theodicy, of justifying the ways of God with humanity. This too is, in human terms, insoluble, but "the bankruptcy of theodicy actually meant the victory of religion."[17] For when explanation fails, trust comes into its own.

But one must act in order to know. Here Söderblom introduces yet another category of mysticism, *livsmystiken*, "the mysticism of life"—activist, involved, questing and questioning, forever striving after distant goals.[18] It is in such a practical commitment that one comes closest to the heart of things, and in a couple of sentences Söderblom comes very close to the central concern of the later phenomenological approach. As they stand they are enigmatic: "The most deeply subjective is the objective. It is a matter of seeking one's way to that which is essential."[19] I am not altogether sure what is meant here, except perhaps that it is in giving oneself most fully that one finds oneself most completely—though not as an isolated individual, but rather as one who accepts being bound up in one bundle of life with others, in a necessary connection.

The last section of the book is entitled "The Verdict of the Comparative Science of Religion." Here the chief "verdict" is that comparative religion must force theology into a much wider frame of reference than that commonly used,[20] especially with regard to the question of revelation. In Söderblom's own view, "something of revelation is to be found everywhere. In higher religion it is purer."[21] He quotes Luther and Kierkegaard in support of this view, but also the *Gita* and the Sufi saint Jalal-uddin, who wrote "you would not seek me if you had not already found me" several centuries before Pascal.[22] There is a certain resemblance here between Söderblom's view and that put forward three or four decades later by Mircea Eliade. True, Eliade was to use the term "hierophany" where Söderblom spoke of revelation, the somewhat impersonal replacing the strongly personal. Söderblom had a respect for history which Eliade did not. But is not the final verdict similar, at least to the extent that it is "the holy" that gives religion its meaning? To Söderblom, "the holy" is least of all an impersonal force, operative largely on other people, but rather "an overwhelming and testing nearness, which the soul cannot avoid."[23] And wherever there are signs in history of human beings bearing witness to that "nearness," however vaguely or incoherently, there is religion, and there is a measure of revelation.

Reading the first part of *Religionsproblemet*, one recognizes that Söderblom had a great capacity in the history of ideas. The second part is less satisfactory. He was never fully at his ease with abstractions, and quite obviously found it hard to explain fully his own position. For the same reason, to summarize the second part of *Religionsproblemet* hardly does justice to any of its arguments. Let us remember, though, that this book was written chiefly for a theological community from whose members he could expect only a limited level of understanding and acceptance.

In 1949 Erland Ehnmark wrote his doctoral dissertation on Söderblom, under the title *Religionsproblemet hos Nathan Söderblom* (The problem of religion in Nathan Söderblom). Let me quote a passage in which Ehnmark characterizes Söderblom's modus operandi in this and other books:

> There is not much in Söderblom's production that is written in cold blood. But sometimes it burns more than on other occasions. The peculiar circumstance that he is criticized at the same time for psychologism and for metaphysics, is perhaps most easily explained by the fact that Söderblom was always

concerned to describe religious reality in experience, his own and other people's, *as* it is experienced—and that includes the "metaphysical" components of faith. He desired to see, and he saw, religion from within, from the point of view of personal experience.[24]

In drawing up his distinction between the mysticism of personality and the mysticism of the infinite, Söderblom was speaking out of his own experience:

> It is the miracle in his own life that he assumes to have a counterpart in the other major forms of religion, and psychological analysis supports his conviction that such is the case. To Söderblom, religion was something real, not only as a psychical phenomenon [*företeelse*] but as a witness to the living God and his acts, as a reflection, obscure and clear, faithful and broken, of the suprasensory reality. This firm conviction explains a good deal of that for which he was criticized. But it had another consequence, in that it gave him a clear eye for differences and types, for the genuine and the false, for life in contrast to doctrine. Nothing was more foreign to his nature than to draw lines of demarcation "in principle" between true religion on his own side and idolatry on the other. He never wrote a single line that would support such an idea. He never, on the other hand, tired of renewing, changing and clarifying his distinctions, and if he is unclear, it is not because he lacked the capacity to hold a firm theological line, but because he had so much respect for historical truth, and for real, empirical distinctions—on which of course principles in the end have to be based, if they are to have any value at all.[25]

The second of Söderblom's major works from the 1910s, *Gudstrons uppkomst* (which can be variously translated as "The origin of belief in God" [literally], "The origin of religion," or "The origin of theism"), is the most extended excursion into the field of comparative religion that he ever undertook, aside from *La Vie future*. It appeared in Swedish in 1914, and was later translated into German, but has never found an English-language publisher.[26] This is a pity since, although by now inevitably dated in some respects, it provides ample proof that Söderblom was nothing if not professional in the field.

In the late nineteenth and early twentieth centuries there was a plethora of anthropological, psychological, and sociological theories, all aiming to account for the origins of religion without (as a rule) recourse to the category of divine revelation. Söderblom, it is safe to say, had all this material at his fingertips. But it is necessary to add that he did not really supplement it: he had no new facts to add to the record. He used the sources the other theorists used, together with their writings. But where most of the works of the period tended sooner or later to assert that religion *must* have originated with one or another human impulse, individual or social, to the exclusion of all others, Söderblom was less easily convinced on that score. Therefore he took the three major theories of origin current at the time—animism, *mana*, and high gods—gave an account of each, and suggested that the three are not so much mutually exclusive as complementary. But first he cleared the ground in a short chapter on "the primitives and we."

Again the theme is the intractability of "reality" (that which is there to be recorded and evaluated), especially where "primitive" peoples are concerned. The material is difficult enough in itself. But there is also the factor of cultural distance to be considered—it is good to see Söderblom recognizing this, at a time when many scholars seemed not to be able to take it into account. "Strangely enough, reality has not been organized for the sake of science."[27] The scientist cannot study sense impressions as experienced by other people; we live in one kind of culture, "the primitives" in another; the barriers to understanding are enormous. But having said that, Söderblom insists that whatever the barriers, the attempt at understanding must be made, almost in the spirit of "if a job is worth doing, it is worth doing badly."[28]

There follow long chapters on animism, on power and *mana*, and on high gods. There would be little point in summarizing them, since for the most part they break little new ground. One might observe, on the other hand, that viewed from a Swedish horizon, most of this material had been totally unknown hitherto, other than through Söderblom's own Uppsala lectures and occasional articles. One should therefore not be too critical of a largely pioneering work in that language. Bearing in mind Söderblom's earlier (1902) essay on Andrew Lang, it is interesting to find him considerably more critical of Lang's "high gods" than on the previous occasion, chiefly on the grounds that such *dei otiosi* do not inspire worship, and therefore are not gods in any strict sense.[29] One cannot speak here of "primitive monotheism," as Wilhelm Schmidt had begun to do, since neither "mono" nor "theism" applies in such cases. Schmidt, Söderblom notes in passing, though antianimist, is strictly evolutionist in his approach.[30] But "reality," he adds, is never as neat as Schmidt would have one believe.[31]

In 1914, incidentally, Söderblom reviewed the first volume of Schmidt's *Der Ursprung der Gottesidee* in the pages of *Deutsche Literaturzeitung*, and had there raised precisely the same objections to the "high god" theory: that it is misleading to speak in this connection of *Urmonotheismus*, since these beings (whatever one may choose to call them) receive no worship; and that Schmidt had carried his passion for systematization too far. The real world had not been organized for the benefit of scientists, being essentially marked by confusion (*Verworrenheit*), in common with all reality. Schmidt, then, had helped to clear away some misapprehensions, but he had not proved his case.[32] (Lang, one might add, had been far more cautious.)

One approaches religion more closely in the realm of *mana*, that catch-all term introduced at the turn of the century by R. R. Marett to denote a species of "fear and trembling" in face of an unknown something hidden in the world, which might be personal or impersonal or both together. At least one can see a line leading from *mana* to holiness—and along that line lies personal religion. But animism is also important, since this too can lead in precisely the same direction, and can explain the origins of a great many deities. In the light of history, "animism signifies the discovery of an agency, a will behind life's expressions. Thus animism is, both for the knowledge of God and for anthropology, an indispensable sense and insight, though its meaning emerges only gradually."[33]

Actually, therefore, Söderblom is able to see the value in all three major theories of the origin of religion. Each represents an angle of approach to the complex reality that is religion. Each illuminates one aspect of the whole, and in later religious life (remote origins aside) each lives on in its own way. As a rule, however, we cannot trace the complex processes that have brought about a clearly individualized idea of deity. What, then, is central? Not surprisingly, Söderblom returns to the concept of holiness.[34] There may be religion without a developed notion of deity or without worship. "But there is no religion [fromhet] deserving of the name, without a sense of the holy."[35] Without an eye to the distinction between the holy and the profane, the student of religion makes all manner of mistakes, separating out from religion phenomena that belong to it on all historical levels. If, for instance, the concept of deity is assumed to be central, then where that concept is absent, what is left must be something other than religion—for instance magic. And magic must be prereligious. But this in Söderblom's view is simply wrong. The question having been dealt with in the wrong terms, faulty results and theories have been the inevitable consequence.[36] Religion *differs* from magic, certainly: in religion there is both fear and reassurance, neither of which is present in magic. In magic one manipulates the supernatural powers, whereas in religion one submits to them.[37] Religion therefore may degenerate into magic; it cannot evolve out of it.

In giving a short account of the "religion and magic" question we have moved into the fifth chapter of *Gudstrons uppkomst*. The sixth chapter is a separate study of a Chinese "high god," *Shang Ti*, and the seventh a similar study of an Indian and an Iranian concept, *Brahman* and *Hvarenah* (both taken here as expressions of "power"). Interestingly enough, the *Hvarenah* section, less than twenty pages in length, is the only passage in this book in which Söderblom makes any use at all of Iranian material, and even so, it is perfunctory. One feels that Söderblom had done all that he needed to do with the Iranian documents more than a decade earlier, and felt little need to rake over the embers of old work.

Chapters eight and nine change gear completely. Here Söderblom moves into the history of ideas in the West, giving an account of Western responses to China and India respectively, to China in the seventeenth and eighteenth centuries, and to India in the eighteenth and nineteenth. Neither chapter is long. Both, however, represent interesting essays, though how they relate to the remainder of the book, the reader is left to decide.

The final chapter shifts ground again, comprising a study of deity in the Old Testament under the heading of "Deity as Will." Here, one might say, Söderblom returns to home base and to his own tradition. But still more he is seeking here to give a scholarly account of that deity who had laid hold on him personally twenty or so years earlier, coupling together scholarship and experience and letting each illuminate the other. Here a slightly longer quotation will emphasize the point:

> The most essential quality of Yahwist religion is not that its great men were Semites, but that they were prophets. Through Moses, Yahweh was lifted out of his natural bonds and became an ethical, judicial will. But the earlier nature of the God of Sinai was not only a hindrance, which had to be swept away before the prophetic Yahweh could emerge. Certainly the theophanies, which still hint at Yahweh's acts, appear to a certain extent in the Old Testament as incidentals. For natural catastrophes are unconditionally related to Yahweh's moral intentions for Israel and the nations. But in the pre-Mosaic Yahweh they already expressed an active and unavoidable violence in his nature, which was of positive importance for Mosaic belief. Intellectualism has often prevented scholars from appreciating in the history of theism that which has not directly served its ethical character, its spiritual quality and its universalism. Is deity ethical, is he spiritual, is he universal? A broad and slow development came in time to answer all these questions in the affirmative. But behind them there nevertheless lies a much more serious question. Is the deity real? Is the deity the first and last reality in the human world? Here the nature-spirit of Sinai occupies an important place. His mighty power and overwhelming majesty were still part of Moses' religion, though his ethical aspect had become richer and the fear of God had acquired a new moral motivation. I do not believe that one can easily overestimate what the overwhelming sense of the deity's power and threatening, but also supportive, nearness has meant for the history of religion. The development has not been unilinear, in the notion of God or elsewhere. A mild and friendly El or a high Original appeals more to the enlightened judgment than does the barbaric Yahweh of the Sinai desert. Nevertheless it is the latter who has meant more to the higher and highest knowledge of God. In the Old Testament the two came together in the religion of revelation. Faith in a high, mild Producer [*frambringare*] and animism's trembling apprehension

and rough shaping of the active nature of the deity combined, and together came to serve the cause of biblical revelation.[38]

What Andrew Lang had called the "high god"—a term thereafter generally germanicized into *Hochgott*—Söderblom transposes as *frambringare* ("Producer," the one who brings forth). By 1914 in Söderblom's case an initial cautious acceptance of Lang's views had become far more critical. This was so chiefly because Söderblom was unable to see the slightest trace of "fear and trembling" in the human response to such deities. Further, their "highness" was open to some question in some instances: "In Australia they evidently began as animals."[39] (This is not necessarily the case, but this was what he wrote.) But lacking the quality of the numinous, there was no revelation in them. Whoever would seek primitive revelation must look rather for that which is "strange, uncontrollable, dangerous, powerful, extraordinary, supernatural," together with a direct involvement in human affairs. Similarly with the Hindu Brahman, who is in all things, but who inspires no "holy trembling" (*helig bäfvan*). Such a concept may intrigue and inspire, but cannot be worshiped. *Mana* and *tabu* bring one closer to the heart of things: "there is no doubt that the hypothesis of power and *tabu* takes us deepest into the inner chamber of primitive religion. . . . Here there awaits the danger that keeps the heart trembling."[40]

What *Religionsproblemet* and *Gudstrons uppkomst* have most clearly in common is that both are books not about the study of religion, but about religion. And whatever else they contain, and however wide the range of material that has gone into them, both in the last analysis are "about" Söderblom's own experience of once having been gripped by *den levande Guden*, "the living God"—which experience provided him with the key (in the musical rather than in the door lock sense) in which to approach and study religion.

The third of the books in the sequence we may pass over more summarily. *Ur religionens historia* (1915) is actually a collection of essays, mostly published previously over the past fifteen or so years. The first three essays (as arranged in the table of contents) have the rubric "The Primitives": the 1902 essay on Andrew Lang, another Australian essay entitled "Mysteries among a Stone-Age People," and a reworked version of an article first published in *The*

International Review of Missions as "Does Primitive Heathenism Present any Points of Contact for Missionary Work?" There are two essays on Chinese subjects, and nine more simply labeled "Comparative," including the essay on intoxication and religion from 1906, one on Nietzsche, one more on Christian missions, and a study of the calling and temptations of the Buddha compared with those of Jesus. There are no grand methodological pronouncements in this book. Rather it corresponds in intention to Max Müller's collection of "chips from a German workshop"—shorter studies completed with a particular purpose in mind and too valuable to be discarded. Dedicated to Anna Söderblom on her forty-fifth birthday (September 24, 1915), a tiny foreword expresses a certain pathos: "Since new official duties now make demands on my time and strength, it was thought appropriate to gather together in one volume a number of minor studies, previously printed or ready for printing. More extensive investigations, not yet in a state to be printed, must be postponed to an indefinite future."

By this time Söderblom had been elevated to the archbishopric of Uppsala. The most horrendous war in human history thus far had been in progress for more than a year already, and had three more gory years to run. Söderblom had in effect entered upon a new career, which was to come to an end only on his death in 1931. But before the decade was out he had, amazingly, produced a fourth large-scale book.

In one of the best books about Martin Luther ever written by a non-Lutheran, Gordon Rupp's *The Righteousness of God* (1953), there is a reference to the role of Scandinavian scholarship in bringing about a renaissance in Luther studies in the early part of the present century. In Rupp's words, "The two great names associated with the beginning of the so-called 'Luther Renaissance' are those of Nathan Söderblom, and of Einar Billing, and it is generally considered to date from the publication of the latter's 'Luthers Lära om Staten' in 1900."[41] On this occasion, however, the otherwise so meticulous Rupp disappoints his readers, giving no indication of what Söderblom's role might have been. There is no book by Söderblom in his bibliography, even.[42] For this we may blame the tyranny of language, since, although Söderblom's massive Luther book of 1919 has been quoted frequently since, it has never been translated.

The thought of Söderblom also having been a Luther scholar will no doubt come as something of a shock to those of a later generation who prefer scholars to be specialists in only one field, and that field to be as carefully circumscribed as possible. It is scarcely necessary to add at this stage, however, that Söderblom's "field" was religion-as-such; that his own religious tradition was Lutheran; and that always Martin Luther was to him an outstanding example of *personlighetsmystik*—that form of communion with deity which he placed highest on his own scale of values. Further, he saw Luther as an outstanding representative of the prophetic tradition, as a powerful personality, and as (in his own special terminology) a "religious genius." Over the years, alongside his other investigations, Söderblom had returned again and again to Luther, in lectures and occasional publications. And during the war years—when otherwise there was a great deal of German writing on the subject of Luther as, among other things, the father of the German nation—he brought together all these impulses into a single study. The four-hundredth anniversary of the Reformation was celebrated in 1917, and a proportion of what the book contains was first presented to various Swedish, Danish, and Finnish audiences in that year in lecture form.

Before the turn of the century, Luther scholarship in Sweden generally had followed in the footsteps of the Germans. Luther was seen as the founder of Lutheranism, and as such was locked into the Lutheran confessions, and made to stand alongside Melanchthon and the Formula of Concord.[43] In a similar manner Jesus had been interpreted in the light (or shadow) of everything that in later years carried his name. The sixteenth-century Luther was largely unknown. The pioneer work in which a return to "the Luther of history" was seriously begun in Sweden was by Einar Billing (1871–1939), in the form of a dissertation, *Luthers lära om staten* (Luther's doctrine of the state, 1900), presented in Uppsala shortly before Söderblom's return. Between 1900 and 1920 Billing taught in Uppsala, first as *docent* and after 1908 as professor; in 1920 he became bishop of Västerås. During these years he and Söderblom became the closest of colleagues and the warmest of friends. In academic terms, however, Söderblom was much Billing's senior, though only five years older, and when eventually Söderblom produced his own extended Luther study, it was of far greater originality.

For one who makes no claim to be a Lutheran specialist, *Humor och melankoli* is hard to evaluate. Hjalmar Lindroth has called it "one of the most distinctive works in the whole of Luther literature."[44] In its twelve chapters, the first two consider Luther's humor (which is not to say that he was a humorist!), and the next four various aspects of his melancholy. The proportions are significant. There follow chapters on the heroic aspect of his journey to Worms, a comparison of Luther and Erasmus, a further consideration of Luther's "mysticism," a "social" analysis of the Peasants' War, and finally an essay on "All Saints' Eve"—the day on which Luther nailed his "theses" to the church door.

Bengt Sundkler has written that there would seem to have been a certain autobiographical element in this book: "In Söderblom, as in Luther, humor and melancholy went together—the bow of humor drawing music from a life made taut by sorrow, and compassion . . . interpreting Luther, he is really writing the story of his own soul. Luther is presented by him as unique in the history of great Christian personalities. While St. Paul and St. Augustine, Calvin and Pascal, lacked humor, Luther alone by this gift could break through the ascetic, well-formed, type of piety. Söderblom himself needed this outlet."[45]

I do not propose to attempt an analysis of this book: merely to make two observations. The first is that it matters relatively little which of Söderblom's books one approaches during the period of his academic maturity: all in the end give the same impression, that the serious business of life has, first and last, to do with the individual's encounter with the living God. Without such an encounter, there can be religion of a kind, but not "real" religion as Söderblom understood it. Whether in a half-formed human response in the dawn of time to the overwhelming mystery of life, in a medieval monk's struggles with a holy and righteous God, in strictly modern attempts to crack the code of religion through layer upon layer of accumulated cipher, always and everywhere the final meaning is the same: that there is a Will and a Power in the universe ready (even if at rare intervals) to break through and take charge. Certainly the scholar's task consists of far more than that, and generally will be conceived in quite other terms: the hackneyed phrase about the 1 percent inspiration that must be completed by 99 percent perspiration still has much to recommend it. But in Söderblom's case, the craft of the professional historian and theologian was learned and applied with that 1 percent in mind.

My second observation therefore must be that, although in a sense Söderblom was clearly one of the last of the encyclopedists in the study of religion (a class of scholar that has practically vanished from the academy), he was least of all a dilettante in the pejorative sense of the word. He was versatile, yes, if for no other reason than that a mind like his would not be imprisoned within the narrow boundaries of any of today's subject specializations. He was a comparative religionist when comparative religion was still a young and somewhat eccentric pastime; a phenomenologist of religion before the label had even been invented; and a scholar for whom the whole of the record of religion in the world had to be taken into account by whoever would explain any part of it. Today, to be a historian of religion(s), a comparative religionist, a religious studies person, or whatever, is frequently taken to indicate a lack of personal involvement (or indeed interest) in anything having to do with the Judeo-Christian tradition. Our minds stocked with bad precedents, we have almost forgotten the generation of which Söderblom was part, and many of us rub our eyes in bewilderment when faced with the extraordinary sight of an Iranist and comparativist writing books on Catholic Modernism and Martin Luther. No matter whether they are good or bad books: we who are comfortable only with that in which we are "qualified" assume almost automatically that to move beyond one's specialization is to commit an act of academic treason.

In Söderblom's case, there may still be those who will be tempted to view his reversion to Luther in 1919 as an act of penance, brought about by his unexpected elevation to a Lutheran archbishopric five years earlier. Nothing could be more mistaken. He wrote his Luther book because he had, at the time, no other choice. He had in a manner of speaking "chosen" Iran as a field of research in the 1890s. He did not, on the other hand, choose religion: it chose him, and he had no other alternative than to follow its imperative in whatever direction it might lead. That it led him in many different directions was only to be expected, because in his private equation, religion equaled reality equaled life. And it was a mark of his breadth of vision that his own private pantheon included so many "geniuses"—all of them in some measure prophetic in that all, having experienced "the living God" in their own lives, could not but act upon what they had experienced. Among the greatest of those geniuses, Luther occupied a notable position.

By 1914 a very little of Söderblom's work had begun to appear in English. To Hastings's *Encyclopaedia of Religion and Ethics* he contributed a number of articles in the Iranian field, and two which we might describe as "methodological." The former show that he was keeping up his reading in the Iranian field, but none of them is in any way innovative.[46] The two latter—on "Communion with Deity" and "Holiness"—appeared in 1910 and 1914 respectively, and gave the English-speaking world its first introduction to Söderblom's distinctive views.

It must be recorded with regret that Söderblom in English seldom reads well, however. Some of his earlier papers (aside from encyclopedia articles) that found their way into English appear terse, abrupt, and almost wooden and convey little impression of either the man or his mind. Even *The Living God* might be reworked with profit, purely with a view to making it more readable for a modern public. Add to that the constraints imposed upon the one commissioned to write for an encyclopedia, and the result is hardly likely to be literature. Doubtless Söderblom wrote in his own English on these occasions, the text being tidied up subsequently by the editorial staff. Nevertheless the major points are there.

Söderblom's "Communion with Deity" article is of interest chiefly because it stated for the first time in English the distinction he had first drawn seven years previously between "the mysticism of the infinite" and "the mysticism of personality."[47] On this occasion, however, he used neither term. One may perhaps conclude that to label both of two fundamental forms of religious expression as variants of "mysticism" had not been really necessary in the first place, and could be extremely confusing. It may well be that this verbal experiment had been prompted in part by the extraordinary vogue of the word "mysticism" in Western religious thought in the years around the turn of the century.[48] On this occasion, Söderblom had been commissioned to write not on mysticism, but on communion with deity—we in our day might prefer the equally imprecise "spirituality." Thus there was no reason for him to elaborate on the range of meanings that the word "mysticism" might carry. He had by no means abandoned his earlier terminology; he did, however, modify it on this occasion. The distinction is still there—between a spirituality that seeks to transcend, and a spirituality that affirms the human personality; between a *via negativa* and a *via positiva* in the world of religion; between the rejection and the affirmation of symbols and values—but it is classified differently. "These two kinds of communion with deity are intermingled and graduated in manifold ways in real religion, but the difference coincides ultimately with the difference between acosmic salvation and prophetic, or revealed, religion."[49] The two differ on the value which each gives to ethics, to history, to authority, and to the kind of union with the Supreme that is sought. The one seeks a union of substance, or that of husband and wife, the other the union of parent and child:

> On the one side there is a higher appreciation of ecstatic states of mind . . . ; on the other side, a higher appreciation of trust and unaffected self-forgetfulness in the presence of the great tasks of life. . . . The gulf to be bridged by communion is considered by the former type mainly as a gulf between the finite and the Infinite, between temporal succession and change, and timeless contemplation and eternity, between complexity and One-ness; on the other side, between what is and what should be, between sinful man and Holy God.[50]

Probably it would not be too much to claim that in English, almost the only words of Söderblom that are widely remembered today are found in the opening paragraph of the second of his *Encyclopaedia of Religion and Ethics* "method" articles, which reads (slightly shortened):

> Holiness is the great word in religion; it is even more essential than the notion of God. Real religion may exist without a definite conception of divinity, but there is no real religion without a distinction between holy and profane. The attaching of undue importance to the conception of divinity has often led to the exclusion from the realm of religion of (1) phenomena at

the primitive stage, as being magic, though they are characteristically religious; and of (2) Buddhism and other higher forms of salvation and piety which do not involve a belief in God. The only sure test is holiness. From the first, holiness constitutes the most essential feature of the divine in a religious sense. The idea of God without the conception of the holy is not religion. . . . Not the mere existence of the divinity, but its *mana*, its power, its holiness, is what religion involves. . . . The definition of piety (subjective religion) runs thus: "Religious is the man to whom something is holy." The holy inspires awe (*religio*).[51]

This article is anything but perfunctory. It is ten pages in length (double column, small print), and passes in review a vast range of material, beginning with primal notions of *mana* and *tabu* as found in the anthropological literature, a discussion of the paradoxical relationship between "holy" and "unclean," purity and impurity, respect and danger, and moving on to Iranian and Indian material, and finally to the concept of holiness in the Christian church.

Although Söderblom here follows a generally evolutionary line, he does not do so rigidly, and indeed observes that "a supposed uniformity must not be allowed to obscure the peculiar features of holiness in particular societies at the lower stages of civilization."[52] Nevertheless the notion develops. It may do so in a wrong direction, for instance in creating a false impression that holiness is little more than a heightened awareness of moral demands, and consequent good behavior (as in the "Holiness movement" of modern Protestantism). But in the church as a whole, "'holy' never became a merely ethical word, but chiefly suggests divine, supernatural power."[53] Thus holiness is a matter of revelation—of divine power—and that revelation may surface "in creative genius, high personal idealism, and ready obedience to the mysteries of divine guidance and to vocation."[54]

Only at the very end of his article does Söderblom mention the sociological theory of holiness (that of Durkheim and the *Année Sociologique* school), and then only to dismiss it somewhat abruptly. In the Durkheimian view, of course, it is a society which decides what is holy, or sacred, and it does so largely in order to preserve its own institutions and values. Here Söderblom wrote only: "The time-honored sociological theory recognizes the momentous importance of society to religion. But, as far as lower culture is concerned, the derivation of the holy institutions and beings from a mysterious apprehension of society seems to be artificial. In the higher culture, holiness and mysticism most consciously put their ideals beyond society."[55] This is not the place to engineer a confrontation between Söderblom and Durkheim on this point. It is fairly evident, however, that the two were approaching the same concept from opposite angles: Söderblom (and subsequently Otto) from the immediate experience of the individual, Durkheim (who would appear never to have had any such experience himself) from the structures of society. Might one perhaps conclude that, verbal coincidences notwithstanding, they were actually not writing about the same thing at all?

Later critics of Söderblom and Otto have generally remarked upon the great leap which needs to be taken by whoever, given a certain human experience, would deduce from it a specific nonhuman cause.[56] For one thing, other explanations are always possible, and none is fully capable of either proof or disproof in rational categories. One suspects, however, that this would not have troubled Söderblom. His own personal experience of the holiness of God had been overwhelmingly self-authenticating—as no doubt Otto's also had been. To comb the evidence of the history of religion in search of proof that others too had experienced that holiness was thereafter natural and inevitable. That human societies have their own ways of speaking of "sacredness" or "holiness," as amply demonstrated by the French sociologists, has no bearing at all on the case, except that there remains a problem of how one group of concepts can carry both an individual and a social meaning. Doubtless each affects the other in countless ways. For Söderblom, however, it was the individual's awe in face of the nameless mystery that had to take precedence over every other phenomenon to which the adjective "holy" may be attached. There, and only there, might the problem of religion find its solution.

8

Archbishop and Scholar

As of the summer of 1914, Nathan Söderblom was no longer a professor of the University of Uppsala, no longer a teaching academic. But the scholarly habit of a lifetime was not to be discarded overnight. Certainly he had new duties and new responsibilities, local, national, and in his case international. Certainly his priorities had to be reassessed. He had fewer contacts than previously with students, and the time available for reading was seriously curtailed. It is perhaps only fair to say, therefore, that his period of creative scholarship had come to an end. Why, then, prolong this study beyond this point?

Because at the time of his consecration in November 1914, Söderblom was less than fifty years old, and still at the height of his powers, he had no intention of abandoning scholarship—nor did he do so. His change in status meant most of all a shift in emphasis from the problem of religion as a theoretical concern to the application in life and work of what his previous experience had taught him. He still had four massive books ahead of him (five, if we reckon the collection *Ur religionens historia*): his Luther volume of 1917, his account of the Stockholm conference of 1925, his devotional book on the sufferings of Christ, which appeared in 1928, and *The Living God*, which he did not live to see in print. There were numerous smaller books and a vast number of articles, pamphlets, and occasional lectures. In the fullest (though still incomplete) bibliography of his publications yet assembled, more than half of the 667 entries date from the period *after* his elevation to the archbishopric.[1] And in this remarkable collection (which it is doubtful whether anyone except Anna Söderblom ever read in full) the incidence of hackwork is very small indeed. Even in the smallest occasional address there is the mind and style of the trained scholar. Perhaps the scholarship is less obtrusive, more "applied" than formerly, but it is there nonetheless.

To attempt in one chapter to do any justice at all to Söderblom's innumerable involvements and initiatives during the last sixteen years and eight months of his life is strictly out of the question. But this study would be incomplete without at least some account of these final years. This must be done chiefly through episodes and vignettes. Into those years Söderblom packed the work of—one feels—several lifetimes. That he was able to sustain the pressure at all was extraordinary, given the serious illnesses he had suffered in earlier years. His health held out for over a decade. But after 1926 the strain began to tell on him. At first the trouble was largely intestinal, but during the last four or five years his heart was increasingly affected. Occasionally he was forced to stop: never to slow down. His final illness lasted for no more than five days, and even then, in the interval between an emergency operation for intestinal obstruction and the onset of heart failure, he worked.

As archbishop, Söderblom was always surrounded by an atmosphere of celebration. It is said that he had an actor's voice and the true actor's ability to grasp and hold an audience. Among his friends were many persons prominent in the arts—all the arts. But liturgical "performances" aside, it was in music that he might well have made yet another career, had he so chosen. At Söderblom's consecration a short cantata was performed, written for the occasion by one of Sweden's most famous romantic composers, Hugo Alfvén.[2]

Alfvén was not one of the most "religious" of men in the formal sense; rather the opposite. Still he and Söderblom had joined forces on one previous occasion. They had first met in Paris in the 1890s, and in April 1913 Söderblom had assembled the texts, and Alfvén had written the music, for *Uppenbarelsekantat* (Revelation cantata), in celebration of the consecration of a new church.[3] Highly praised at the time, for many years this cantata languished unperformed, though it has recently been resurrected. A second cantata, *Reformationskantat* (Reformation cantata)—again with part of the text by Söderblom—followed in connection with the Luther celebrations of 1917 and an honorary doctorate conferred upon Alfvén himself.[4] It was probably in connection with the preparation for this work that there took place a bizarre episode, totally irrelevant to the subject of this book, but worth retelling nonetheless.

The year was 1917, and in wartime Sweden there was no hard

liquor (*brännvin*) to be had—much to Alfvén's distress and disgust. He was at the time university director of music, and lived in Linnaeus's old house on the corner of Svartbäcksgatan and Linnégatan in Uppsala. On the basis of the old proverb that "necessity is the mother of invention" he had joined forces with two scientist-students to do a little home distilling in the kitchen, and the apparatus had just started to function when Söderblom was announced, in company with a Polish visitor. "So there sat the archbishop in the sitting-room with the bootlegger and made conversation, in his usual cheerful and witty manner, while a meter from him as the crow flies, on the other side of the wall the liquor poured out of its tube. . . . The visit lasted no more than an hour but for me one hour was as long as a whole day."[5] Söderblom had never been noted for keeping company only with the conspicuously godly. As archbishop he had to be somewhat more circumspect, but the collaboration with Alfvén continued. He was one of Sweden's best composers and a personal friend of long standing. Who better to be enrolled on such occasions?

Söderblom's first publication as archbishop, in 1914, was the customary book-length Pastoral Letter (*Herdabrev*) to the ministers and churches in the archdiocese. Eivind Berggrav was later to call it "the most epoch-making letter of its kind ever in Lutheranism."[6] Over a quarter of the letter Söderblom devoted to the question of the war. In the late months of 1914 theologians on both sides of the North Sea spilled mountains of paper and oceans of ink to help justify the actions of their respective countries—a vast and extraordinary literature, it now seems. Söderblom at least attempted to be analytical. The war he saw as an unmitigated tragedy in most respects, while still hoping that some good might somehow come of it. Already he could see with crystal clarity that the outbreak of war had brought to an end the era during which the West had believed in the inevitability of social progress. War reduces human life to its essentials: "Reality awakens the race from the dream of automatic improvement. The nuances of culture are as it were swept away by a hard hand."[7] Rationality itself vanishes, and with it the capacity to judge as scholars judge. Calm judgment is elbowed out by bombast, hysteria, and hatred, and even the great academics join in the chorus of condemnation of "the enemy":

We recognize the famous names. But are these the same men who exercised criticism and judgment primarily over their own scholarship, and were shining examples of free and noble humanity? Some proclaim aloud their disgust. Others shout them down with insults. Others again prove, in learned and refined terms, the devilish wickedness of the enemy. Those who were accustomed to turn a text this way and that a hundred times, now believe blindly in idiotic accusations and rumors. What has happened to rationality?[8]

Rationality had been proved to be a broken reed—but then Söderblom's interpretation of religion had never rested on rationality. And in the meantime, even the horrors of war (which Söderblom did not for one moment play down, as some firebrands were prone to do) might lead indirectly to positive results, since in war "everything becomes more basic."[9] Still Söderblom was prepared to declare his admiration for the German people and their unity under arms, while allowing that much the same unity had been created in France and England.[10] His love of Germany was still very great. In 1914 it was far too early to predict the outcome, but almost at once Söderblom threw himself into the ministry of reconciliation among warring Christian factions—a labor described in great detail by Nils Karlström in an almost six-hundred-page book published in 1947.[11] That, however, falls outside the range of this study to consider further.

The impact of the war on Söderblom's interpretation of religion and culture is best seen in a little pamphlet produced after the armistice, *Gå vi mot religionens förnyelse?* (Are we moving toward the renewal of religion?, 1919). In the past five years, he said, people had aged fifteen years. Before the catastrophe everyone believed that culture would make people happier and better, trusting in rationality, enlightenment, and organizations. So strong had been the belief in rationality that the essential irrationality of religion had been excluded from most people's minds. But now, "This belief has been discarded. . . . We no longer believe in culture. We believe only in love and righteousness."[12] In the fires of war, evil had been proved to be far stronger than anyone had previously believed, and the world's suffering "has compelled us to a faith in the future, beside which many of the futuristic images of the past golden age, well-being, and cultural security appear poverty-stricken."[13] The age of idealism was past and gone: "Can anyone really still harbor the illusion that everything is as it once was?"[14]

The intellectual, spiritual, and ideological turmoil of the wartime years and their aftermath must not be underestimated by anyone who would grasp the intellectual dimension of the twentieth-century European experience. In comparison, world conflicts since 1945 have been more remote and often far more theoretical, only Vietnam biting into the heart of a people as the two world wars had done. But whereas a generation and more of European intellectuals had their minds thrown utterly into disarray by the 1914–18 conflict, Söderblom was one of those whose thinking was better able to cope with the pressure. Idealism in its smoother forms he had abandoned years before others had it torn away from them. He never felt himself to live in a well-ordered and suffering-free world. Hence where a proportion of the postwar generation retreated abruptly into wild experiments in existential irrationality and formlessness, Söderblom's mind maintained its balance—and its religious priorities. No one who revered the prophetic tradition as Söderblom did could really be taken by surprise by events having about them the flavor of the Apocalypse.

Söderblom's longtime "brother-in-arms" Samuel Fries was already seriously ill at the time of Söderblom's return to Uppsala. Early in December 1914 he died after six months' illness, and on December 20 Söderblom conducted his funeral.[15] The circle of *Samfundet fritt ur hjärtat* was broken after more than twenty-five years. Fries had always been an enigma—a strange combination of the most radical scholarship and the most childlike orthodox piety. Those who had known him only slightly saw him as the aggressive radical and the hammer of old-style biblical orthodoxy. Söderblom knew the other side, and in his funeral oration apostrophized not his troublesome writings, but the depth and sincerity of his Christian faith. In one of the last letters Söderblom had written to him, only a few days before he suffered his fatal stroke, he had said that he would have felt far more secure as archbishop with Sam Fries to turn to for advice and encouragement. But this was not to be. Again a support had been removed at a critical moment.

Being archbishop in no way severed Söderblom's connections with the University of Uppsala. On the contrary, he was now pro-chancellor ex officio (in today's Sweden this is no longer the case, it should be added), and as such was closely involved with policy on the highest level. His new residence lay beside the main university building, and although he was no longer able to lecture regularly, he was always available for academic consultation. Former students now occupied numerous academic posts in various parts of the world, and their number was increasing year by year.

The chair occupied by Söderblom since 1901 and vacated in 1914 was filled initially by a pupil of his, Edgar Reuterskiöld, a solid scholar whose area of specialization was the religion of the Lapps (Sami), and who was ultimately appointed bishop of Växjö (1929), when he was succeeded by another Söderblom disciple, Tor Andrae (1885–1947).[16]

Andrae was by no means a carbon copy of Söderblom. He did, on the other hand, carry forward the Söderblom line into a new generation. Andrae's own area of specialization was Islamic studies, though he had a second string to his bow in the psychology of religion. It was, however, as an Islamist that he achieved an international reputation, first with his dissertation *Die person Muhammeds in lehre und glauben seiner gemeinde* (1917; the missing German capitals were intentional), the subject of which Söderblom had suggested, and later with *Muhammed: hans liv och hans tro* (Muhammad: His life and his faith, 1930; translated into many languages).[17] With this book Andrae achieved a wider international reputation than even Söderblom himself had enjoyed. In 1931 Andrae became Söderblom's first biographer; he succeeded him as a member of the Swedish Academy, and might well have succeeded him as archbishop. Andrae gained second place in the election of 1931; again the choice fell upon the one who came third, Erling Eidem. In matters of scholarship Andrae was very much Söderblom's man. He was not, on the other hand, a slavish imitator, but a powerful and independent mind and (it may be added) in Swedish a brilliant stylist. In 1937 Andrae became bishop of Linköping. Thereafter the Uppsala line moved in an increasingly anti-Söderblom direction, for reasons that need not here concern us.

The Söderblom theological line in the 1920s and 1930s was carried on more in the sister-university of Lund than in Uppsala. Here the impulse was twofold: partly from such works as Söderblom's *Uppenbarelsereligion* (1903) and partly from the new impulse which he had helped to give Luther studies, especially after the publication in 1919 of *Humor och melankoli*. One of my own teachers of many years ago, the Swedish-American Nels Ferré, wrote in 1939 that "the Lundensian theologians claim Söderblom as the source of the Lundensian system."[18] Hjalmar Lindroth has pointed to the formal resemblance between Anders Nygren's celebrated distinction between *agapé* and *eros* as two "types" of love and Söderblom's two "types" of communion with deity.[19] But the living link between Uppsala and Lund was provided by Gustaf Aulén, who had been a student in Uppsala at the time of Söderblom's celebrated inaugural lecture of 1901 and who worked under Söderblom for several years. Aulén carried his "style" southward in the 1920s. Thereafter the Söderblom approach was applied and elaborated by Aulén himself, and at a certain remove by Anders Nygren, Ragnar Bring, and others.[20] It is part of a much later history that in a book published in 1981, *Interpreting Religious Phenomena*, Olof Pettersson and Hans Åkerberg of Lund regretted the later neglect of Söderblom in Uppsala, and suggested that the succession had in fact passed to Lund.[21]

We may now retrace our steps. Outside Sweden, disciples of Söderblom were most likely to be found among the small number of students he had begun to train in Leipzig between 1912 and 1914. These were relatively few, but they included some outstanding scholars. F. R. Lehmann's investigations into the question of the *real* (as opposed to the supposed) meaning of the Melanesian/ Polynesian word *mana* were inspired by Söderblom.[22] So too was H. W. Schomerus's masterly study of Saiva Siddhanta[23]—still the best account we have of that most subtle and sophisticated South Indian variant of Hindu philosophy. In the 1920s, however, Söderblom's "man in Germany" was not one of his Leipzig students, but a troubled Roman Catholic from München, Friedrich Heiler.

Even reluctant soldiers in modern wars would be unlikely to take with them into the trenches (were there trenches in modern wars) textbooks in comparative religion. Friedrich Heiler was one who did. As a medical orderly in the German army he had practically learned by heart the Tiele-Söderblom *Kompendium*. This had whetted his appetite for more from Söderblom's pen, and he had learned Swedish in order to be able to pursue his new master's thought further.[24] But Heiler was a Catholic with Modernist leanings, who had been deeply disturbed by what had happened to the Modernists since 1907. During the war he had written a large comparative study on prayer, *Das Gebet* (1918; English translation, *Prayer*, 1932). This he had sent Söderblom on its publication as a mark of indebtedness. There followed an invitation to Sweden, which was duly accepted. So it was that in the summer of 1919 Heiler and Söderblom met for the first time, and Heiler established himself as the most enthusiastic of Söderblom's personal disciples.

Already Heiler was looking for a way to extricate himself from the Roman Catholic fold. At a church conference in Vadstena (which he addressed in his own limited Swedish) he took part in a Lutheran Eucharist in the ancient church of St. Birgitta. This he was convinced was tantamount to a self-excommunication, and a formal declaration of his conversion to Protestantism.[25] Possibly it separated him from Rome in the legal sense; alas, it did nothing official to make him a Swedish Lutheran. Far more important was the fact that the visit brought him under Söderblom's personal canopy. Söderblom's first thought was that Heiler might find a position as *Privatdozent* in Leipzig. Alternatively, he might consider going to China to take charge of a projected Lutheran college. In the end, though, we find Söderblom negotiating with Rudolf Otto to have Heiler appointed to a post in Marburg. This was ultimately accomplished, though not without various questions being asked about his church affiliation. Söderblom assured Otto that Heiler actually was a Protestant—or at least that in Swedish terms there was no way in which he could become *more* Protestant than he was. Actually this was somewhat irregular, amounting to little more than an act of intention on Heiler's part in sharing in a Swedish Eucharist. But it satisfied the authorities.[26]

Thereafter Söderblom was to have no more devoted disciple than Heiler. During the war Heiler had encountered Söderblom through the medium of the fourth (1912) edition of the Tiele *Kompendium*. The fifth edition (1920) he helped Söderblom revise and see through the press, only a year after their first meeting.

Over the next few years, beginning in 1921 with the publication of a little book by B. H. Streeter and A. J. Appasamy, *The Sadhu*, Heiler was to become more and more drawn into a protracted debate about the life and work of a young Indian Christian, Sadhu Sundar Singh, a preacher and visionary. Söderblom, too, was interested in Sundar Singh, and for several years Heiler and he stood

180 *Archbishop and Scholar*

together in the forefront of the Sadhu's defenders. We shall return to that intriguing episode shortly. But first, a glimpse farther afield still, to China.

One of Söderblom's many ex officio positions from 1914 on was that of chairman of the board of the Church of Sweden Mission. Hitherto the mission's major fields had been in South India and in southern Africa, but in the years following the Chinese revolution of 1911 the interest of the West began to turn more and more in the direction of China, where there was a modest Scandinavian presence, Swedish and Norwegian. Söderblom's interest in missionary work and in the encounter of religious traditions in the modern world we have mentioned before, as dating back to his early student days. Now, however, he was in a position to exercise direct influence on the course of events, more especially in China. Unlike a John R. Mott or a modern missionary leader, Söderblom was not a world traveler. But we may take two examples of his "style" in such questions.

Karl Ludvig Reichelt (1877–1952) had been in China under the auspices of the Norwegian Missionary Society since 1903, at first as a fairly run-of-the-mill village missionary.[27] At an early stage, however, he had been deeply impressed by the spirituality of Buddhist monasticism, and sought ways and means by which to approach the monks with the Christian message while preserving as much of their Chinese Buddhist heritage as possible. In 1919 Reichelt had met a young Buddhist monk, Kuantu, whom he instructed and baptized, and the two together proposed the setting up of a specialized mission to other Buddhist monks. By this time, it might be added, Reichelt had made himself a considerable authority on the Chinese variants of Mahayana Buddhism, and especially on the Pure Land sect. His approach to the encounter of religions he derived in large measure from his reading of Söderblom, and shared with him the view that there is revelation in *all* religions, though revelation reaches its fullest expression in and through Jesus Christ. The Christian message therefore may be seen as the fulfillment and crown of all religion—including in this case Mahayana Buddhism.

On furlough in 1920, seeking support for his new initiative, Reichelt contacted Söderblom, who it would seem already knew of him as the author of *Kinas religioner* (The religions of China, 1913; English translation, *Religion in Chinese Garment*, 1951). The two met in Uppsala in 1920, and Reichelt was invited back to deliver the Olaus Petri Lectures in the spring of the following year on Mahayana Buddhism.[28] The result was a 350-page book, *Fra Østens religiøse liv* (From the religious life of the East, 1922), dedicated to Söderblom "in gratitude for brilliant contributions to the study of the history of religion." Thereafter the history of "Reichelt's mission" was a stormy one, partly due to compact opposition from Norway's conservatives, who saw Reichelt's approach as "syncretistic," and partly because of the violent political climate of China at the time. I have written at length elsewhere about these developments, and will say only that the Mission to Buddhists would perhaps never have begun at all without Söderblom's support and that of the Swedish board.

At this same time a somewhat different initiative was being started in China under another of Söderblom's disciples, Knut B. Westman.[29]

If Aulén represents the Söderblom line in theology and Andrae the line in the history of religion, Westman carried on the succession in mission and international affairs. Westman had graduated in 1905, and in 1911 had gained his doctorate with a dissertation on St. Birgitta of Vadstena. At first, therefore, he was a medievalist professionally, while being deeply involved in the Christian movement among students. In 1914 he became Söderblom's international secretary, and Söderblom was anxious that he should gain the Uppsala chair of church history. The choice went elsewhere. However, when after some years of negotiation it was determined to start a Lutheran "college" in China, at Tao Hwa Lun (Hunan), Westman was persuaded (for once, against Söderblom's wishes) to accept a post as its first principal. Westman left for China early in 1923, and at first the situation appeared promising. But after the death of Sun Yat Sen in 1925 the country fell into a period of escalating conflict and civil war, and in November 1926 the school was forced to close, and Westman returned to Sweden. There, like Reichelt (whose mission in Nanking was likewise destroyed in March 1927), he lectured for the Olaus Petri Foundation, on the history of Chinese civilization.[30] At the end of the civil war he returned to China briefly, but in 1929 was appointed to a personal chair in missionary and church history in Uppsala, which he occupied with great distinction for the remainder of his active life. In 1931 he placed first in the election for Söderblom's successor as archbishop, with Tor Andrae second, but as we have seen, the appointee was the one who came third by popular choice, Erling Eidem.

Westman was by far the more careful and meticulous scholar than was Reichelt. Reichelt on the other hand knew the Chinese language far better than did Westman, and was unparalleled in his firsthand knowledge of Buddhist practice and piety. Westman was the scholar-pastor, Reichelt the evangelist who used scholarship as a tool. Both, however, were Söderblom's emissaries in China, whose successes and failures, hopes and disappointments, Söderblom followed with the liveliest interest.

In the 1920s, the Far East notwithstanding, the interest of the world of religion was in large measure centered upon Gandhi's India. For Sweden's part, India had come to popular attention a few years earlier, as a result of Rabindranath Tagore's Nobel Prize for Literature in 1913. For a century, India had been close to the heart of the comparative study of religion on the one hand, and to the heart of the Protestant missionary enterprise on the other. Hindu scriptures were read as a matter of course by every student of religion—translations of the Vedas, Upanishads, and especially the *Bhagavad Gita* were on every student bookshelf. But whereas in the nineteenth century the West regarded Hinduism as a phenomenon belonging mainly to the past, in the early twentieth century Hinduism was showing remarkable signs of new life under a succession of gifted leaders, none more outstanding than the fiery and eloquent Swami Vivekananda, whose oratory at the Chicago World's Parliament of Religions in 1893 had in a manner of speaking brought "Neo-Hinduism" to birth. Thereafter the movement spread like wildfire, fed from diverse sources. It was political and religious in almost equal measure, but before the 1920s its religion was almost exclusively Hindu. Indian Christianity was pulled in two directions. Desiring to be universally Christian and patriotically Indian, it ran a serious risk of being neither. In the West since the 1880s Christian leaders had expected great things from the Indian church, if only it could steer clear of partisan politics and bring "the heart and mind of the East" to bear on the most central of Christian questions. Again, before about 1920 it had shown little sign of even wanting to do this, much less of being capable of fusing together East and West into a strong and flexible alloy. In the 1920s, finally, there appeared a man who seemed capable of fulfilling the hopes of generations in his own unique person. His name was Sundar Singh. Having chosen the path of the solitary wanderer in his youth, he took (or was given) the appellative of "Sadhu"—one who is on the right path, the path that leads to enlightenment. It was, then, as Sadhu Sundar Singh that he came to be known to the Christian world.

We cannot here tell the story of his life.[31] Suffice it to say that he was born in the Punjab in 1889 of a fairly Hinduized Sikh family; that he was converted to Christianity and baptized on his sixteenth birthday; and that between then and 1916, when the first book about him appeared, he was a peripatetic and mostly solitary Christian evangelist who had traveled far and wide in the service of the Gospel. But where had he traveled? In later accounts (of which there were many), Sundar Singh's "mission field" had been Tibet, and there had been many hair-raising adventures. He had many times been on the verge of martyrdom. He had discovered a secret Christian brotherhood among Hindu holy men, and had met a Christian *Maharishi* of vast age. It was around such stories as these that most of the bad-tempered discussions of the later 1920s circled.[32] None of these episodes could be proved actually to have taken place; therefore Sundar Singh might be dismissed as either a dreamer or, at worst, as a pathological liar.[33] In 1920, however, these objections had not yet begun to be raised. In that year Sundar Singh visited the West for the first time, and in Oxford met the noted British theologian and New Testament scholar B. H. Streeter and Streeter's young Indian student A. J. Appasamy. They interviewed Sundar Singh at length, and in 1921 published a book about him, entitled simply *The Sadhu: A Study in Mysticism and Practical Religion*. This had the effect of announcing to the Christian world that Sundar Singh was that *rara avis*, an actual living "mystic." He had seen visions and heard voices; he spent long hours in prayer and meditation; he fasted; and yet his message was clearly Evangelical to the core. Was the Sundar Singh phenomenon, then, proof that at long last Christianity had taken root at the deepest level of

Indian spirituality? Many in the Christian world *wanted* to believe that, and easily allowed themselves to be persuaded that such was indeed the case.

But the Streeter-Appasamy book, though it spoke at length of Sundar Singh's mystical and ecstatic experiences, sought in the end to explain them away in rationalistic terms.[34] One who was infuriated by this approach was Friedrich Heiler, who was convinced that Sundar Singh was all that he appeared to be. And when Sundar Singh began to be attacked from diverse quarters, Heiler rallied to his defense. Over the next few years, the "Sadhu affair" was to become something of an obsession on Heiler's part, the more so from about 1926 on, when Sundar Singh's credentials and honesty began to come under attack. In 1922, however, the storm had not yet broken, and Söderblom was as yet uninvolved in it.

Söderblom had, however, also read Streeter-Appasamy, and had been sufficiently impressed to incorporate a summary of Sundar Singh's life and work into a lecture delivered in Sigtuna in August 1921 and in Uppsala in October of the same year, and subsequently published in Swedish, Norwegian, and English. Streeter's book he described as "exemplary as a concise, well-organized and expressive narrative."[35] Among the things which Söderblom said about Sadhu Sundar Singh on this occasion were that he was a "genuine Hindu," and an equally genuine Evangelical (i.e., Protestant) Christian; that he was a "typical mystic," with a developed tendency toward vision and ecstasy remarkable even in an Indian; but that his visions and ecstasies were in no way induced (as in the case of those connected with the practice of Yoga) but came to him spontaneously. On the whole, though, Söderblom was disposed to interpret the Sadhu's witness as welcome evidence of the universality and adaptability of the Christian message, rather than as a textbook example of mysticism in practice: "Unconsciously Sundar Singh bears witness in his life and teaching to a Christianity which in India is not changed or brought to perfection but purified, revealing out of its innermost nature that which has been obscured in the West."[36]

In April 1922 Sundar Singh undertook a second preaching tour to the West, and on this occasion visited Sweden, where he spent a few days as Söderblom's guest in the Archbishop's House. He preached in the cathedral, and addressed a large audience in the

Great Hall of the University. This was the first and last time the two were to meet face to face. They were photographed together in Söderblom's study, Söderblom with his black frock coat and pectoral cross, Sundar Singh with his short hair and neatly pointed black beard, dressed in a flowing robe with wide sleeves. Another photograph of the Sadhu taken on the same occasion shows him seated in a deep leather armchair, his hands folded. But most striking of all was his profile, resembling as it did so many conventional images of Jesus in all save the length of his hair, while being almost military in its bearing and expression. Here clearly was a man to be treated with the utmost respect.

The Sadhu was in Uppsala for only three days, April 21–23, 1922. It was perhaps fortunate that the Sadhu did not read Swedish, for the local press was by no means unanimous in welcoming either him or his public addresses, and one newspaper in particular took the opportunity to use the Sadhu's visit as an excuse for an attack on Söderblom himself. On Monday, April 24, *Upsala Nya Tidning* lamented that Sundar Singh's performance in the Great Hall of the University on the previous Saturday had been a disappointment: "His delivery was strikingly simple and in no way supported either by ethical or aesthetic pathos. Unless the Indian apostle's uniqueness is at a deeper level, one must express one's surprise at the way he has been exploited for the sake of the Christian public in Sweden."[37]

But worse was to come, for the writer went on to register his personal protest that the Great Hall of the University was being thrown open (in this case by Söderblom) to what he insultingly called "diverse charlatans, frauds, and imbeciles"; why, he asked, should "every new film in which the Church's Primate [Söderblom] plays a leading role" be exhibited in this milieu?[38] The report also noted with some satisfaction that very few students or other academics were present, and ended by expressing the hope that those who had come expecting a sensation had gone away disappointed.

Naturally enough there was an immediate and scandalized reply from the vice-chairman of the Uppsala Student Christian Movement, to which was added a retort from the editor of *Upsala Nya Tidning* that the question was not whether Sundar Singh was an honest man and a sincere Christian, but whether the Great Hall of the University was the appropriate place for him to appear. The editor also hinted that episodes of this kind set a question mark against the appropriateness of retaining the archbishop as pro-chancellor of the university. Other Swedish newspapers joined in. *Svenska Morgonbladet* called the original report an example of adolescent bad manners, though typical of the left-wing "culture-radical" group associated with the *Verdandi* society, but concluded that an attack from that quarter was more to be welcomed than lamented, the *Verdandi* clique being what it was. *Stockholms Tidningen* noted the Uppsala debate, and warned the people of the capital city not to expect too much from the Sadhu. Perhaps, its correspondent noted, it had been a very dangerous mistake to bring Sundar Singh to Europe in the first place: "On the whole one must seriously doubt the suitability of removing an Indian, just because he happens to be a Christian, from the natural milieu in which his personality has its roots, and instead parading him around in America and Europe as a curiosity [*sevärdhet*]."[39] It would have been far better for him to have stayed at home than that he should have been subjected in this way to expectations which could not possibly be fulfilled. *Socialdemokraten* urged under the headline "A Burnt-Out Sensation" that Sundar Singh ought to return to India as soon as possible, though the fault lay more in Western culture than in the Indian Christian: "Sundar Singh must forgive those who are kicking his shins. Perhaps he will also be able to forgive the business man who drew him in one of his advertisements, barefoot and dressed in pajamas, smiling delightedly at the excellent X soap being offered him by the hotel pageboy; if he can, then he must be a real Christian!"[40]

A few days later, the leading Stockholm newspaper *Svenska Dagbladet* printed an article by a Major Oswald Kuylenstierna, comparing Sundar Singh with none other than the celebrated Emanuel Swedenborg—a matter on which there will be more to say later. Alas, the major's article had been supplied—doubtless by some anonymous subeditor—with the provocative headline "A Christological Swindle." This appears to have been a matter of either pure malice or pure editorial sensationalism. The expression was that of a well-known academic, Professor Emanuel Linderholm, and had been used a few days previously by him. It had no real relevance to Kuylenstierna's article, which was appreciative of Sundar Singh and which pointed out the resemblance between his visions and those of Swedenborg, without suggesting that there was any "swindle" involved in either.[41]

After a couple of weeks, Sundar Singh had moved on, and the debate came to an end. Despite the initial attack on him in the pages of *Upsala Nya Tidning*, Söderblom appears to have made no public reply. Two Uppsala professors, Erik Stave and Adolf Kolmodin, gave statements to *Svenska Morgonbladet*, Stave pointing out that Tagore had previously spoken in the Great Hall of the University without anyone complaining, and that the only thing which might have made the university senate refuse permission in this case would have been the suspicion of politics being involved in the lecture. Kolmodin, one of the most conservative of the faculty members, simply noted that Sundar Singh's personality was such as to disarm all criticism and to convince everyone of his genuineness—except presumably the radicals of *Verdandi* and *Upsala Nya Tidning*.[42]

Söderblom (who did not agree with Kolmodin on many things) would certainly have concurred on this point. He had better reason to do so. Whereas most of the disputants had seen and heard Sundar Singh either at a distance, or not at all, Söderblom had spent as much time as possible in his company. He had taken him on a sightseeing tour of the town, and had shown him the cathedral. The two had had long conversations on a variety of subjects, and approximately a year later, Söderblom published a book in which he summed up his impressions and memories.

Sundar Singhs budskap utgivet och belyst (Sundar Singh's message expounded and illustrated, 1923) comprises, first, a Swedish translation of an earlier book by Sundar Singh, *Maktib i Masih* (1921; in English, *At the Master's Feet*, 1922), and secondly, a sequence of seven chapters about Sundar Singh—chapters on visions and parables, the text of his sermon in Uppsala Cathedral on April 23, 1922, a record of Söderblom's conversations with Sundar Singh, and finally a chapter on "Modern India's Three Great Men [Tagore, Gandhi, Sundar Singh] and Religion." As such it is rather a conglomerate of impressions and studies, the work of a busy man who has had little time to digest a multitude of powerful impulses but who nevertheless feels a certain compulsion to write about them. The most valuable material is that contained in the "conversations" chapter.[43] Little time was taken by Söderblom to reflect on the

Sadhu's public appearances in Uppsala, though he did admit that for many, Sundar Singh's public lecture in the Great Hall of the University had been somewhat of a disappointment. "He showed no bleeding feet. There was nothing striking, exotic, or exciting in his appearance and his speech. He was not even found to be sufficiently emotional."[44] Even so, those who knew something about Indian religion found his lecture instructive—a tiny trace of academic one-upmanship which even Söderblom could display on occasion. Söderblom had shown Sundar Singh around Uppsala Cathedral, and there Sundar Singh had, he wrote, been impressed by three things—the shrine of Sweden's patron saint, St. Erik; a medieval cope bearing an embroidered picture of the birth of Christ; and the tomb of Emanuel Swedenborg, "for Swedenborg like him was a visionary."[45]

I have written at length elsewhere about the curious consequences of this encounter of the two visionaries, the eighteenth-century Swede and the twentieth-century Indian. The essentials were these: Sundar Singh had already read a little Swedenborg (very possibly *Heaven and Hell*),[46] and over the next few years was to read much more; meantime his own visionary experiences continued, and he gradually became convinced that he was conversing with the spirit of Swedenborg in heaven, who was instructing him and in all essentials acting as his guru. In 1926 Sundar Singh published a little "visionary" book, *Visions of the Spiritual World*, to the Swedish translation of which Söderblom supplied a tiny foreword, noting a certain resemblance to Swedenborg, but without implying anything more than that.[47] Not until November 1928 did Sundar Singh write to Söderblom, revealing that he had been "conversing" with Swedenborg and asking whether he might be able to publish the record of those conversations in book form.[48] Söderblom was not in any way ill-disposed toward Swedenborg as a significant figure in Swedish religious history: rather the opposite. But the Sadhu's proposal went too far altogether. There is no record that Söderblom ever replied to this letter, and only five months later Sundar Singh, desperately ill, left his home in Subathu on a final missionary tour to "Tibet," never to be seen or heard of again.

This episode suggests that despite his lifelong interest in "mysticism," Söderblom was somewhat at a loss to know how to evaluate a living visionary, particularly one whose visions took such forms as those experienced by Sundar Singh. During the 1920s there were few Sadhu enthusiasts who were prepared to acknowledge the vast religious, cultural, and psychological distance that separated them from the object of their affections, "the Master's Indian Apostle." In this regard Söderblom was neither better nor worse than most of those who were writing about the Sadhu, though some—notably Eivind Berggrav in Norway—were more cautious than others. But Söderblom's Sadhu book remains an intriguing document for all that, and perhaps also a mild warning to those who assume too lightly that phenomenological *Verstehen* is easily arrived at, merely through the exercise of what it is fashionable to call "sympathy." Sympathy he certainly possessed; understanding on this occasion proved elusive.

No one could seriously argue that in the early 1920s the question of mysticism stood uppermost on the Söderblom agenda. Chiefly he was concerned with the problem of Christian unity after the trauma of the first world war. And to the world at large, Söderblom's incomparable achievement of the 1920s was the Life and Work conference held in Stockholm in August 1925. It was for this effort that he gained the Nobel Peace Prize in 1930, and not for anything he had achieved in the world of religiohistorical scholarship.

I do not, however, propose to discuss Stockholm 1925 here. The ecumenical movement has had its notable historians, and Söderblom's work for the cause of Christian unity is therefore known to all who care to read the literature.[49] It may, on the other hand, be necessary to emphasize once more that Söderblom the scholar and Söderblom the world churchman were not two persons, but one. To my mind the most impressive achievement of the whole of his career as a *writer* was his personal account of Stockholm 1925—an astounding 964 pages in length, an extraordinary tour de force by anyone's standards, and well-nigh incomprehensible in that it was published only fifteen months after the conference! This was hardly a work of scholarship in the fullest sense, being almost devoid of those references that make the historian's work so much easier, yet in another sense it represents a highly valuable document of modern Christian history. The Stockholm proposal, wrote Berggrav, had been trampled under foot for eleven years, and officially condemned to death three times.[50] And yet the conference took place. Few in Sweden knew precisely why, or what it was intended to achieve—hence the need Söderblom felt to explain himself to his people at length, offering an *apologia pro vita mea* to those who objected that he had neglected his church and his diocese in the pursuit of an impossible (and in the eyes of many, an undesirable) dream.[51]

To one who reads the Stockholm book in sequence with Söderblom's other writings, the signs are unmistakable. This is still the scholar at work—albeit a scholar in a hurry. The great Söderblom themes recur throughout: the need to return to the creative sources, the danger of regarding religion under the aspect of culture, the socioethical imperative, the complementarity of visions, the centrality of the Christian message of the Kingdom of God (almost a hundred pages are devoted to this theme), and at the heart of all, holiness and worship. One feels almost that where modern conference reports are largely committee work and put together on word processors, this had almost been written in blood.

Two years later there appeared yet another massive book from Söderblom's pen, *Kristi pinas historia* (The story of the sufferings of Christ, 1928), subtitled "A passion book for Holy Week and other weeks," again almost five hundred pages in length. This is a work of devotion, following the six "acts" of the Christian drama, from Jesus' entry into Jerusalem, through his trial, crucifixion, and death, to the resurrection on the third day. It has little enough to do with the *study* of religion, everything to do with its practice. But again one must not fall into the trap of assuming that this book represented no more than a belated retreat into orthodoxy on the part of one whose orthodoxy was still greatly suspect in certain parts of Sweden. Never for one moment did Söderblom doubt that the key to what he had once called "the problem of religion" was to be found here, and only here, in the *mysterium Christi*. This was the solution of the problem that had been forced upon (or revealed to) him in his student days, and world traveler as he was, this was the center to which he always returned—or rather, which he never left.

In 1929, a group of Swedish parliamentarians, led by the same K. G. Westman who had once been responsible for appointing Söderblom archbishop, submitted to the Nobel Committee of the Norwegian *Storting* the name of Söderblom as a candidate for the Nobel Peace Prize. The chief motivation was his work for international reconciliation as symbolized by the Stockholm conference of four years earlier. "Here we have an initiative for peace and international understanding which has already led to notable results."[52] No Peace Prize was awarded in that year, but in 1930, amid growing international support, Söderblom was awarded the prize—the 1929 prize going belatedly to the American diplomat Frank Billings Kellogg.

What no member of the Norwegian Nobel Committee knew at that stage was that Söderblom, alone among prizewinners, had actually known Alfred Nobel personally, and indeed had conducted his funeral service in San Remo thirty-three years earlier, in 1897.[53] Nobel, a strange and reclusive man with few friends, had taken the young pastor somewhat into his confidence. So it was that in Oslo to receive the prize in December 1930, Söderblom was able in his acceptance speech to recall the paradox of the armaments and explosives manufacturer who nonetheless sought to further the cause of peace, while at the Nobel banquet he delivered a speech "which it is certain no other than he could have given on such an occasion: full of personal reminiscences and observations, now lighthearted, now serious as a sermon."[54]

What the Nobel Peace Prize was in the world of international relations, Scotland's Gifford Lectureship was in the smaller world of religious scholarship. Since its inception in the 1880s this annual lectureship had been awarded only to the greatest scholars in the field. Previous lecturers had included Friedrich Max Müller, C. P. Tiele, Andrew Lang, William James, J. G. Frazer, and Henri Bergson, and in 1930 the lectureship for the two following years, 1931 and 1932, was offered to and accepted with gratitude by Söderblom. Since 1914 he had published very little in the history of religion, and despite his remarkable achievements as an international church leader, it is very obvious that still he looked back on the professorial years with a certain nostalgia. Now there had come the opportunity to complete a trilogy of substantial scholarly works: *La Vie future* in French, *Gudstrons uppkomst* in Swedish and German, and now a summing-up in English, the end product of almost half a century of study and reflection. As a provisional title he chose "Basal Forms of Personal Religion." "Basal forms" was an attempt to translate the Swedish *grundformer*, and could have been more happily chosen: though correct, it sounded a trifle contrived. The title "The Living God" was, it seems, not originally contemplated.

Over the past three or four years, Söderblom had been suffering more and more from angina, and his doctors had dissuaded him from unnecessary traveling. But on this occasion he was adamant. Even for a man in perfect health it would have been difficult to have written twenty entirely new lectures for the two series, given the countless other calls upon his time. There was, however, no real reason why he should. What he was attempting was a summing-up, a single concentrated statement, after all. Therefore he did what others have done in similar situations, and assembled from his own extensive writings whatever suited his purpose. For those who are interested in such details, in 1937 Folke Holmström assembled a list of Söderblom's sources as used in *The Living God*.[55] And certainly the reader familiar with Söderblom's earlier production will find little in *The Living God* that is new. But again, this is hardly to be expected. As it stands in the Swedish version of 1932 and the English version of 1933, the final text has undergone a certain amount of editorial revision, largely from the Swedish side by Tor Andrae, while the English version called for a good deal of discreet polishing: though good, Söderblom's English was far from perfect.

Ten lectures were actually delivered in May and June 1931. Beginning with "primitive religion," Söderblom dealt in turn with Yoga, Jainism and early Buddhism, Bhakti in the *Bhagavad Gita*, Mahayana Buddhism, Zarathustra, Socrates, Mosaism, "The Religion of Incarnation," and "Continued Revelation." The scheme is historically developmental, in that it moves step by step from "lower" to "higher" forms of personal religious experience and awareness. It is not, on the other hand, crudely evolutionary: higher forms are superimposed upon lower forms rather than emerging out of them; higher insights and fuller responses to revelation are not achieved without a struggle; and the possibility of regression is ever-present.

On the very first page of the lectures as published, Söderblom stated his well-established priorities: to seek for characteristic *differences* between forms of individual religious expression, rather than superficial and misleading similarities; and to state his own deep conviction that religion must be personal before it can become social: "It must be found in the individual before it becomes the concern of the community."[56] Söderblom might have been wholly a theologian or wholly a historian; he could never have become a sociologist of religion. Arguably his lack of interest in sociology was his chief weakness as a student of religion. His own argument, broadly speaking, was that "behavioral" religion, though common and not without interest, is not "true" religion at all, since it substitutes conduct and performance and acquiescence for the firsthand encounter with the living God. In this he was wholly consistent. But in relegating "religion as method" (in Swedish, *övningsreligion*) to a lower stage of religious awareness, he may have been in danger of underestimating the purely social pressures that help to shape religious traditions. Stated presuppositions must always be accepted, however, and in Söderblom's case his major premise was expressed with total clarity: "If we want to study the essence and elementary forms of religion, we must study the soul-life of the individual."[57]

To attempt a summary of the contents of an almost four-hundred-page book would be quite impracticable here. Nor is it necessary. Rather we may draw attention to a few of the characteristic Söderblom "touches" that appear throughout. A long chapter on Yoga and ecstatic religion generally is especially interesting in the light of what we have previously said about Söderblom's encounter with Sadhu Sundar Singh, who was a Christian *and* an ecstatic. Ecstatic religion as such never appealed to Söderblom, any more than it appealed to the liberal generation of which he was part. Ecstatic experiences may be blissful, but they *teach* nothing. Ecstasy "differs from what we call intuition and inspiration in not solving any riddles or problems. It does not widen the intellectual sphere."[58] Many ecstatic experiences, further, "are due neither to vigour of faith or mind, nor to the earnestness of the blissful ecstasy, but to a peculiarity in the organism of man."[59] Not surprisingly, the name of Sadhu Sundar Singh is nowhere mentioned in this connection, perhaps because Söderblom had come to believe (rightly or wrongly) that in his case what began as vision had slipped into the regions of pathology.[60] Nevertheless, the goal of religion is not here, but in the encounter with the living God, and that encounter "is unattainable by training or by human art." But, he concludes, "alas, when

God draws nigh to man, the normal state of man is far from being one of bliss. God is a consuming fire. And in man there is much to be burnt away."[61]

The fourth lecture, on "Religion as Devotion: Bhakti," is mainly an analysis of the *Bhagavad Gita*, the most important and best loved of all Hindu scriptures, and one which took on fresh importance after the 1880s as, in a manner of speaking, the all-sufficient scripture of "Neo-Hinduism." Here Söderblom expresses himself warmly, commending the democratic aspect of *bhakti* piety and the elevation of the principle of the love of Deity above that of knowledge on the one hand and asceticism on the other. And he attests: "Nowhere else in India do we meet as here the living God. . . . God has made himself known. He comes close to men. . . . Love towards God is here to fill the whole life of man, his daily work as well as his devotional exercises."[62] But has it not been India's problem that she has never had the capacity to say *No*? Tolerance is one thing (though historically speaking, Hindu India has been far less tolerant than the Vivekananda tradition has asserted), but one may not tolerate the intolerable: "India has allowed low, cruel, sensual, and brutal figures and rites to flourish beside high manifestations of religion. The Avatara doctrine has made this eminently possible. Thus it is the tragedy of India that it has never been able to say *No*, however lovely and sublime we deem that wide-heartedness which acknowledges the divine wherever and however it may appear."[63]

In the course of his lecture on Mahayana Buddhism, Söderblom digresses on the problem of gaining assurance in religion. One may attempt to follow "the Jacob's ladder of mysticism," or trust in one's own powers of reasoning. But, he goes on, the soul craves more: "On the approach of doubt, when the world and all that happens seem grimly to contradict the assurance of a divine power and a divine mercy, one's own experiences do not suffice. And the conclusions of reason may collapse like a house of cards."[64] There follows a moment of testimony, in which Söderblom is in effect saying that this is what he has experienced, let others attempt what solutions they will: "When all else breaks down, the pious gaze at the Cross which is the everlastingly valid proof of the unsearchable mercy of God."[65] Thereafter he returns at once, without further elaboration, to the Mahayana theme.

The lecture in *The Living God* devoted to Zarathustra/Zoroaster is notable chiefly for being an indirect tribute to the memory of the one who in the 1890s had inspired Söderblom to take up the study of Iranian religion in the first place, James Hope Moulton, and to his major work, *Early Zoroastrianism* (1913).[66] Söderblom feared that this lecture might prove "more prosaic and less interesting from a general point of view." So perhaps it was. It was notably more detailed than some of the other lectures, for one thing, and represented something of a reversion to an intricate style of presentation which Söderblom had had little occasion to use in recent years. Most of what it contained was already there in *La Vie future* of thirty years earlier, though complemented by a certain amount of later reading, refined and condensed.

The seventh lecture centers on Socrates, being based largely on unpublished lectures of years earlier. Söderblom might well, had he so chosen, have become a Socrates scholar of note.[67] To Söderblom, Socrates was primarily the great ethicist, but also one whose life and work was based "not upon a deduction, a calculation, or an idea, but upon something secret which did not admit of analysis and explanation by the reason; upon a mystical experience, an irrational or super-rational apprehension which carried with it an inward compulsion, an unconditional obligation."[68] In other words, there was that in Socrates which Söderblom immediately recognized as "true religion" within the category of *personlighetsmystik*. For the nonclassicist, Söderblom's image of Socrates—which otherwise had appeared on numerous occasions in his earlier work—is impossible to evaluate. But it is at least significant that here, the Socrates lecture comes immediately prior to the three on the Judeo-Christian prophetic tradition, as in effect the highest point attained outside that tradition.

The last three lectures delivered in Edinburgh were on Old Testament prophecy, the Christian view of Incarnation, and "Continued Revelation" respectively. None broke any new ground. Indeed, the last lecture had been in print in Swedish since 1911.[69] It argued that revelation continues in human experience in three forms: first, through the works of genius; secondly, through the processes of history; and thirdly, through the spiritual personality and the regeneration of the individual. Rather than summarize further, let me quote two passages which contain the heart of the matter. The first comes at the end of the section on "revelation in history:"

> The certainty of God's creation cannot be given to men and preserved in men, when they need it, by any inference from or reflections upon civilization [culture] or history, but only by God first taking men out of civilization and history to be alone with him, revealing himself to them and continuing his revelation in their lives. . . . We must ourselves possess a hidden life with God in order to discern clearly for ourselves and believe thoroughly in his continued Revelation in history.[70]

The second—and again it is interesting that these words, written for an Uppsala doctoral graduation twenty years earlier, should have been reproduced unaltered in 1931 in Söderblom's last public lecture—concerns "comparative religion" and theology:

> The difference between religious research in general and Christian theology in particular consists in the fact that the belief in revelation is an essential part of the latter. For Christian theology the history of religions is a divine self-communication. The comparative study of religions in general leaves the question of revelation open. He who practices it may be inspired by the conviction that a supernatural reality is lying behind the phenomena of religion. Or he may deny the belief in the spiritual which is fundamental for religion. Or he may remain inquiring and uncertain about the revelation, certain only of the impossibility of knowing anything about it. Or he may lack interest in the question about the truth of religion. Different views as regards the idea of revelation may of course not influence the method of research and the historical and psychological investigations in such a way that these are displaced in one direction or another by dogmatism. The remedy against such mistakes (faults) is not to forbid the investigator to have a certain conviction, but solely to carry out the investigation rightly, conscientiously, and seriously, and to submit readily to perceived truths.[71]

Söderblom of course had every intention of delivering a further series of Gifford Lectures in the following year, 1932. These were planned to concentrate on mysticism and sanctity, and to lead finally to the interplay of human and divine activity, the nature of prayer, and "the living God." It was in anticipation of this series that his last two sentences—repeating yet again his most distinctive idea and personal conviction—were: "a saint is he who reveals God's might. Saints are such as show clearly and plainly in their lives and deeds and in their very being that God lives."[72]

Söderblom had been both stimulated and cheered by the reception he had received in Scotland, but one suspects even more so by having been able to "play professor" for a time and to return in spirit to a simpler and less troubled period in his life. He looked forward to returning to Scotland in the following year to give a second series of lectures. Back again in Sweden, there was much awaiting his attention.

For a while, all went well. But on July 8 he collapsed. On the previous day he had attended an Anglo-Scandinavian conference of theologians at Sparreholm Castle and, although not on the official list of speakers, was persuaded by the chairman, Gustaf Aulén, to deliver an impromptu address. In the evening he also gave an afterdinner speech in his usual witty style. These were his last two speeches; unfortunately, no record was kept of either. In conversation with Aulén he spoke of his Gifford Lectures, and revealed that he planned to call the two volumes together "The Living God."[73] Contrary to later impressions, he did not decide on this title on his deathbed.

Söderblom returned to Uppsala by train early on the following day. He had a number of interviews scheduled, but between two of them began to suffer severe abdominal pain. He completed his final interview—with a minister working among Swedes in Poland—prostrate in bed, bathed in sweat, but in full possession of his faculties, alert and encouraging.[74] On July 10, two days later, he was taken to the university hospital, where intestinal obstruction (ileus) was diagnosed. An emergency operation was clearly necessary, and since the senior surgeon was on holiday and could not be reached, it was carried out by his assistant, Dr. Sölve Richter. The operation was wholly successful, and had Söderblom's heart been stronger, all would have been well. Indeed, for a time he seemed to have stood the operation well. But in the middle of Sunday, July 12, heart failure set in, and soon it was clear that he had little time left.

Most of what he said during the last couple of hours was heard, remembered, and recorded by one member or another of his family, or by Dr. Richter.[75] He insisted that his vast library was not to be sold, but passed on to future theologians in the family. (In the event, it was cared for by Anna until her death in 1955, when it passed to a foundation; none of Söderblom's eight sons became a theologian, though all three daughters married future bishops.) He spoke the enigmatic words: "I know that God lives. I can prove it by the history of religion." Refusing morphine to ease his pain, he remained fully conscious to the last. Anna kept repeating to him: "Blessed are the pure in heart, for they shall see God." His last words were hardly audible. They may have been "This is eternity," "This is life," or "Eternal life." Shortly thereafter he passed away. The date was July 12, 1931, and he was sixty-five years old.

A memorial service was held in Uppsala Cathedral on July 15, at which his son-in-law Algot Anderberg told the congregation a little of what Söderblom had said on his deathbed.[76] The funeral took place three days later, but on this occasion there was no sermon, nor was the name of the deceased mentioned even once. The music was by Bach, Schütz, Cherubini—and Söderblom, for the congregation sang the hymn "I denna ljuva sommartid" to Söderblom's own tune. And two passages from Söderblom's writings were read: two paragraphs from an essay-sermon on "the inner guest" and four from *Kristi pinas historia*.[77] After these, there followed two Bible verses:

> So likewise ye, when ye shall have done all those things which are commanded you, say, We are unprofitable servants: we have done [in Swedish, only done] that which was our duty to do.
> [Luke 17:10]

> For none of us liveth to himself, and no man dieth to himself. For whether we live, we live unto the Lord; and whether we die, we die unto the Lord: whether we live therefore, or die, we are the Lord's.
> [Romans 14:7–8]

By special royal permission, Söderblom was laid to rest in the northeast corner of the sanctuary—the first person to be buried within the cathedral since 1786. Later the grave was covered with a magnificent granite block bearing the "slave-saying" (as Söderblom had once called it), Luke 17:10. Twenty-four years later, Anna joined him.

A brief word, finally, about those twenty-four years. Anna Söderblom, née Forsell, was a remarkable person in every way.[78] Always she had been her husband's closest confidante and best critic, the mother of twelve children, loyal and independent at one and the same time. Her long years of widowhood (during which she always wore black widow's weeds in public) she devoted to Nathan Söderblom's memory. She took up residence in the ancient building, *Domtrapphuset*, east of the cathedral, less than a hundred yards from his grave, and there she began the task of organizing his library, his letters, and papers, with the most meticulous care and accuracy. In 1932 she published a devotional book entitled simply *Ett år* (One year), with daily readings for every day in the year, taken from Söderblom's writings—assembled, it may be added, with great skill and sensitivity. Thereafter she was to publish several more volumes of Söderblom's writings, some previously printed, some not, and in 1948 a volume of reminiscences of her own, *På livets trottoir* (On the sidewalk of life). A second volume appeared in 1956, in the year after her death, assembled from her drafts and notes.

But chiefly the historian-biographer must acknowledge a vast debt of gratitude to Anna Söderblom for systematizing Nathan Söderblom's letters and papers. Some she determined not to make public, insisting that her family's privacy needed to be respected. But so far as one is aware, nothing was destroyed, as in other such cases. And even with certain gaps, her labors have meant that Söderblom is accessible as many other great scholars and church leaders of the past are not.

That over the half-century that has passed since his death the name and reputation of Nathan Söderblom have fluctuated in scholarly esteem is perhaps no more than one can expect. In a postscript I shall attempt to give a brief sketch of some of those fluctuations. It is remarkable nevertheless that during that half-century even in Sweden there have been only two biographical studies of any consequence, those of Tor Andrae and Bengt Sundkler, thirty-seven years apart. Had Söderblom been prominent in some other field, like an August Strindberg; had he been a theologian belonging to a different period and a different climate of opinion, like a Karl Barth or a Dietrich Bonhoeffer; or had he written in a less inaccessible language his name and personality would have been better known. As it is, despite the vast amount of material available, no definitive Söderblom biography has ever been written. Still, the first three decades of our century have finally begun to emerge out of a long period of eclipse. When the emergence is complete—and perhaps when a long-overdue work of translation, comparable to that carried out in respect of Søren Kierkegaard, has been undertaken—the history of religion and culture and international relations in the twentieth century will have a new great name.

This has been a book about the *study* of religion. But inevitably it has slipped into being also a book about religion itself. This was not altogether intentional, but having happened, it may be appropriate to close with a short quotation from the only other international personality of comparable stature Sweden has known this century, Dag Hammarskjöld. In the fall of 1961 Hammarskjöld's body lay in state only a few yards from Söderblom's grave. He had grown up in Uppsala, and clearly had learned much from Söderblom—though that is not a matter we can pursue further. Hammarskjöld's diary, published posthumously as *Vägmärken* (Markings), contains much to remind one of Söderblom. Thirty years on from Söderblom's death, Hammarskjöld wrote:

Weep
if you can,
weep,
but do not complain.
The way chose you—
and you must be thankful.[79]

Nathan Söderblom, archbishop and scholar, would surely have understood.

Postscript

As the writing of this study has proceeded, I have come more and more frequently to feel that in terms of today's presuppositions and debates, it might in the end satisfy no one. To try and combine narrative and analysis is difficult enough. That, however, is more a matter of technique than of substance. More serious has been the problem posed by the man himself and the period (and country) in which he lived and worked. There is a triple barrier to overcome: a barrier of language, a barrier of period, and a barrier of personality. Phenomenology, whatever else it may attempt to do, claims to seek "understanding" (*Verstehen*). Alas, it would seem that phenomenologists of religion are seldom at their best when it comes to understanding one another—and this may raise certain doubts about their ability to understand peoples and cultures of the remote past. In Söderblom's case, even in his own country (where one naturally expects there to be a measure of such understanding) opinion as to the extent and importance of his contribution to the study of religion has fluctuated greatly over the half-century that has passed since his death. Outside Scandinavia these fluctuations have hardly been noticed. But they are not without interest.

Söderblom's reputation in the world of scholarship would appear to have passed through four more or less well-defined stages since his death. The first lasted until the late 1940s and early 1950s. Both in Sweden and on the Continent influential positions were occupied by scholars who had been his pupils and friends, and who shared his ideals—an Andrae, an Aulén, a Heiler, a van der Leeuw. At the same time, the gradual coming to fruition of the ecumenical movement in the immediate postwar period tended to give the impression that whatever Söderblom might or might not have achieved as a scholar, his lasting reputation would be as an international church leader. This first period tailed off as the members of the Söderblom generation passed away, and came symbolically to an end with the death of Anna Söderblom in 1955.

By that time, however, a sharp reaction had already begun to set in, nowhere more markedly than in Söderblom's Uppsala. Its causes were and are complex. On the one hand, theology in Sweden came under bitter attack from the direction of a new generation of "antimetaphysical" empiricists, led by the analytical philosopher Ingemar Hedenius, whose polemical book *Tro och vetande* (Faith and knowledge) appeared in 1949, and who later accused certain of Söderblom's arguments of being "confused to the point of unintelligibility."[1] But the attack did not stop there; the ultimate objective was to secure the abolition of faculties of theology altogether, on the grounds of their "unscientific" methods and procedures. All this was of course highly reminiscent of the situation as it had been at the end of the nineteenth century. In the interim, however, the relative positions of the combatants had changed radically. The church was no longer in the position of power and privilege it had enjoyed half a century earlier. Under Social Democracy (in power in Sweden since 1932) the church was not persecuted, but neither was it favored. Whether or not the disestablishment of the church and the abolition of Sweden's two faculties of theology was ever really likely is of no consequence. It was far more important that those who occupied teaching positions in those faculties were forced to defend themselves against shrill charges of "unscientific" methods and procedures, "subjectivism," and an unhealthy taste for "metaphysics" by insisting on their own scientific standards, chiefly as historians, though in a subsidiary sense also as "phenomenologists."

The full force of the "antimetaphysical" onslaught was borne by those who had learned their theology from Söderblom, notably Anders Nygren and Torsten Bohlin, Gustaf Aulén and Gustaf Wingren. Ironically, one of those who led the attack—though in far less extreme terms than those often used by Ingemar Hedenius—was Samuel Fries's son Martin Fries.[2] But the overall impact was temporarily devastating. Söderblom, and the generation to which he belonged, virtually disappeared from the records. Even the Nathan Söderblom Society in Uppsala, set up in 1941 to honor his contribution to the history of religion, moved after about 1950 into empirical—or at least explicitly nontheological—channels, to judge from the papers published in the society's yearbook. By the late 1950s religiohistorical research in Uppsala had distanced itself altogether from the Söderblom heritage, and especially so in the faculty of theology, where "the Uppsala school," led by Ivan Engnell and Geo Widengren, were concentrating their efforts on the Ancient Near East generally, and on such specific historical questions as the myth and ritual pattern, the character of Israelite kingship, and the oral transmission that had preceded the literary phase in the religious history of the area.[3] No one would wish to question the degree of philological and other expertise which the Uppsala school of the late 1950s and early 1960s brought to bear on some areas of the study of religion. Nevertheless, while the affirmations of the history of religion in Uppsala in the early 1960s were well marked, their antipathies were even more so: "evolutionism," "subjectivism," and theological and philosophical "speculation" among them. In these circles it was more or less taken for granted that the Söderblom heritage was a thing of the past. How far this was a conscious reaction to the state of siege brought upon the faculty of theology by the constant attacks of the "antimetaphysicians," we may leave an open question. But there is a very strong prima facie case that the empiricism of the Uppsala faculty of theology in the 1950s and early 1960s was brought about in part by the need to defend its right to exist in an unfriendly academic environment. Söderblom had been "subjectivist," "individualist," "evolutionist," and a man who had never been able to hold the history of religion and theology in decent isolation from each other. If, as van der Leeuw had said in the late 1930s, he actually had been the father of the phenomenology of religion, the sons had accomplished a deed of which Freud himself might well have been proud, consigning him to that particular limbo reserved for those whose insights have outlived their usefulness.

And so the matter rested until 1968, when the World Council of Churches chose to hold its fourth seven-yearly assembly in Uppsala. The name of Nathan Söderblom never having been other than highly honored in ecumenical circles, it was appropriate that 1968 should have seen the publication of Bengt Sundkler's English-language biography and, among other things, the renaming of the square in Uppsala between the Archbishop's House, the cathedral, and the old faculty of theology building as *Nathan Söderbloms plan* (formerly *Odinslund*). By now the antitheological animus of the late 1940s and early 1950s had largely disappeared, and a third period in Söderblom studies was well under way.

If the first period had been one of adulation and the second a period of impatient rejection, the third was one of cautious recovery. Scholars began to find their way to the Söderblom collections in the Uppsala University Library. Historians of ideas began to realize that the period in Western thought between the 1880s and the 1930s could not just be erased from the records, and that the secular 1950s had perhaps been something of a parenthesis in the modern religious history of the Western world. In the late 1960s and early 1970s the West went through a time of extraordinary religious and social upheaval, of frantic experimentation in a number of areas simultaneously, of realignment in patterns of world power, and much else. Everywhere there emerged "new religious movements," new gurus, new prophets, new disciples. A generation and more lost whatever trust they might still have had in established authority, and in the unaided human reason as an adequate key with which to unlock life's mysteries. Students took to the streets and besieged university administrations, bent on reconstructing the world in their own unstable image. This generation was well on the way to losing one thing altogether: it had little or no sense of history. To the powerful "youth element" at Uppsala 1968, the Stockholm conference of 1925 no doubt seemed inconceivably remote. Nevertheless, there was that in Söderblom with which religion's new age in the West had a certain assonance, namely, his insistence that the heart of religion is to be found not in doctrines, dogmas, or even morals, but in an ineffable experience. This every last member of every new religious movement believed—and sought.

During the third period, however, there was no real question of Söderblom's being "updated," or being made a participant in an ongoing contemporary debate. The task was essentially one of recovery, and of rescuing "the living Söderblom" from the 1930s hagiographers on the one hand and the later detractors on the other. For this work, two senior Uppsala scholars were largely responsible: in the history of religion, Carl-Martin Edsman, and in ecumenical theology, Bengt Sundkler. Edsman's essay *Ur Nathan Söderbloms arbetsverkstad* (From Nathan Söderblom's workshop) appeared in 1966, and showed what might be found in the manuscript collections by anyone who would take the time and trouble to look, and how much more valuable such collections are to the history of scholarship than printed finished products.[4]

Bengt Sundkler, in addition to his English-language biography of

1968, published in 1975 in Swedish a collection of "by-products"—ten independent essays, six of them previously published in Swedish journals between 1967 and 1973.[5] This collection, again, is so much more than a mere repetition of what had been written in the 1930s. It is based on an unrivaled knowledge of the manuscript sources—not only the Söderblom collection, but the letters and papers of those who were Söderblom's contemporaries.

However, Sundkler quite deliberately did not, as we said at the beginning of this study, tackle the question of Söderblom's scholarship, other than incidentally.[6] It happened that in 1975 a scholar in the sister-university of Lund, Hans Åkerberg, published his dissertation *Omvändelse och kamp* (Conversion and struggle), subtitled "An empirical religiopsychological investigation of the young Nathan Söderblom's religious development, 1886–1894."[7] This was something new in Söderblom studies. To be sure, already in 1931 Tor Andrae had begun to speculate somewhat about the psychological aspects of Söderblom's personality, and especially about his relationship to his father. Sundkler had also brought up this difficult question on various occasions. But between 1931 and 1975 the psychology of religion had changed radically. During "the empirical years" in Uppsala there was only one psychologist of religion of any stature in Sweden, Hjalmar Sundén, and the overlap with the history of religion was slight.[8] In Uppsala it was virtually nonexistent, despite the fact that the chair once occupied by Söderblom actually at the time carried the title "the history and psychology of religion"—which suited Tor Andrae perfectly, but not his successor Geo Widengren. Not having the expertise to judge Åkerberg's thesis professionally, I will suggest only that it might be seen as marking the first cautious beginning of a fourth phase of Söderblom study. From adulation, rejection, and recovery we have begun to move toward a reassessment.

In 1981 the Nathan Söderblom Society in Uppsala mounted a symposium on the occasion of the fiftieth anniversary of Söderblom's death, at which four lectures were given, by Bengt Sundkler, Åke Hultkrantz, and Sven Hartman of the older academic generation and by Carl Fredrik Hallencreutz of a younger generation. I was unfortunately not able to be present, but was privileged—also as a member of the "younger" generation—to contribute an essay to the volume *Nathan Söderblom and His Contribution to the Study of*

Religion (1984). Again it would seem appropriate to speak of the beginnings of a reassessment under the aegis of the history of ideas.

By this time, a few of Söderblom's writings in Swedish were beginning to be reissued in new editions. In 1974 one of Sweden's most celebrated literary figures, Sven Stolpe, had published a selection of *Tal och essayer* (Speeches and essays), and in 1975 Åkerberg had republished *Uppenbarelsereligion* (1903, 1930) and *Tre livsformer* (1922) under the composite title of *Till mystikens belysning* (Toward the illumination of mysticism). In 1982 he suggested, in an essay published in the Nathan Söderblom Society journal *Religion och Bibel*, that it was high time for a reexamination of Söderblom's contribution to the study of mysticism, since his distinction between "the mysticism of the infinite" and "the mysticism of personality" fitted the facts of the experiential case far better than most other later attempts to come to grips with the subject.[9] He argued persuasively that Söderblom—because he had *not* been in bondage to an a priori theory—had hit upon precisely the distinction that the study of mysticism needs if it is to avoid squashing *all* intensive religious experience into only one category (usually nontheistic). This distinction "remained his most outstanding contribution to the psychology of religion."[10]

I would agree—though it still seems to me that more would be achieved if the notoriously slippery word "mysticism" could be deleted from the records altogether.[11] Words come trailing clouds of associations, not all of them helpful, and the aura around the word "mysticism" is more unhelpful than most. What we actually have in Söderblom's work is a fundamental distinction between theistic and nontheistic forms of human response to the riddle of the world, and that distinction he saw and mapped out in its nature and implications. That was a lasting contribution to the study of religion—and as Åkerberg points out, he was disinclined to pin it down to a firm and fixed terminology. *Verklighet* (reality) he knew to be highly resistant to pigeonholing—and that is a lesson of which we all need to be constantly reminded.

Few, even in his own day, understood Nathan Söderblom. Certainly he was Swedish, but in many ways he was such an untypical Swede as to confuse and baffle his contemporaries. On reading Tor

Andrae's 1931 Söderblom biography, the noted literary historian and critic Martin Lamm wrote to Andrae: "Might he not have achieved more if he had had time for less, if on an occasion he had been stopped in his tracks, had had less success and been forced to put down roots? That he moved forward with determination, you have convincingly demonstrated—his attitude to death shows that. But does a flame need to flicker so much in order to shine?"[12]

In one of the most insightful short studies published in the year of Söderblom's death, the Norwegian writer and churchman Eivind Berggrav quoted the words of an Oslo newspaper. What had been Söderblom's secret? "The secret was primarily that the archbishop was a simple and happy man."[13] Nonsense, said Berggrav. He was anything but simple and happy; on the contrary, his life was full of tension—between what he owed to his Pietist father and what he owed to scholarship, between the conservative and the liberal in his own makeup, between confessionalism and liberalism in the world of religion. His depressions remained largely concealed from the world around him, it is true, but they were there for all that. The last big book he published in Swedish was about the *sufferings* of Christ.

Berggrav, an astute psychologist, could see how vulnerable Söderblom had been. He trusted everyone—or almost everyone—even those untrustworthy enough in themselves. During his lifetime an anonymous novel was in circulation, spreading rumor and innuendo about him.[14] The mounting of the Stockholm conference in 1925 had brought him to the verge of personal bankruptcy, from which he sought to extricate himself—according to Berggrav—as Sir Walter Scott had done a century earlier, by constant writing and publishing: "When his friends, walking the town at night, saw the lamp lit in his study, they felt the pressure of the burden under which the great man now sat and wrote."[15]

And when he received the Nobel Prize in 1930, within a month he had also received 20,000 begging letters![16] To quote Berggrav again: "No one was allowed to notice the wrong and hurt that there had been. It would have eased the burden if he had been able to talk. It must have helped. The most serious attacks on him never ceased. . . . Nathan Söderblom was never fully accepted in the Scandinavian churches; always he was suspected by many, and at best tolerated."[17]

That, however, was precisely what also happened to other members of Söderblom's generation who did what he had done, questioning the traditional seat of authority in the church, realigning Christianity on a fresh ground plan, and finding a generous place in that plan for religious traditions other than Protestant Christianity. Even though the European battle line was less crude than that between the Fundamentalists and the Modernists in America, and though Lutherans were less apt to mount heresy trials than were many in the Calvinist world, the struggle was no less intense. The tension between conservative and liberal factions was especially marked in Norway in the late 1920s, where Karl Ludvig Reichelt in 1926 had been forced to sever his connections with the Norwegian Missionary Society on account of what the conservatives called his "syncretism" in introducing Chinese Buddhist elements into the work of his minute mission.[18] As archbishop, Söderblom was less vulnerable in the legal sense than was Reichelt; emotionally he was equally vulnerable—perhaps more so, since it was that much more difficult for him to respond as he perhaps would have wished.

Ever since the 1890s, when Söderblom had been one of Fredrik Fehr's young men, alongside the beleaguered Samuel Fries, he had been branded a "Ritschlian" and therefore a dangerous radical. That he had soon moved away from Ritschl and taken Schleiermacher as his guide had improved matters not at all. Like Fries he had remained a Pietist at heart. But to a certain kind of Evangelical, to arrive at the right results along the wrong course of reasoning is as suspect as to reach no result at all. And to attempt to introduce these dangerous methods and approaches into faculties of theology dedicated to the training of young men (not as yet women: that for Sweden's part came along only in the late 1950s) for the work of the Lutheran ministry could not but be resisted. Gradually of course the opposition was worn down, and by the 1930s the kind of academic controversy that had exercised students in the 1890s was largely a thing of the past. But for Sweden, that change would not and could not have come about without Söderblom's constant urging and his personal example.

On that level, then, this study will have achieved its major objective if it has rendered intelligible something of what took place in and around the University of Uppsala between the 1880s and the outbreak of the first world war—how from being almost entirely confession-bound, deductive, and dogmatic, the study of religion became "scientific," historical, inductive, and human. However, we would do well to remember that Söderblom never either studied or taught in a "secular" university or in a department of religion, comparative religion, or religious studies in such a university. His three faculties, in Uppsala, Paris, and Leipzig, were all faculties of theology, Lutheran in the first and last cases and generally Protestant in the case of Paris. His task therefore was to liberate the study of religion not from the grasp of theology as such, but from a narrow and stifling confessionalism which would lead only to predetermined results.

Part of what was involved in this program was to persuade those engaged in the study of religion that they face not neatly sorted and packaged fragments of human experience, but "reality" (*verklighet*) in all its intractable variety. Christianity is not a special case in the history of religion that needs to be approached using totally different methods from those the student otherwise uses. Humanly speaking, religion is all of a piece: one long and complex story branching out into innumerable subplots. In the drama of religion there are great and small actors, the Prophets in Söderblom's view being the greatest of all, but none of them ultimately unimportant. In Söderblom's judgment Jesus Christ occupied a wholly unique place in the prophetic tradition, and no amount of selective interpretation of Söderblom's writings will, or should, change that. But that being so, it must be allowed that today's empiricists will very likely lose interest just as soon as they discover that the "phenomenologist" Söderblom was "just another theologian after all." If that is the case, then so be it. The empiricist voice needs to be heard, provided that it is prepared to deal empirically even with the "theological" evidence—which it has not always done hitherto, let it be added. All too often empiricists of a certain kind seem to argue as they do chiefly out of fear of precisely the kind of deductive confessionalism *against* which Söderblom and his generation waged tireless war. Not for the first or last time, it is the "liberal" evidence that has proved to be the hardest to read.

Today a considerable part of the world of religion has come to separate itself into two vast blocks, ultraconservative (in popular parlance, "fundamentalist") on the one hand, ultraradical on the other. Each has its package of values, its bogeymen, its conventions, its jargon, and its deplorable tendency to interpret deviation from its own norm as a sign of complicity with "the enemy," on the principle of "those that are not for us are against us." Thankfully, the process is far from complete. But when and where this polarization has happened, almost always the consequence has been the same: the emptying out of the middle ground where the courtesies and generosities of liberalism once had their place, where men and women could discuss and not merely denounce, and where it was believed that the acquisition of sound knowledge had its own liberating quality. Of course liberals in this sense have not vanished from the face of the earth, though for the most part they have been most effectively silenced. A consequence—one among many—has been to place the period during which liberalism flourished out of reach of all save a minority among historians—and that minority can all too easily be dismissed as nostalgic romantics, especially should they seek to exhibit the virtues, and not only the failings, of the period. In other branches of history and letters, that period is now open to fresh examination, but scarcely as yet in religion and theology, and least of all in those regions in which religion and theology intersect, where passions run high and where pious ignorance masquerades as a virtue.

There, then, is one of Söderblom's contributions to the study of religion: that he and the generation of which he was a part subjected the study of religion to the best thinking of which they were capable on a basis of the best and most accurate information available to them. That he, Fehr, Fries, Sabatier, Moulton, Lehmann, and the rest persisted in believing that the world of religion had a meaning and focus beyond the exercise of human reason does nothing at all to spoil the quality of their work; those who dismiss the possibility of revelation a priori or discount it as a "scientific" irrelevancy may have the greater problem. That, however, is by the way.

In Sweden, Söderblom lifted the study of religion, almost singlehandedly as far as the university world was concerned, out of one era into another, and did so, moreover, in little more than a decade as a full-time teacher. Internationally, though at the end of his life Söderblom was undoubtedly far more widely known as an ecumenical leader than as a scholar, he was never other than a scholar forced by an imperative sense of duty into the service of his church.

What, then, of his scholarship? As an Iranist, his contribution has been practically forgotten today. The only one of his larger books ever published in English, *The Living God*, is seldom or never read today. Nor, I suspect, would it be greatly appreciated were it to be read afresh: quite apart from its stodgy English, it would no doubt fall between the customary stools of theology and "religious studies." The English-speaking student, cheated by modern educational theory out of all but the faintest chance of ever learning enough of any other language to be of use, is separated from such as Söderblom by a well-nigh impenetrable barrier. Why, then, did a committee of the American Council of Learned Societies in 1973 place Söderblom uppermost in their list of scholars of the past who ought to be better known? Almost certainly because Gerardus van der Leeuw once called him, in effect, the "father" of the phenomenology of religion. And because it was embarrassing in 1973—as it is still embarrassing today—to have to admit that one knows so little of one's roots: especially so, if one has pretensions to be a "phenomenologist of religion" oneself.

The ACLS committee in 1973 was, however, wiser than it knew. In uncovering the "roots" of the phenomenology of religion, one finds not a "value-free" exercise in the suspension of belief, but a "value-rich" exercise in devotion, discipline, and learning. Not a gaunt empiricist, passionate only in denial, but a generous, open, flexible mind that knew where its own center lay, and therefore was able to enter into dialogue with the whole of the world of religion, past and present, remote and proximate, on a basis of a shared experience of "that which is holy." In the last resort that experience is inaccessible to rational analysis. But if it has any meaning at all, *det heliga, das Heilige*, "the holy" provides the one key by which the earliest phase of the phenomenology of religion is to be grasped. Rudolf Otto's English translator was foolish (or at least unwise) to render *Das Heilige* as "The *Idea* of the Holy." An imperative does not become an idea without losing much of its force. Söderblom had experienced the imperative. He knew that "It is a fearful thing to fall into the hands of the living God." Nothing could ever obliterate the memory of the day in 1893, eight years before he became a professor, twenty-one years before he became archbishop, when he had fallen into the hands of the holy and righteous God—or to give an alternative interpretation its due, had collapsed in fear at the thought of his inability to meet the impossible demands of his holy and righteous father.

Interpret the 1893 crisis how we will (though phenomenologically speaking, is there any other religious reality than the faith of the believer and the consequences to which that faith leads?), it is in the *experience*, and not merely in the *idea* of "the holy" that we have the key to how and why Söderblom studied religion. Religion to Söderblom was not organization, not ethics or morals, not "self-realization," not doctrine or dogma. Each of these has its place, but that place is not at the center. At the center there is an encounter, in face of which the only proper human response is worship. And wherever in history the student finds people at prayer, in an attitude of submissive expectancy and obedience to a power and a will—there is revelation, and there is religion.

In December 1925 Söderblom spoke at the consecration of the Swedish church in Oslo. He said, among other things:

> Before the holy God we miserable humans who dare to approach him and build sanctuaries for his holy presence feel our own unholiness. Before him, the pure one, we feel our own impurity. Our hearts sink to the dust in contrition and adoration . . . [but] . . . the holy does not only inspire fear. From the beginning it has another quality. It attracts human beings to itself. For the holy, in all its fearful mystery, is at the same time the only agency that can give life real value. This mighty dual assonance in the heart—trembling and devotion—cannot be separated. Should there be a separation, although the fear may remain, or a kind of familiarity with the supernatural may be there, religion will have departed.[19]

As to those who have responded fully to this "dual assonance," he had this to say: "A saint is one who, in his or her life, in active love, in the consecration of gifts to God and the community, in the inwardness and warmth of prayer and worship, shows that God lives, and one who thus helps others to believe in the majesty of the Holy One. Holy is the one who belongs to God and thus in experience and conduct reveals something of the power of God."[20]

In the end, therefore, the study of religion as conceived and practiced by Söderblom was devoted wholly to the investigation of this question. Addressing an audience of Danish students in 1920, he said: "Most of my spiritual strength has been spent in the study of religion. No part of my far too diverse, and yet, perhaps, basically concordant work has given me a purer sense of satisfaction."[21] The study of *religion* is not the study of heterogeneous fragments but of a line of revelation and response, discernible to whoever will accept the *verklighet*, the "reality" of religious phenomena as they are.

Religious experience to Söderblom was an experience sui generis, to which human beings had always been open. It had begun, so far as our records are capable of knowing, with notions akin to those of *mana* and *tabu*. The search for self-realization and self-fulfillment had been a digression—gnosticism had few attractions to him. Religion had reached its fullest expressions in the prophetic consciousness of an Isaiah, a Micah, an Amos, to continue wherever individual response reached the pitch of genius. He was not setting up a new theory of religion against existing theories. What he was doing was attempting to establish a category under which religious experience could be viewed in its own right, as a focal point for the religious interpretation of history. In all his work on religious phenomena, "primitive," ancient, or modern, he was constantly asking three questions. First, what is religion? Secondly, what, within the category of religion, is Christianity? And thirdly, what, within the category of Christianity, is Protestantism?

He answered all these questions *both* as a historian *and* as a theologian, and there is no way in which we are at liberty to divide his mind into two separate compartments. Theology and scientific study overlap in his work, and to isolate the one arbitrarily from the other is to draw an artificial distinction. The compatibility of the two, which he had asserted in his 1901 inaugural lecture, he bore out in every aspect of his subsequent writings. Whether he was expounding Iranian eschatology, primal taboos, the Sermon on the Mount, Catholic Modernism, the experience of Europe, Martin Luther, Andrew Lang's theory of primeval "high gods," or his own concept of "Evangelical Catholicity," he never lost sight of what were, to him, the primary and irreducible categories of all religion: not his own theories, but the experience of human beings on the verge of the unknown and in the grip of an imperative.

Appendix 1:
To the Students of Theology (1901)*

Before leaving this platform, I wish finally to greet those with whom I shall be mainly concerned in Uppsala, those whose servant I have been called to be. I greet the students of theology at Uppsala University.

You will, gentlemen, hear many commiserations in these days. I must congratulate you.

People pity you because you serve what is supposed to be an outdated cause, that of Christianity, or at least—and the distinction must be carefully drawn—because you serve an outdated church. People pity you because you have to wear the yoke of the church's confession around your necks. Others pity you because you live in a period when accepted opinions, particularly concerning the origin of certain books of the Bible and one or other detail in the sacred history of God's dealings with humanity, have been challenged and altered; and these persons believe the study of theology to be fraught with new and great spiritual peril. Others of your friends pity you on account of the lamentable—though with God's help improvable—external circumstances which weigh hard and mercilessly on a proportion of the clergy of our church.

Now, gentlemen, I wish to congratulate you with all my heart on your present studies, on studying theology at this time, and on your coming vocation.

Certainly there are in studies as well as in work difficult crises and narrow gates to be passed through, abysses to cross, where no routine, no human help, but only the wings of faith can carry us; and I believe with Luther that anyone who has experienced crises of conscience and the distress of captivity has a priestly guarantee of the value of his dearly-bought salvation and freedom. But if my words were to be a lament rather than a congratulation, I should be untrue to my own most precious experiences in the study of the-

*Om studiet av religionen (Lund: CWK Gleerups förlag, 1951), 44–48.

ology and in the service of the church, as well as to what since my childhood I have seen to be achievable.

I congratulate you on your studies here at the university and beyond it: carry on studying without fear of offending anyone. I congratulate you on those who will be your companions: an Amos, a Hosea, an Isaiah, a Jeremiah, a Paul, an Augustine, a Francis, a Luther, a Pascal, a Kierkegaard. And high above all of these the Master, the Lord Jesus, who grows before our eyes the closer we come to him. He is the one whom you, yourselves set free by submitting to his yoke, are to present to your brethren. In the history of religion the human heart will reveal its deepest secret: its longing for God. This longing will shine out toward you, even in dark times, in the darkness of ignorance and sin, like a sacred fire, in the light of which you will glimpse or understand much of that which before was contradictory or obscure to you. In the superstitious rituals of savages and the confusions of animism, which ignorance merely despises, you will sense the infinite. In the Christian church's doctrinal statements, which our contemporary world finds most foreign, you will recognize comforting and saving truths.

In the universally recognizable longing for the divine you will see the reflection of a heavenly light. If it should appear dimmer here, brighter there, this is due not to the insufficiency of the source of light, but to the position and receptivity of the receiver. But you will find more than that reflection. You will also look into the eyes that have themselves seen the divine light and hear voices that are able to tell of its glory.

You will see the universality of religion, discern the laws of its progress among a people, and of its effect upon a human heart. But when you have been blinded by its wonderful power and progress; when you have admired the loftiest, boldest speculations produced by a human reason permeated by Christianity: even then you will count this as nothing compared to the great and ineffable secret, which no statistics can measure, no psychology analyze, no speculation fit into its systems—namely, the fellowship of the chosen ones, the prophets and witnesses, with God, and especially the hidden life of Jesus with his heavenly Father.

I congratulate you on studying theology in these days. No higher position or insight is won without increased risk. And it would be thoughtless to deny the seriousness of the great crisis into which the conflict between theological research and traditional doctrine is carrying us—but a crisis the dangers of which may be due more to the dogmatic obscurantism, the struggle for power, the well-meaning foolishness, the indiscretions and human passions, on both sides, which worsen the crisis and obscure its real meaning, than to that meaning itself. It would be lamentably shortsighted to deny the invaluable benefits which the church has already gained from this so widely decried theological science, or to close one's eyes to the Lord's wonderful guidance. When one or other thing of which I have been fond has been removed in the course of research, I have said to myself: look at what we have already gained; wait, be faithful, here too you shall see light. And when I have felt myself doubting or uneasy in the face of an analysis which seemed to dissolve into nothing facts which appeared essential to my Christian faith, I have always found that the fault lay, not in science itself, but in a denial of the spirit of *true* science, an inadequate sense of reality and life, of the reality of history, of the real life of human beings. Therefore, gentlemen, I can say to you with confidence, out of my own experience: not less science, but more science, a deeper sense of reality, more serious research: for with it will come new clarity, new humility, and new strength. In the trouble and distress, into which your youthful love of truth may have brought you in face of the real or falsely contrived contradictions between age-old faith and theological research, I shall not warn you by holding up to you Peter on the water, ready to sink; but encourage you by pointing to Paul, storming toward the goal, reckoning all things—even opinions hallowed by time—as loss in comparison with the overwhelming fact of the knowledge of the Lord Jesus Christ. I must congratulate you on the great privilege of being allowed at this time to work with those questions which concern human life most deeply.

In particular I congratulate you on your coming vocation as the servants of religion among our people. You are to be witnesses of the power of the Gospel to judge, crush, and humble; to raise up, to help where there was no other help, to give comfort where all other comfort had come to an end, to give the courage to live and the courage to die. You are to be the interpreters of truth, without fear or favor, and the spiritual guides of our people, not intrusive, not ingratiating, but available to all—for if you are too great to concern yourself with the smallest person, you are too small to be a minister—loving not comfort but people, not humanity but people, our brothers and sisters who struggle around us and who conceal behind barriers, behind sensitivity or the armor of inaccessibility, hearts which can live only on love. When you have experienced this, you will find a genuine concern for all human occupations and activities, sorrows and joys.

Do not seek any power or party, but the salvation of souls. Do not, I pray you, shut yourself up within any circle of persons or ideas, but desire to understand people and try constantly to learn to write a few new letters in the copybook of life. When you meet with rebuffs, ask yourselves whether you have found the right key to those hearts and whether you have made the right use of that key which the word of God provides. Remember this—that your true happiness and the happiness of your churches will depend on whether you take seriously Paul's rule: Not as lords over the faith of the church, but as helpers of the church's joy. Not lords but servants—not servants of a party or faction, but servants of the church, creating joy, pouring out joy, by your life in love and your proclamation of the pure Gospel, from the eternal source of joy for the refreshment of thirsting souls.

You are to be the servants of all but the slaves of none: not the slaves of any sin, of any individual, of any class. You are natural peacemakers in the class wars, natural helpers of the weak and the deceived. We may confidently leave in your hands the social problems of our country—not to be dealt with as a challenge in the political arena, but as a privilege for you who in your ministry will be with our people day in and day out, in town and country, not as members of one or other social class, not as employers or employees, not as citizens of a legally constituted state, or in any other function, but simply as individual human beings.

As the servants of Jesus you have an ally in every human being. You will experience opposition, hard opposition, if you otherwise live up to the truth: first and last the same kind of opposition that you must constantly combat in yourselves through daily repentance and renewal in vigilance and prayer—the ingenious pride and rebellion of the human heart. But you have a secret confidant in every person, provided that you otherwise serve the cause of Christ. Through the revealing of the truth you will recommend yourself before God to every human conscience.

May the Lord light the sacred fire in your hearts and preserve it!

Appendix 2: Method in the History of Religion (1908)*

It has been of inestimable benefit to the study of religion, and to religion itself, that the scriptures of Christianity—and subsequently those of other religions—have been extracted from the isolation to which the doctrine of inspiration had consigned them, and subjected to the same treatment and methods as other historical documents. This type of biblical research is not new, strictly speaking. It was pursued with great freedom in the early church, and, by the Antiochines, with a sense of history. It is part of the principle of the Reformation. But only during the last century, with impulses from the much-criticized Enlightenment, but with a hard-fought liberation at a later stage from its unhistorical and dull rationalism, has it reached such proportions and such independence that no historical documents can be compared with the Bible in respect of historical analysis.

However, the old isolation has sometimes reemerged, though in an opposite direction. Formerly it was a matter of *noli me tangere*. Now, here and there among biblical scholars, it has become a "critical"—actually an uncritical—arbitrariness, or a formal and formalistic cleverness which has taken leave of all reality and which, if applied to other historical documents, would place historical certainty out of reach. It is easily forgotten that tradition, whether written down at an earlier or later stage, is part of that which the historian must explain. Some biblical scholars treat tradition as a sort of malicious power which, in a spirit of Protestant zeal, must always be profoundly mistrusted, fought, and rearranged. However psychologically understandable this attitude may be as a reaction to the intolerable rigidity of a previous age, it is not scientific. Fortunately, though, the one who goes out looking for donkeys

---

Studiet av religionen, 3rd ed. (Stockholm: Norstedt, 1916), 54–59.

may find a king's crown. However crazy one's methods and objectivity, energy and talent can produce excellent results. There are still honorable people around who consider a statement more scientific, the farther it departs from what the sources say, and the later it dates the books of the Bible. It is as though a historical innovation would be the more easily grasped if it were placed a century or so nearer our own day. This is as unhistorical and as unscientific as the attempt elsewhere to explain a new spiritual discovery by claiming it to have emerged out of a hypothetical primeval wisdom, learned by all. The unique does not become any more easily understood by being redated in either direction. And tradition is there to be explained, not to be refuted. Nothing arises out of nothing. The simplest explanation is: this is what happened. We know of traditions that have survived, purely orally, for centuries, and which later research has proved true. But there may be a statement in the documents or a tradition which has a better or a more probable explanation than that. If the scholar should find such a clue, he must not allow himself to be inhibited by the nearest approximation, or by consideration for the current traditional or "critical" dogma—it is contradictory to talk about critical dogma, but opinions and hypotheses which have gained a certain acceptance among scholars have a dangerous tendency to stick fast and prevent work from proceeding freely. The golden middle way gives protection against dangerous precipices and steep hills. But it will never lead to the final destination. Every new discovery, every new insight, must be produced directly and without fear of current opinion. That is genuine critical radicalism. It recognizes only one corrective, namely, respect for reality.

But this respect presupposes a sense of historical and psychological reality, which is part of that artistic equipment necessary for all higher historical research. History is not taking photographs of past events, but comes into being through the medium of the historian's personality, which in turn is shaped by his state of mind and heart. History is not an assembly of isolated events, but a connection between them. We believe that the connection lies in the events themselves, and we are trying constantly to approach the real meaning of the historical process. In the last resort the connection belongs to the divine factor in history. It is a divine purpose which is glimpsed in the great moments of history by the eye of devotion and genius. But this is not to say that this divine purpose should be understood as a Deus ex machina. The great drama has not been put together that badly. But we cannot stand outside ourselves. It is the spirit of the historian which combines and interprets. There is a subjective element in the very selection of facts from among all the confusing mass of contemporary events. There is even more in their connection and evaluation. History, like every other activity of the human spirit, exists in order to help human beings to cope with their world and reach self-realization. History is the work of the spirit toward the gaining of clarity and orientation in the present situation of society and the individual, and thus courage and direction for action. That is why different cultures [literally, culture-circles] interpret the same events so differently. To us, Marathon and Poitiers are inestimably positive as turning points in the history of civilization and religion. From the Persian-Islamic point of view both were tragic hindrances to the victory of a purer religion and a freer culture. In our image of history, Luther and the Reformation occupy a central position, and in accordance with the deplorably general law of human limitations, the Middle Ages have been left in undeserved obscurity. For us, Kant ushered in a new and higher epoch. From a Catholic, Thomistic point of view, on the other hand, the Middle Ages were the classical epoch of religion and thought, which at most can be resurrected and continued. Horizons and patterns of light and shade vary according to the spiritual vantage point one occupies. We [in Sweden] who have just lived through a national crisis can see how previously unquestioned dogmas having to do with our national consciousness have collapsed. The human spirit realizes itself in the labors of the historian. But the saying is true even here that he must lose himself in order to win himself. No well-meaning enthusiasm, no cautious or bold construction with a conscious end in view is capable of creating history which is worthy of the name, and which renders its healthy service to the liberating and strengthening of the spirit; only pure devotion to reality will suffice.

The more the scholar forgets his most cherished opinions and desires, the more impartially he allows the sources and the human life which flows out of them to affect him, the greater guarantee he has that his work will be rich, meaningful, and beneficial, the more purely will it express the highest aspirations of his soul. For the hidden world of the heart is revealed in acts, and even in the works of the historian. Where difficult subjects are concerned, the truth of the historical picture presupposes a soundness and an eye for what is essential in the spirit of the author, and this can never be replaced by mere virtuosity.

The difficulty in the study of the Bible is connected in the last resort with the uniqueness of the personality of Jesus, and with the unique place he claims for himself in the world of religion. At this high point in the study of religion, a modicum of understanding for such genius and artistic imagination is even more indispensable than it might otherwise be. Lives of Jesus are dangerous, often compromising, either revealing their authors' intelligence, depth of understanding, feeling for essentials, and their spiritual freedom; or betraying their imprisonment in dogmatism, bitterness, partisan feeling, and philistinism.

It is one of the maddest aspects of the madness of our day, that there are those who would concern themselves with the methods and results of biblical scholarship, and discuss its justification and value, before getting to know the Bible. If some people have become separated from nature, and from an appreciation of the beautiful silent friends who would gladden, comfort, and exhort us, we do not need to blame Linnaeus's artificial system and try to replace it with a natural classification. First we must go out among the flowers and herbs on a fresh spring morning or on a glorious summer evening—from here I can hear the song thrush, which is singing late in our flower garden this year. The Bible is the soul's garden. It is shameful that so many people read our sacred book so seldom. A very famous and gifted classical actor, who knows every line of Ibsen and Bjørnson, and a great deal else besides, wondered whether he had heard correctly, that that beautiful passage about love [1 Cor. 13] which the minister had read was actually by Paul. What a happy discovery, that the Bible is part of literature.

Appendix 3:
Söderblom on His Father (1914)*

I have been into cottages far away in the forests. I have met farmers and "gentlemen." I have spoken with townsmen and fishermen. Everywhere the name of my father opens people's hearts to me. It is no wonder that his passionate restlessness, his mixture of openness and suspicion, sometimes gentle, sometimes rough, and his many eccentricities meant that opinions of him were divided. But during his time of penitence and in his enthusiastic revivalist preaching he felt the threat of the law over him, even to the point of mental unbalance—so much so, that later, when he had dared to believe in Christ's atonement, he ceaselessly proclaimed the message of joy, until the time when even his disciplined bodily forces failed him. No hour was too early or too late, no road was too hard or too long, no tiredness or illness might stand in his way, when it was a matter of comforting the sick or the dying, of helping the poor or proclaiming the word. Still, when the infirmity of old age had begun to leave its mark on him, a Trönö parishioner said to me, "No one gives words of comfort like the old rector." When I sat on the back of his buggy and we met someone he did not at once recognize (which was not often), he would not give up until he had found out from which village and farm the stranger came—using a memory and a capacity for making connections which he could also apply to the Hebrew Old Testament and in other branches of knowledge, and which put the student to shame. Once he had placed the individual, there followed long monologues on that farm and that village and that family, and how things might work out for one person or another. Certainly he knew their troubles and their life-style. And certainly he was deeply concerned for their spiritual well-being. When Landgren was asked for his advice about the

---

*Herdabref till prästerskapet och församlingarna i Uppsala ärkestift (Uppsala: Askerberg, 1914), 79–81.

election of a rector for Bjuråker, and had said all that he could about the good qualities of the two other candidates, he added: "But if you want a man who can show you the way to heaven, choose Söderblom." A wise and thoughtful man close to him, a man of impeccable character and a great deal of personal dignity—and a man who was in many ways my father's opposite, who often criticized my father in my hearing for pointless effort or dangerous submissiveness—said to me after my father's death, "They never understood him. His way of going about things always reminded me of the words, 'Seek first the kingdom of God.'"

In time he was overtaken by an illness against which his otherwise unfailing medicines, fasting and water, were of no avail. Twelve years later I came home from the center of German Lutheranism [Leipzig] to hear my dear mother's last tender words. To my father's deathbed the way home was even longer: from my work at the Swedish church in Paris. During the last days he had been unable either to speak or to see anything. But he knew that I was on my way. And the ascetic discipline of his will accomplished one last miracle. Toward morning I entered his sickroom and approached his bed: the room was bare of even the most elementary comforts. Now he was ready to speak. For two hours he talked about all manner of things, great and small, about cares, wishes, hopes, memories, and plans; it all poured out of him, and even at times he managed a joke or an epigram. But this, first and last, was what he said: "You must have the same rule that I have always followed. My rule has always been: not as lords over the congregation, but as helpers of your joy."[1] In this way he combined in his memory the two texts from Paul and from the First Letter of Peter. After that he said nothing more, and a few hours later in the day he fell asleep.

Appendix 4:
Söderblom's Honorary Doctorates

Doctor of Theology/Divinity

Geneva, 1909
Kristiania (Oslo), 1911
St. Andrews, 1911
Glasgow, 1921
Greifswald, 1922
Dublin (Trinity College), 1926
Sopron, 1928
Copenhagen, 1929

Doctor of Philosophy

Uppsala, 1917
Greifswald, 1922
Bonn, 1924

Doctor of Law(s)

Berlin, 1921
Oxford, 1923

Doctor of Medicine

Greifswald, 1922

Notes

Abbreviations

Abbreviations have been used wherever possible, especially to Söderblom's own writings, to a few works of reference, and occasionally to journals.

BSM   Bengt Sundkler, *Nathan Söderblom och hans möten* (Stockholm: Gummesson, 1975).
BSNS   Bengt Sundkler, *Nathan Söderblom: His Life and Work* (London: Lutterworth, 1968).
CRH   Eric J. Sharpe, *Comparative Religion: A History* (London: Duckworth, 1975, 2d ed. 1986).
EBNS   Eivind Berggrav, *Nathan Söderblom: geni og karakter* (Oslo: Aschehoug, 1931).
ER   Mircea Eliade, ed., *The Encyclopedia of Religion* (New York: Macmillan, 1987).
ERE   James Hastings, ed., *The Encyclopaedia of Religion and Ethics* (Edinburgh: T. & T. Clark, 1908–21).
FRU   Nathan Söderblom, ed., *Främmande religionsurkunder i urval och öfversättning* (Stockholm: Gebers, 1908).
GU   Nathan Söderblom, *Gudstrons uppkomst* (Stockholm: Gebers, 1914).
HB   Nathan Söderblom, *Herdabref till prästerskapet och församlingarna i Uppsala ärkestift* (Uppsala: Askerberg, 1914).
HLI   Sven Thulin, ed., *Hågkomster och livsintryck av svenska män och kvinnor*, vols. 12, 14, 15 (Uppsala: Lindblad, 1931, 1933, 1934).
HML   Nathan Söderblom, *Humor och melankoli och andra Lutherstudier* (Stockholm: SKDB, 1919).
IRM   *The International Review of Missions*
JB   Nathan Söderblom, *Jesu bärgspredikan och vår tid: en undersökning* (Stockholm: Haeggström, 1898).
KMS   Nathan Söderblom, *Kristenhetens möte i Stockholm* (Stockholm: SKDB, 1926).
LF   Nathan Söderblom, *Les Fravashis: Étude sur les traces dans le Mazdéisme d'une ancienne conception sur la survivance des morts* (Paris: Leroux, 1899).

LG	Nathan Söderblom, *The Living God: Basal Forms of Personal Religion* (London: Oxford University Press, 1933, reprint, 1939; reprint, Boston: Beacon Press, 1962).
LVF	Nathan Söderblom, *La Vie future d'après le Mazdéisme* (Paris: Leroux, 1901).
NRRH	Nathan Söderblom, *Naturlig religion och religionshistoria: en historik och ett program* (Stockholm: Bonnier, 1914).
NSIM	Nils Karlström, ed., *Nathan Söderblom in memoriam* (Stockholm: SKDB, 1931).
NSSR	Eric J. Sharpe and Anders Hultgård, eds., *Nathan Söderblom and His Contribution to the Study of Religion* [Horae Soederblomianae VII] (Uppsala: Söderblom Society and Leiden: Brill, 1984).
NSVS	Nathan Söderblom, *När stunderna växla och skrida*, 4 vols. in 2 (Stockholm: SKDB, 1935).
OSR	Nathan Söderblom, *Om studiet av religionen*, ed. Erland Ehnmark (Lund: Gleerup, 1951).
PLT I,2	Anna Söderblom, *På livets trottoir* 1,2 (Lund: Gleerup, 1948, 1956).
RGG	*Die Religion in Geschichte und Gegenwart*
RP	Nathan Söderblom, *Religionsproblemet inom katolicism och protestantism* (Stockholm: Gebers, 1910).
RSU	Nathan Söderblom, "Religionen och den sociala utvecklingen," in *Religionsvetenskapliga Kongressen i Stockholm 1897*, ed. Samuel A. Fries, 76–143 (Stockholm: Bohlin, 1898).
SAR	Nathan Söderblom, *Studiet av religionen* (Stockholm: Norstedt, 1908).
SF I,2	Nathan Söderblom, *Svenskars fromhet* 1,2, ed. Anna Söderblom (Stockholm: SKDB, 1933, 1941).
SM	Nathan Söderblom, *Sommarminnen*, ed. Anna Söderblom (Stockholm: SKDB, 1941).
SSB	Nathan Söderblom, *Sundar Singhs budskap utgivet och belyst* (Stockholm: Gebers, 1923).
TANS	Tor Andrae, *Nathan Söderblom* (Uppsala: Lindblad, 1931).
TLF	Nathan Söderblom, *Tre livsformer: mystik (Sundar Singh), förtröstan, vetenskap* (Stockholm: Gebers, 1922).
TLZ	*Theologische Literatur-Zeitung*
TOS	Nathan Söderblom, *Tal och skrifter*, 6 vols. (Malmö: Världslitteraturens förlag, 1930–31).
UR	Nathan Söderblom, *Uppenbarelsereligion: några synpunkter i anledning af Babel-Bibeldiskussionen* (Uppsala: Schultz, 1903 and later editions).
URH	Nathan Söderblom, *Ur religionens historia* (Stockholm: Norstedt, 1915).

UUL   Uppsala University Library, Nathan Söderblom Manuscript Collection.
VK   Nils Lövgren and Edvard Rodhe, eds., *Vår Kyrka*, 4 vols. (Stockholm: SKDB, 1912–26).
WRIL   Nathan Söderblom, *Waldemar Rudins inre liv* (Stockholm: Norstedt, 1923).

Preface

1. In the nineteenth century, the name of the town was spelled "Upsala." Today, with one or two exceptions, the spelling is "Uppsala." In this book, to avoid confusion, I have used the more modern spelling throughout.

Introduction

1. Van der Leeuw 1938, 694.
2. *LG*, xxviii.
3. *HLI*, 15:12
4. *TLF*, 97.
5. *TLF*, 106–7.
6. *TLF*, 111.
7. *TLF*, 120.
8. *BSNS*, 59.
9. Otto 1923, 8.
10. See Chapter 3.
11. *SAR*, foreword to 1st ed., dated Oct. 7, 1907, unpaginated.

Chapter 1

1. *SF*, 2:17.
2. On Jonas Söderblom, see *SF*, 2:9–41; *TANS*, 24–42.
3. *SF*, 2:23.
4. *SF*, 2:23–24. The names "Lauritz" and "Olaus" were later simplified into the Swedish "Lars" and "Olof" and generally appear only in these forms.
5. Söderblom 1923(1), 3.
6. Söderblom 1923(1), 4.
7. *HB*, 80.
8. *TANS*, 57.

9. Elsa Englund (Söderblom's youngest sister), in *HLI*, 15:52.
10. *TANS*, 57.
11. *TANS*, 58.
12. Åkerberg 1975.
13. Hartman 1968, 160.
14. *TANS*, 38.
15. *TANS*, 42.

Chapter 2

1. For Söderblom's own reminiscences of the 1880s and 1890s, see *SF*, 2:129–52.
2. Rodhe 1935, 295–347 (Pontus Wikner) and 349–90 (Viktor Rydberg).
3. *SF*, 2:130.
4. See most recently Hultkrantz 1983, 31–41.
5. Lindroth 1976, 196.
6. Fjellstedt 1880, 466.
7. Chesterton 1961, 9–12.
8. *VK*, 2:447–48.
9. *SF*, 2:140.
10. *TANS*, 69–70.
11. *SF*, 2:138.
12. Richter 1935, 17–18.
13. *SF*, 2:145.
14. *TOS*, 5:9–37.
15. *TOS*, 5:25.
16. See below, Chapter 5.
17. *TANS*, 69–70.
18. Söderblom to Harnack, May 2, 1923, UUL.
19. Söderblom 1900, vi–xi.
20. Quoted in Holmström 1937, 28.
21. *TANS*, 113–14; Holmström 1937, 47 at n. 2.
22. Boschwitz 1968, 5–18.
23. Fries 1945, 115. For the influence of Wellhausen on Nietzsche, see Boschwitz 1968, 30–31, 82–83.
24. On Fehr, see *SF*, 2:42–90.
25. On Ritschl, see, for the earlier literature, *RGG*, 4:2326–33, and more recently Richmond 1978.
26. See the essay on Anna Söderblom in *BSM*, 80–95, and cf. *SF*, 2:42–90.
27. *PLT*, I:55.
28. *BSM*, 86–87.

29. *PLT*, I:132.
30. *BSNS*, 23.
31. *TANS*, 102.
32. On December 20, 1921, Söderblom succeeded Rudin as a member of the Swedish Academy, and according to custom delivered an inaugural address on his predecessor, *Minne av Waldemar Rudin* (Stockholm: Norstedt, 1923). This he then expanded into a book, *Waldemar Rudins inre liv* (*WRIL*).
33. *WRIL*, 78.
34. Fries 1945, 191, cf. 211, 249–50.
35. *TANS*, 101.
36. Söderblom 1925, 22.
37. *BSNS*, 30.
38. *BSNS*, 30.
39. Karl Fries, in *HLI*, 12:171.
40. *SM*, 10–103.
41. *SM*, 61.
42. *SM*, 97.
43. *BSNS*, 38.
44. On an American government mission to Russia in 1917, Mott addressed a gathering of Cossacks and was reported as having insulted Germany, though whether he actually did in so many words must remain an open question. True or not, he lost the trust of many Christians in Germany at this point. For details, see Hopkins 1979, 498–501.
45. Fries 1945, 239.
46. Ibid., 240.
47. Ibid., 241–42. Söderblom thought Fehr had overreacted: Söderblom to Göransson, May 25, 1892, UUL.
48. Fries 1945, xxii–xxiii.

Chapter 3

1. On the "history of religion school," see below, Chapter 5.
2. Sharpe 1975, 119–43.
3. *TANS*, 158.
4. Briem 1927, 46.
5. Ibid., 48.
6. Andrae, in *NSIM*, 46–48.
7. F. Max Müller, ed., *The Sacred Books of the East*, vols. 4, 23, 31 (Oxford: Clarendon Press, 1883–87).
8. Published in an English translation by Rasmus B. Anderson as *Teu-*

tonic *Mythology* (London: Swan, Sonnenschein, 1891).
   9. On Moulton, see Sharpe 1980, 144–50.
   10. Ibid., 150.
   11. Moulton 1919, 136.
   12. Hartman, in *NSSR*, 36–37.
   13. Ibid., 37.
   14. Söderblom to Göransson, Feb. 18, 1893, UUL.
   15. Andrae (*TANS*, 34) thought his knowledge adequate, but Nyberg, who actually was an Iranist, knew it to be rather superficial (Nyberg 1943, 10).
   16. Andrae, in *NSIM*, 45: "His own statements bear witness that he did not go off to Iran merely in order to be able to report the way things once were."
   17. Estborn 1944, 24–25.
   18. *PLT*, I:143–49.
   19. *TANS*, 157.
   20. *BSNS*, 33.
   21. *TOS*, 3:17.
   22. *TOS*, 3:18.
   23. Söderblom to Göransson, Sept. 10, 1893, UUL.
   24. Söderblom to Göransson, Sept. 29, 1893, UUL.
   25. Söderblom to Göransson, Oct. 24, 1893, UUL.
   26. Söderblom to Göransson, Dec. 11, 1893, UUL.
   27. *SM*, 150–51.

Chapter 4

   1. Sharpe 1975, 122–23.
   2. Söderblom to Göransson, Jan. 24, 1894, UUL.
   3. Anna Söderblom called the Paris period "our seven-year honeymoon," *SF*, 2:49.
   4. Hartman, in *NSSR*, 38.
   5. *NSSR*, 39.
   6. Söderblom to Göransson, July 13, 1894, UUL.
   7. Söderblom to Göransson, Aug. 7, 1894, UUL.
   8. Söderblom to Göransson, Sept. 21, 1894, UUL.
   9. Söderblom to Fries, July 12, 1893, UUL.
   10. Details from *The New Schaff-Herzog Encyclopedia of Religious Knowledge* (New York: Funk & Wagnalls, 1911) 10:133–34.
   11. *RP*, 397.
   12. Söderblom to Göransson, Dec. 19, 1894, UUL.

13. Söderblom to Göransson, Jan. 11, 1895, UUL.
14. Söderblom to Göransson, Dec. 19, 1894, UUL.
15. Söderblom to Göransson, Jan. 28, 1895, UUL.
16. *BSNS*, 44–45.
17. *BSNS*, 45.
18. Söderblom to Fries, May 28, 1895, UUL.
19. *SF*, 2:57–59.
20. *SF*, 2:59–61.
21. Söderblom 1926(2), 7.
22. *SF*, 2:83–84.
23. Söderblom to Göransson, Oct. 29, 1895, UUL.
24. *BSNS*, 48.
25. The third edition (the first edited by Söderblom) appeared in 1903, the fourth in 1912, and the fifth in 1920.
26. Lehmann to Söderblom, Feb. 3, 1900, UUL.
27. Hartman, in *NSSR*, 39.
28. *NSSR*, 40.
29. "Christian Socialism" was the original term, as used in Britain in the 1840s and 1850s. By the end of the century it had become more usual to speak of "Social Christianity." In Germany there were various branches and terminologies, that with which Söderblom was associated generally being called *Evangelisch-sozial*. See *RGG*, 2:759–66.
30. Massey 1983, 81–112.
31. Boschwitz 1968, 30–31, 82–83.
32. Söderblom to Göransson, Jan. 11, 1895, UUL.
33. Karlström 1947, 178.
34. Söderblom to Fries, May 28, 1895, UUL.
35. *TANS*, 187.
36. Karlström 1947, 178.
37. Ibid., 179.
38. Herz 1929, 357.
39. Karlström 1947, 179.
40. Fries 1898(1). Present-day congresses in the history of religions are numbered in a sequence beginning not with Stockholm 1897 but with Paris 1900, perhaps because of the high level of church involvement in the Stockholm assembly. See *CRH*, 138–42.
41. Williams 1906, 345.
42. Ibid., 346.
43. Ibid., 348.
44. Barrows 1893, 1492–95.
45. Williams 1906, 354.
46. *The Church Missionary Intelligencer* (1894):170.

47. Fries 1895, 64.
48. Fries 1898(2), 8–9.
49. Söderblom 1898(3) (*RSU*) takes up pages 76–143, the discussion pages 143–95 in the printed proceedings, Fries 1898(1).
50. *RSU*, 99.
51. *RSU*, 114.
52. *JB*, 30.
53. *JB*, 31.
54. *JB*, 33.
55. *JB*, 38.
56. *JB*, 39.
57. *JB*, 42.
58. *JB*, 43.
59. *JB*, 45.
60. *JB*, 46.
61. *TANS*, 204.
62. *BSNS*, 56.
63. Söderblom to Göransson, Sept. 3, 1898. Cf. Söderblom to Harald Hjärne, Sept. 4, 1898: "His [Ekman's] appointment has disturbed the peace in our home. . . . I shall oil my boots too. After all, one can only fail." UUL.
64. Söderblom to Göransson, Sept. 3, 1898, UUL.
65. Söderblom to Göransson, Sept. 3, 1898, UUL.
66. Söderblom to Göransson, Jan. 23, 1899, UUL.
67. Fries to Söderblom, June 25, 1899, UUL.
68. Fries to Söderblom, Nov. 22, 1899, UUL.
69. Malmeström 1950, 184–90.
70. Zaehner 1961, 76, 146–48.
71. *LF*, 27.
72. *LF*, 31.
73. *LF*, 75.
74. Hartman, in *NSSR*, 40–41.
75. Söderblom 1899(1), 6.
76. Ibid., 8.
77. Ibid., 10.
78. Ibid., 13.
79. Ibid., 14–15.
80. Ibid., 15.
81. See below, Chapter 6.
82. Söderblom 1899(1), 20.
83. Ibid., 29.
84. Ibid., 32.
85. Barbe de Quirielle, in *HLI*, 14:47.

86. On the uses and misuses of the word "eschatology," see Carmignac 1971, 365-90.
87. *BSNS*, 49.
88. *LVF*, 320-21.
89. *LVF*, 422.
90. *LVF*, 427.
91. Andrae, in *NSIM*, 45.
92. Widengren 1954, 424. Hartman, in *NSSR*, 40.
93. Van Veen 1940, 25.
94. Zaehner 1961, 343.
95. Hartman, in *NSSR*, 45.
96. Brandon 1961, 269-75.
97. Anna Söderblom to Göransson, Jan. 26, 1901, UUL.
98. A. Sabatier to Söderblom, Jan. 20, 1901, UUL.
99. Lehmann to Söderblom, Feb. 25, 1901, UUL.
100. Tiele to Söderblom, Apr. 1, 1901, UUL.
101. P. Sabatier to Söderblom, Feb. 27, 1901, UUL.
102. Fries to Söderblom, Jan. 25, 1901, UUL.
103. Bousset, in *TLZ* (May 1901): 517-22.
104. Bousset, in *TLZ* (May 1901): 522.
105. Mme Sabatier to Söderblom, Feb. 21, 1901, UUL.
106. Fries to Söderblom, Feb. 13, 1901, UUL.
107. Fries to Söderblom, Mar. 17, 1901, UUL.
108. Fries to Söderblom, Mar. 27, 1901, UUL.
109. Fries to Söderblom, June 9, 1901, UUL.
110. Fries to Söderblom, Oct. 6, 1901, UUL.
111. *PLT*, 2:18-19.
112. Söderblom diary, Apr. 19, 1901, UUL.
113. Tiele had in fact previously offered the revision of his *Kompendium* to Lehmann, who had turned it down. Lehmann to Söderblom, Feb. 25, 1901, UUL.
114. Tiele to Söderblom, May 14, 1901, UUL.
115. Lehmann to Söderblom, Aug. 7, 1901, UUL.
116. Söderblom to Göransson, June 23, 1901, UUL.
117. Söderblom diary, June 27, 1901, UUL. Cf. *HB*, 80-81.
118. Söderblom to Rabbi G. Klein, Aug. 4, 1901, UUL.

Chapter 5

1. Söderblom to Göransson, Sept. 11, 1901, UUL.
2. *BSNS*, 61-62.

3. Söderblom's last book, *The Living God* (1932–33), contains, albeit in a revised form, lecture material from these years. Cf. below, Chapter 8.
4. Söderblom to Göransson, Oct. 27, 1901, UUL.
5. Harnack 1904, 159–90.
6. Ibid., 167.
7. Ibid., 176.
8. Ibid., 182.
9. Ibid., 183.
10. *OSR*, 21.
11. *OSR*, 23.
12. *OSR*, 19.
13. *OSR*, 24.
14. *OSR*, 28.
15. *OSR*, 34.
16. Moulton 1913, 122–23. Cf. Sharpe 1965, 329–45.
17. *OSR*, 44.
18. Aulén 1939, 146.
19. *HLI*, 14:39.
20. *BSNS*, 64. Years later, Söderblom's youngest sister recorded a fragment of conversation from about this time. He had been under attack again, and said to her: "But you know, I am really entirely orthodox." "I know you are," she replied. Elsa Englund, in *HLI*, 15:55.
21. *OSR*, 44.
22. H. Gunkel, quoted in Verheule 1973, 306.
23. Verheule 1973 is the best account of which I am aware. But see also K. Rudolph, in *ER*, 12:293–96.
24. Verheule 1973, 295.
25. *OSR*, 24.
26. Söderblom to Göransson, July 7, 1902, UUL.
27. Söderblom to Göransson, Jan. 24, 1902, UUL.
28. Lang's *The Making of Religion* had been reviewed in the French journals *Mélusine* and *Revue de l'Histoire des Religions*, and it may well have been this which had attracted Söderblom's attention. See De Cocq 1968, 102.
29. Reprinted in *URH*, 71–98, with the simplified title, "Andrew Lang and Baiami."
30. *URH*, 92–93.
31. *URH*, 93.
32. *URH*, 95.
33. Hultkrantz, in *NSSR*, 25. The term "Producer," which has a slightly odd sound as an English equivalent of the Swedish *frambringare* (and German *Urheber*), would seem to have been Söderblom's own. In an article published in the *International Review of Missions* in 1915 he wrote about "the

exalted ancient beings that I call Producers." *IRM* 4 (1915): 531.

34. O. Weber 1904, 11, made the curious comparison of Israel and Babylon with Switzerland and Germany!
35. T. Weber 1903, 6.
36. Finkelstein 1958, 432.
37. O. Weber 1904, 4.
38. Jeremias 1903, 37.
39. *UR*, 8.
40. *UR*, 11.
41. *UR*, 25.
42. See Sharpe 1965, 39–56, 94–108, 329–45.
43. *UR*, 43–44, and compare the Sundar Singh episode in Chapter 8, below.
44. *UR*, 55.
45. Cf. Sharpe 1981, 19–37.
46. *Mystik* is a less pejorative term than *Mystizismus*, but in the nineteenth century many Protestant theologians disapproved of the "non-rational" forms of religion which both denoted. See Ritschl 1880, 1:28.
47. Söderblom to Göransson, Mar. 1, 1897, UUL. *TANS*, 27.
48. *RGG*, 5:1721–25.
49. Söderblom had, however, written one of the *Volksbücher*. See below, Chapter 6, at n. 8.
50. Lehmann to Söderblom, Dec. 26, 1902, UUL.
51. Lehmann to Söderblom, July 15, 1903, UUL.
52. Söderblom to Göransson, Aug. 11, 1902, UUL.
53. Söderblom to Göransson, May 8, 1903, UUL.
54. Söderblom to Göransson, Nov. 2, 1903, UUL.
55. Söderblom to Göransson, Nov. 2, 1903, UUL.
56. *SM*, 168.
57. *SM*, 169.
58. *SM*, 170.
59. *SM*, 170–71.
60. *SM*, 172.
61. *SM*, 173.
62. *SM*, 173.
63. *SM*, 174–81.
64. *URH*, 31–56.
65. *URH*, 56.
66. Anna Söderblom to Göransson, Mar. 6, 1906, UUL.
67. Söderblom to Göransson, Aug. 11, 1906, UUL.
68. *TANS*, 221–22.
69. *RP*, 157–58.

70. *BSNS*, 70–71.
71. *RP*, 160. *BSNS*, 71.
72. Pages 76–98 in the 1916 edition.
73. *FRU*, I:131.
74. Söderblom 1912(2), 81.
75. Emilia Fogelklou-Norlind in *HLI*, 12:241–55; Anna Söderblom in *PLT*, 2:82–109; Gabrielsson in *HLI*, 12:256–65.
76. *PLT*, 2:87.
77. *PLT*, 2:82–97.
78. *PLT*, 2:96–97.
79. *PLT*, 2:97.
80. Lehmann to Söderblom, Aug. 12, 1908, UUL.
81. *BSNS*, 91–93.
82. Söderblom 1903(1), a fifty-page essay.
83. Söderblom 1908(3), 391–410.
84. Reprinted in *SM*, 182–242.
85. *SM*, 184.
86. *SM*, 202.
87. *SM*, 236.
88. *SM*, 238.
89. *SM*, 238.
90. Söderblom 1911(1).
91. Söderblom 1911(1), 65, 69, 71–72. The final chapter of *The Living God* (1932–33) is a modified version of this 1911 lecture.
92. *SM*, 244.
93. Söderblom to Rabbi G. Klein, Aug. 21, 1911, UUL.
94. Lehmann to Söderblom, Feb. 28, 1912, UUL.
95. Söderblom to Anna Söderblom, June 25, 1912, UUL.

Chapter 6

1. Bailey 1978, 111, 172.
2. Rudolph 1962.
3. Kittel, in *HLI*, 14:112.
4. *HLI*, 14:113.
5. *HLI*, 14:113.
6. *PLT*, 2:110–11.
7. *BSNS*, 84.
8. *RGG*, 5:1725.
9. Söderblom to Anna Söderblom, June 25, 1912, UUL.
10. Following the pattern of Söderblom 1912(2), 166–88.

11. Fries to Söderblom, July 27, 1912, UUL.
12. Söderblom to Göransson, Aug. 17, 1912, UUL.
13. Lehmann to Söderblom, June 8, 1913, UUL.
14. Lehmann to Söderblom, Nov. 9, 1913, UUL.
15. Hempel, in *HLI*, 14:123.
16. Söderblom to Fries, May 30, 1913, UUL.
17. Söderblom to Fries, Oct. 28, 1913, UUL.
18. Page references are to the Swedish edition (*NRRH*).
19. *NRRH*, 78–79.
20. *NRRH*, 82–83.
21. *NRRH*, 82, footnote. In the German edition (Söderblom 1913) the equivalent note is on p. 77.
22. *NRRH*, 84.
23. *NRRH*, 110.
24. *NRRH*, 112.
25. Barbe de Quirielle, in *HLI*, 14:49.
26. *HLI*, 14:128.
27. Söderblom to Fries, Nov. 23, 1913, UUL.
28. Söderblom to Fries, Dec. 9, 1913, UUL.
29. Söderblom to Göransson, May 9, 1914, UUL.
30. *BSNS*, 101–6.
31. *BSNS*, 104.
32. Söderblom to Fries, May 28, 1914, UUL.
33. Rosenstock-Huessy 1966, 158, was entirely mistaken when he wrote that Söderblom gave up his professorship out of disgust at "the emasculate mind of scholarship and the stagnation and nationalism of the Churches," and "sacrificed his academic idol in time, when he was still free to act with conviction, not as a mere opportunist." After all, he did not elect himself archbishop, and had he not been elected, he would certainly have remained in his academic post.
34. *PLT*, 2:115–18.
35. Cumont to Söderblom, June 20, 1914, UUL. Cf. Edsman 1966, 35–37.
36. Söderblom diary, July 31, 1914, UUL.
37. Söderblom to Göransson, Aug. 5, 1914, UUL.
38. Söderblom to Fries, Aug. 12, 1914, UUL.

Chapter 7

1. See above, Introduction.
2. *CRH*, 220–50. Cf. Hultkrantz 1970, 68–88.
3. See above, Chapter 5.

4. Berggrav 1931, 51, suggests that Söderblom was somewhat careless in the way in which he put his books together.

5. *BSM*, 67.

6. *SF*, 2:147.

7. Bohlin 1956, 176.

8. Heiler 1967, 5.

9. Paul Sabatier's *Vie de S. François d'Assisi* was first published in 1894, went into no less than forty-five editions, and was translated into many languages. It is generally agreed that the appearance of this book marked the beginning of modern Franciscan studies. Paul Sabatier and Söderblom corresponded for many years.

10. *RP*, 375–76.

11. *RP*, 382.

12. *RP*, 400.

13. *RP*, 413–14.

14. *RP*, 417.

15. *RP*, 419.

16. *RP*, 415.

17. *RP*, 433.

18. *RP*, 434–35.

19. *RP*, 436.

20. *RP*, 443.

21. *RP*, 446.

22. *RP*, 446.

23. *RP*, 465.

24. Ehnmark 1949, 216.

25. Ibid., 216–17.

26. A German edition, *Das Werden des Gottesglaubens*, was published in 1916, and an English translation was made but failed to find a publisher. See Edsman 1966, 44.

27. *GU*, 6.

28. *GU*, 8.

29. *GU*, 145.

30. *GU*, 149.

31. *GU*, 152.

32. *Deutsche Literaturzeitung* (June 20, 1914):1553–56.

33. *GU*, 359.

34. *GU*, 180.

35. *GU*, 181.

36. *GU*, 182.

37. *GU*, 183. "Magic" is a word almost impossible to define with precision, but I agree with Cavendish 1978, 7, that "magic is an attempt to exert

power through actions which have a direct and automatic influence on man, nature and the divine." The operative word is "automatic."

38. *GU*, 357–58.
39. *GU*, 365.
40. *GU*, 367.
41. Rupp 1953, 33.
42. In a letter to the present writer, dated March 31, 1959, Rupp acknowledged that the only Söderblom book he had ever read was *The Living God*.
43. Wingren 1968, 20.
44. Lindroth 1941, 14.
45. *BSNS*, 155.
46. The articles in question were: (1) "Ages of the World (Zoroastrian)," in I:205–10; (2) "Ardashir I," in I:774; (3) "Asceticism (Persian)," in 2:105–6; (4) "Creed (Parsi)," in 4:247–48; (5) "Death and Disposal of the Dead (Parsi)," in 4:502–5; and (6) "Incarnation (Introductory; Parsi)," in 7:183–84, 198–99.
47. See above, Chapter 5.
48. Sharpe 1981, 20–21.
49. *ERE*, 3:738.
50. *ERE*, 3:738.
51. *ERE*, 6:731.
52. *ERE*, 6:732.
53. *ERE*, 6:740.
54. *ERE*, 6:741.
55. *ERE*, 6:741.
56. Cf. *CRH*, 165.

Chapter 8

1. The bibliography in *NSIM*, 391–451 has 305 entries down to the end of 1914, and 361 thereafter. But this list, comprehensive as it is, is still not altogether complete.
2. Alfvén 1949, Hedwall 1973.
3. Alfvén 1949, 51–56; Hedwall 1973, 67–69, 289–92.
4. Alfvén 1949, 120–25; Hedwall 1973, 297–300.
5. Alfvén 1949, 114.
6. Berggrav 1931, 35.
7. *HB*, 53.
8. *HB*, 56.
9. *HB*, 67.
10. *HB*, 54–55.

11. Karlström 1947.
12. Söderblom 1919(2), 3.
13. Ibid., 8.
14. Ibid., 17.
15. For his memorial oration, see *TOS*, 4:248–55.
16. On Andrae, see Widengren 1947, Hassler and Murray 1947, and Sharpe 1987.
17. Andrae, *Muhammed* (1930). Later editions of 1950 and 1967 contain some eighty pages by Widengren. The English edition of 1935 (and later reprints) is by way of a German translation of the 1930 Swedish original.
18. Ferré 1967, 10.
19. Lindroth 1941, 14.
20. Ibid., 33, 92.
21. Pettersson and Åkerberg 1981, 86.
22. F. R. Lehmann (a German) was no relation to Edvard Lehmann (a Dane). See F. R. Lehmann, 1922.
23. Schomerus 1912.
24. Heiler, in *HLI*, 14:209–32.
25. *HLI*, 14:213.
26. Misner 1981, 305, 309, 317.
27. Sharpe 1984(1).
28. Ibid., 69–70.
29. *BSM*, 110–34.
30. Westman 1929.
31. The only reasonably complete biography available is Appasamy 1966, but this is uncritical.
32. Sharpe 1976, 48–66.
33. Ibid., 60–63.
34. Streeter and Appasamy, 1921, 115.
35. *TLF*, 52.
36. *TLF*, 13.
37. *Upsala Nya Tidning*, April 24, 1922.
38. *Upsala Nya Tidning*, April 24, 1922.
39. *Stockholms Tidningen*, April 26, 1922.
40. *Socialdemokraten*, May 2, 1922.
41. *Svenska Dagbladet*, May 8, 1922.
42. *Svenska Morgonbladet*, April 26, 1922.
43. *SSB*, 124–67.
44. *SSB*, 126.
45. *SSB*, 129.
46. Streeter and Appasamy 1921, 18. On this strange subject, see Sharpe 1984(3), 5–28.

47. Sharpe 1984(3), 17.
48. Ibid., 23. Sundar Singh to Söderblom, Nov. 13, 1928, UUL.
49. One wishes, all the same, that the history of the ecumenical movement would attract historiographers other than those writing, in the last resort, to further (or denigrate) the cause.
50. *EBNS*, 36.
51. *KMS*, 6.
52. *TANS*, 294–95.
53. His funeral oration on that occasion appears in *TOS*, 4:217–22.
54. Brun, in *HLI*, 14:43.
55. *BSNS*, 424. Söderblom 1932, 6.
56. *LG*, 1.
57. *LG*, 2.
58. *LG*, 74.
59. *LG*, 75.
60. Sharpe 1981, 30. It is, however, far more likely that Söderblom planned to discuss Sundar Singh in his 1932 lecture series, which of course was never delivered.
61. *LG*, 80.
62. *LG*, 133.
63. *LG*, 135.
64. *LG*, 158.
65. *LG*, 159.
66. *LG*, 167.
67. I have not ventured in these pages to discuss Söderblom's interpretation of Socrates. See, however, Rudberg 1942, 49–57, and Rudberg 1951, 20–28.
68. *LG*, 236.
69. Söderblom 1911(1). See above, Chapter 5, n. 91.
70. *LG*, 380.
71. *LG*, 384.
72. *LG*, 386.
73. Aulén, in *HLI*, 12:400.
74. Hellquist, in *HLI*, 12:404–10.
75. S. Richter 1950, 66–70.
76. Anderberg, in *HLI*, 12:411–14. Neither Richter nor Anderberg mentions the "history of religion" saying, which appears to have been transmitted only by Brilioth, in *LG*, xxviii.
77. *NSVS*, I:42–43. Söderblom 1928, 429–30.
78. *BSM*, 80–85.
79. Hammarskjöld, *Vägmärken* (Stockholm: Bonniers/Delfin, 1966) 171.

Postscript

1. Hedenius 1959, 84–85, commenting on *Religionsproblemet*, accuses Söderblom of "anti-intellectualism," brought about by the a priori assumption that all religious statements are self-contradictory, and therefore cannot be dealt with "logically." On this view science and religion are totally incompatible.
2. M. Fries 1948. For an analysis of the debate, see Hemberg 1966.
3. Widengren 1953.
4. Edsman 1966.
5. *BSM*.
6. See above, Introduction, n. 8.
7. Åkerberg 1975.
8. Sundén 1960 contains a number of references to Söderblom's development. One might add that during these years the psychology of religion was passing through a very difficult period, due mainly to the suspicion with which it was regarded by the behavioral majority.
9. Åkerberg 1982, 60–65.
10. Åkerberg 1982, 57.
11. Sharpe, in *NSSR*, 89–92.
12. Quoted in Widengren 1947, 187–88.
13. *EBNS*, 5.
14. *EBNS*, 26.
15. *EBNS*, 27.
16. *EBNS*, 27.
17. *EBNS*, 28–29.
18. Sharpe 1984(2), 84–90.
19. *TOS*, 4:166, 168.
20. *TOS*, 4:170.
21. *TLF*, 97.

Appendix 3

1. In the King James Version, "not as lords over God's heritage" (1 Peter 5:3), and "but as helpers of your joy" (2 Cor. 1:24).

Bibliography

Books and Articles by Söderblom

For the fullest available Söderblom bibliography, see Nils Karlström, ed., *Nathan Söderblom in memoriam* (Stockholm: SKDB, 1931), 391–451.

1889	"Om Sveriges förste kristne lärare." In *Tal och skrifter*, 5:9–37. Malmö: Världslitteraturens förlag, 1931.
1893	*Ritschls åskådning af kristendomen.* Stockholm: Norstedt.
1898(1)	*Jesu bärgsprediken och vår tid: en undersökning.* Stockholm: Haeggström.
1898(2)	*Jesu kläder.* Stockholm: Palmquist.
1898(3)	"Religionen och den sociala utvecklingen." In *Religionsvetenskapliga Kongressen i Stockholm 1897*, edited by S. A. Fries, 76–143. Stockholm: Bohlin.
1899(1)	*Betydelsen af Schleiermachers "Reden über die Religion": ett hundraårsminne.* Uppsala: Schultz.
1899(2)	*Les Fravashis: Étude sur les traces dans le Mazdéisme d'une ancienne conception sur la survivance des morts.* Paris: Leroux.
1900	Foreword to *Kristendomens väsende*, by Adolf Harnack. Swedish translation by A. F. Åkerberg. Stockholm: Seligmann.
1901	*La Vie future d'après le Mazdéisme: à la lumière des croyances parallèles dans les autres religions: étude d'eschatologie comparée.* Paris: Leroux.
1903(1)	*Treenighet.* Uppsala: Upsala Nya Tidnings AB.
1903(2)	*Uppenbarelsereligion: några synpunkter i anledning af Babel-Bibeldiskussionen.* Uppsala: Schultz.
1904	*Kristendomen och religionerna.* Stockholm: Norstedt.
1908(1)	*Främmande religionsurkunder i urval och öfversättning.* Stockholm: Gebers.
1908(2)	*Studiet av religionen.* Stockholm: Norstedt.
1908(3)	"The Place of the Christian Trinity and the Buddhist Triratna amongst Holy Triads." In *Transactions of the Third International Congress for the History of Religion*, 2:391–410. Oxford: Oxford University Press.
1910	*Religionsproblemet inom katolicism och protestantism.* Stockholm: Gebers.

1911(1) "Does God Continue to Reveal Himself to Mankind?" In *Report of the Conference of the World's Student Christian Federation . . . April 24–28, 1911*, 59–78. New York: WSCF.
1911(2) *Tre heliga veckor*. Uppsala: Norblad.
1912(1) *Tiele's Kompendium der Religionsgeschichte*. 4th ed. Berlin: Biller.
1912(2) *Översikt av allmänna religionshistorien*. Stockholm: Gebers.
1913 *Natürliche Theologie und allgemeine Religionsgeschichte*. Stockholm: Bonnier and Leipzig: Hinrichs.
1914(1) *Gudstrons uppkomst*. Stockholm: Gebers.
1914(2) *Herdabref till prästerskapet och församlingarna i Uppsala ärkestift*. Uppsala: Askerberg.
1914(3) *Naturlig religion och religionshistoria: en historik och ett program*. Stockholm: Bonnier.
1915 *Ur religionens historia*. Stockholm: Norstedt.
1916 *Svenska kyrkans kropp och själ*. Stockholm: Norstedt.
1919(1) *Humor och melankoli och andra Lutherstudier*. Stockholm: SKDB.
1919(2) *Gå vi mot religionens förnyelse?* Stockholm: Sveriges kristna studentrörelsens förlag.
1920 *Tiele-Söderbloms Kompendium der Religionsgeschichte*. 5th ed. Berlin: Biller.
1922 *Tre livsformer: mystik (Sundar Singh), förtröstan, vetenskap*. Stockholm: Gebers.
1923(1) "Hemma i Hälsingland." In *Svenska Turistföreningens Årsskrift 1923*, 1–12. Stockholm: Wahlström and Widstrand.
1923(2) *Sundar Singhs budskap utgivet och belyst*. Stockholm: Gebers.
1923(3) *Waldemar Rudins inre liv*. Stockholm: Norstedt.
1925 *Från Upsala till Rock Island*. Stockholm: SKDB.
1926(1) *Kristenhetens möte i Stockholm*. Stockholm: SKDB.
1926(2) "Vid Pariskyrkans trehundraårsjubileum." In *Minnesskrift vid Svensklutherska Parisförsamlingens 300-års jubileum*, edited by F. U. Wrangel, 1–11. Stockholm: SKDB.
1928 *Kristi pinas historia: en passionsbok*. Stockholm: SKDB.
1930–31 *Tal och skrifter*. 6 vols. Malmö: Världslitteraturens förlag.
1932 *Den levande Guden: grundformer av personlig religion*. Stockholm: SKDB.
1933(1) *The Living God: Basal Forms of Personal Religion*. London: Oxford University Press, reprint, 1939; reprint, Boston: Beacon Press, 1962.
1933(2) *Svenskars fromhet*. Edited by Anna Söderblom. Stockholm: SKDB.
1933(3) *Ett År: ord för varje dag samlade ur Nathan Söderblom skrifter*. Edited by Anna Söderblom. Stockholm: SKDB.
1933(4) *The Nature of Revelation*. Translation by Frederic E. Pamp of 1930 edition of *Uppenbarelsereligion*. London: Oxford University Press.

1935	När stunderna växla och skrida. 4 vols. in 2. Stockholm: SKDB.
1941(1)	Svenskars fromhet: Ny följd. Edited by Anna Söderblom. Stockholm: SKDB.
1941(2)	Sommarminnen. Edited by Anna Söderblom. Stockholm: SKDB.
1951	Om studiet av religionen. Edited by Erland Ehnmark. Lund: Gleerup.
1963	Uppenbarelsereligion. 1930 ed. Edited by Erland Ehnmark. Stockholm: Prisma.
1974	Tal och essayer. Edited by Sven Stolpe. Stockholm: Rabén and Sjögren.

Other Books and Articles

In Swedish, the letters Åå, Ää, and Öö come at the end of the alphabet, after Xx, Yy, and Zz. Here they will be treated as though they were the unmodified letters Aa and Oo, though it should be pointed out that they are pronounced entirely differently.

Åkerberg, Hans. 1975. *Omvändelse och kamp: en empirisk religionspsykologisk undersökning av den unge Nathan Söderbloms religiösa utveckling*. Lund: Gleerup.

———. 1982. "Oändlighetsmystik och personlighetsmystik: Till belysningen av premisser och möjligheter i Nathan Söderbloms mystikdistinktion." *Religion och Bibel* 40:49–73.

Alfvén, Hugo. 1949. *I dur och moll: från Uppsalaåren*. Stockholm: Norstedt.

Andrae, Tor. 1930. *Muhammed, hans liv och hans tro*. Stockholm: Natur och Kultur.

———. 1931(1). *Nathan Söderblom*. Uppsala: Lindblad.

———. 1931(2). "Nathan Söderblom som religionshistoriker." In Karlström 1931, 25–62.

Appasamy, A. J. 1966. *Sadhu Sundar Singh: A Biography*. Madras: Christian Literature Society.

Aulén, Gustaf. 1931. "Den teologiska gärningen." In Karlström 1931, 63–104.

———. 1939. *Spaningstjänst*. Stockholm: SKDB.

Bailey, Charles E. 1978. "Gott mit uns: Protestant Theologians in the First World War." Ph.D. dissertation, University of Virginia.

Barrows, John H. 1893. *The World's Parliament of Religions* 2 vols. Chicago: The Parliament Publishing Company.

Berggrav, Eivind. 1931. *Nathan Söderblom: geni og karakter*. Oslo: Aschehoug.

Bohlin, Anna, ed. 1956. *Anna Söderblom: en minnesbok*. Uppsala: Lindblad.

Boschwitz, Friedemann. 1968. *Julius Wellhausen*. Darmstadt: Wissenschaftliche Buchgesellschaft.
Bousset, Wilhelm. 1903. *Die jüdische Apokalyptik*. Berlin: Reuther & Reichard.
Brandon, Samuel G. F. 1961. *Man and His Destiny in the Great Religions*. Manchester: Manchester University Press.
Briem, Efraim. 1927. "Religionshistoriens ställning vid våra universitet." In *Religionshistoriska studier tillägnade Edvard Lehmann*, 45–76. Lund: Gleerup.
Brilioth, Yngve. 1931. "Den ekumeniska gärningen." In Karlström 1931, 273–347.
———. 1933. "Biographical Introduction." In Söderblom 1933(1), xi–xxix.
Carmignac, Jean. 1971. "Les Dangers de l'Eschatologie." *New Testament Studies* (July 1971):365–90.
Cavendish, Richard. 1978. *A History of Magic*. London: Sphere.
Chesterton, Gilbert K. 1961 (1908). *Orthodoxy*. London: Collins.
Curtis, Charles J. 1966. *Nathan Söderblom: Theologian of Revelation*. Chicago: Covenant Press.
De Cocq, Antonius P. L. 1968. *Andrew Lang: A Nineteenth-Century Anthropologist*. Tilburg: Zwijsen.
Edsman, Carl-Martin. 1966. "Ur Nathan Söderbloms arbetsverkstad." *Religion och Bibel* 23:18–44.
Ehnmark, Erland. 1949. *Religionsproblemet hos Nathan Söderblom*. Lund: Gleerup.
Eliade, Mircea, ed. 1987. *The Encyclopedia of Religion*. New York: Macmillan.
Estborn, Sigfrid. 1944. *Under Guds grepp: en studie i Nathan Söderbloms förkunnelse*. Stockholm: SKDB.
Ferré, Nels F. S. 1967. *Swedish Contributions to Modern Theology*. New York: Harper Torchbooks.
Finkelstein, Jacob J. 1958. "Bible and Babel." *Commentary* (November 1958):431–44.
Fjellstedt, Peter, ed. 1880. *Concordia Pia*. Stockholm: EFS-Förlaget.
Fries, Karl. 1939. *Mina Minnen*. Stockholm: Triangelförlaget.
Fries, Martin, ed. 1945. *S. A. Fries: Vår kärleks historia: ett bidrag till teologiens historia*. Stockholm: Natur & Kultur.
———. 1948. *Metafysiken i modern svensk teologi*. Stockholm: Natur & Kultur.
Fries, Samuel A. 1895. *Betydelsen av Religionskongressen i Chicago*. Stockholm: Bohlin.
———. 1898(1). *Religionsvetenskapliga Kongressen i Stockholm 1897*. Stockholm: Bohlin.

———. 1898(2). "Der religionswissenschaftliche Kongress in Stockholm." *Zeitschrift für Missionskunde und Religionswissenschaft.*
Hallencreutz, Carl F. 1984. "Nathan Söderblom, Mission and the History of Religions." In Sharpe and Hultgård 1984, 52–67.
Harnack, Adolf. 1904. *Reden und Aufsätze.* Giessen: Ricker.
Hartman, Olov. 1968. *Earthly Things.* Translated by Eric J. Sharpe. Grand Rapids: Eerdmans.
Hartman, Sven S. 1984. "Nathan Söderblom and the Religion of Ancient Iran." In Sharpe and Hultgård 1984, 17–34.
Hassler, Ove, and Robert Murray. 1947. *Tor Andrae in memoriam.* Stockholm: SKDB.
Hastings, James, ed. 1908–21. *The Encyclopaedia of Religion and Ethics.* Edinburgh: T. & T. Clark.
Hedenius, Ingemar. 1959. *Tro och livsåskådning.* Stockholm: Bonniers.
Hedwall, Lennart. 1973. *Hugo Alfvén: En svensk tonsättares liv och verk.* Stockholm: Norstedt.
Heiler, Friedrich. 1967. *Die Passion des mystischen Christus.* Typescript.
Hemberg, Jarl. 1966. *Religion och metafysik.* Stockholm: SKDB.
Herz, Johannes. 1929. "Der Protestantismus und die soziale Frage." In *Der Protestantismus der Gegenwart,* edited by G. A. Schenkel, 338–82. Zürich: Bohnenberger.
Holmström, Folke. 1937. *Uppenbarelsereligion och mystik: en undersökning av Nathan Söderbloms teologi.* Stockholm: SKBD.
Hopkins, C. Howard. 1979. *John R. Mott, 1865–1955: A Biography.* Geneva: World Council of Churches and Grand Rapids: Eerdmans.
Hultkrantz, Åke. 1970. "The Phenomenology of Religion: Aims and Methods." *Temenos* 6:68–88.
———. 1979. "Nathan Söderblom och indianernas frambringare." *Religion och Bibel* 38:17–25.
———. 1983. "Viktor Rydberg och religionshistorien." *Svensk religionshistorisk Årsskrift* 1:31–41.
———. 1984. "Concept of God in the Making: 'Primitive Religion' in Nathan Söderblom's Interpretation." In Sharpe and Hultgård 1984, 17–34.
Jeremias, Alfred. 1903. *Im Kampfe um Babel und Bibel.* Leipzig: Hinrichs.
Karlström, Nils, ed. 1931. *Nathan Söderblom in memoriam.* Stockholm: SKDB.
———. 1947. *Kristna samförståndssträvanden under världskriget 1914–1918 med särskild hänsyn till Nathan Söderbloms insats.* Stockholm: SKDB.
Leeuw, Gerardus van der. 1938. *Religion in Essence and Manifestation.* London: Allen & Unwin.
Lehmann, F. Rudolf. 1922. *Mana: Der Begriff des "ausserordentlich Wirkungsvollen" bei Südseevölkern* 2 vols. Leipzig: Hinrichs.

Lindroth, Hjalmar. 1941. *Luther-Renässansen i nyare svensk teologi*. Stockholm: SKDB.
Lindroth, Sten. 1976. *A History of Uppsala University, 1477–1977*. Stockholm: Almqvist & Wiksell.
Lövgren, Nils, and Edvard Rodhe, eds. 1912–26. *Vår Kyrka*. 4 vols.
Malmeström, Elis. 1950. *J. A. Eklund: en biografi*. Stockholm: SKDB.
Massey, Marilyn C. 1983. *Christ Unmasked: The Meaning of the Life of Jesus in German Politics*. Chapel Hill: University of North Carolina Press.
Minnesalbum över Ärkebiskop Nathan Söderblom. 1931. Malmö: Världslitteraturens förlag.
Misner, Paul. 1981. *Friedrich von Hügel, Nathan Söderblom, Friedrich Heiler: Briefwechsel*. Paderborn: Bonifatius.
Moulton, James H. 1913. *Religions and Religion*. London: Epworth.
Moulton, William F. 1919. *James Hope Moulton*. London: Epworth.
Murray, Robert, ed. 1947. *Tor Andrae in memoriam*. Stockholm: SKDB.
Neander, Herman. 1932. *Med Nathan Söderblom: krigsfångvård och ekumenisk gärning*. Stockholm: Wahlström & Widstrand.
Nyberg, Henrik S. 1943. "Nathan Söderblom insats i utforskandet av den iranska religionshistorien." *Religion och Bibel* 2:1–13.
———. 1966. "Nathan Söderblom och studiet av religionen." *Religion och Bibel* 25:3–13.
Nystedt, Olle. 1931. *Nathan Söderblom: en levnadsteckning*. Stockholm: SKDB.
Otto, Rudolf. 1923. *The Idea of the Holy* (English translation by J. W. Harvey of *Das Heilige*, 1917). London: Oxford University Press.
Pettersson, Olof, and Hans Åkerberg. 1981. *Interpreting Religious Phenomena: Studies with Reference to the Phenomenology of Religion*. Stockholm: Scandinavian University Books.
Richmond, James. 1978. *Ritschl: A Reappraisal*. London: Collins.
Richter, Julius. 1935. *Das Buch der deutschen Weltmission*. Gotha: Klotz.
Ritschl, Albrecht. 1880. *Geschichte der Pietismus*. Vol. 1. Bonn: Marcus.
Rodhe, Edvard. 1930. *Svenska kyrkan omkring sekelskiftet*. Stockholm: SKDB.
———. 1935. *Den religiösa liberalisman: Nils Ignell, Viktor Rydberg, Pontus Wikner*. Stockholm: SKDB.
Rosenstock-Huessy, E. 1966. *The Christian Future*. New York: Harper & Row.
Rudolph, Kurt. 1962. *Die Religionsgeschichte an der Leipziger Universität*. Berlin: Akademie-Verlag.
Rupp, Gordon. 1953. *The Righteousness of God*. London: Hodder & Stoughton.
Schomerus, Hilko W. 1912. *Der Çaiva-Siddhanta*. Leipzig: Hinrichs.

Sharpe, Eric J. 1965. *Not to Destroy but to Fulfil: The Contribution of J. N. Farquhar to Protestant Missionary Thought in India before 1914*. Uppsala: Studia Missionalia Upsaliensea V.

———. 1969. "Nathan Söderblom and the Study of Religion." *Religious Studies* 4:259–74.

———. 1975. *Comparative Religion: A History*. London: Duckworth.

———. 1976. "Sadhu Sundar Singh and His Critics." *Religion* 6:48–66.

———. 1980. "Comparative Religion at the University of Manchester, 1904–1979." *Bulletin of the John Rylands University Library of Manchester* 63//1:144–70.

———. 1981. "Christian Mysticism in Theory and Practice: Nathan Söderblom and Sadhu Sundar Singh." *Religious Traditions* 4//1:19–37.

———. 1984(1). *Karl Ludvig Reichelt: Missionary, Scholar and Pilgrim*. Hong Kong: Tao Fong Shan.

———. 1984(2). "Nathan Söderblom, Sadhu Sundar Singh and Emanuel Swedenborg." In Sharpe and Hultgård 1984, 68–95.

———. 1984(3). "Sadhu Sundar Singh and the New Church." *Studia Swedenborgiana* 5//2:5–28.

———. 1987. "Tor Andrae." In Tor Andrae, *In the Garden of Myrtles*. Translated by Birgitta Sharpe, xiii–xxiii. Albany: SUNY Press.

Sharpe, Eric J., and Anders Hultgård, eds. 1984. *Nathan Söderblom and His Contribution to the Study of Religion*. Uppsala: Söderblom Society; Leiden: Brill.

Söderblom, Anna. 1948. *På livets trottoir*. Lund: Gleerup.

———. 1956. *På livets trottoir 2*. Lund: Gleerup.

Södergren, Viktor. 1945. *Vågen vi gått och vågen fram*. Stockholm: SKDB.

Streeter, Bernard H., and A. J. Appasamy. 1921. *The Sadhu: A Study in Mysticism and Practical Religion*. London: Macmillan.

Sundén, Hjalmar. 1960. *Religionen och rollerna*. Stockholm: SKDB.

Sundkler, Bengt G. M. 1968. *Nathan Söderblom: His Life and Work*. London: Lutterworth Press.

———. 1975. *Nathan Söderblom och hans möten*. Stockholm: Gummesson.

———. 1984. "Nathan Söderblom—a Complex Personality." In Sharpe and Hultgård 1984, 6–16.

Thulin, Sven, ed. 1931, 1933, 1934. *Hågkomster och livsintryck av svenska män och kvinnor*. Vols. 12, 14, 15. Uppsala: Lindblad.

Transactions of the Third International Congress for the History of Religion. 1908. Oxford: Oxford University Press.

Veen, J. M. van. 1940. *Nathan Söderblom: Leven en Denken van een Godsdiensthistoricus*. Amsterdam: H. J. Paris.

Verheule, Anthonie F. 1973. *Wilhelm Bousset: Leben und Werk*. Amsterdam: Ten Bolland.

Waardenburg, Jacques. 1973. *Classical Approaches to the Study of Religion.* Vol. I. The Hague: Mouton.
Weber, Otto. 1904. *Theologie und Assyriologie im Streite um Babel und Bibel.* Leipzig: Hinrichs.
Weber, Theodor. 1903. *Kaiser Wilhelm II und Admiral Hollman über "Babel und Bibel."* Gotha: Perthes.
Westman, Knut B. 1929. *Den kinesiska odlingens huvudepoker.* Stockholm: SKDB.
Widengren, Geo. 1947. *Tor Andrae.* Uppsala: Lindblad.
_____. 1953. "Die religionswissenschaftliche Forschung in Skandinavien in den letzten 20 Jahren." *Zeitschrift für Religions- und Geistesgeschichte* 5:193–222, 320–34.
_____. 1954. "Nathan Söderblom." In *Svenska män och kvinnor,* 7:424–27. Stockholm: Bonniers.
Williams, R., ed. 1906. *The New Church and Chicago: A History.* Chicago: Conkey.
Wingren, Gustaf. 1968. *Einar Billing.* Lund: Gleerup.
Zaehner, Robert C. 1961. *The Dawn and Twilight of Zoroastrianism.* London: Weidenfeld & Nicolson.

Index

Åkerberg, Hans, 178, 205, 206
Alfvén, Hugo, 173, 174
Almkvist, Herman, 33, 34, 102
Anderberg, Algot, 198
Andrae, Tor: on Söderblom, 6, 8, 10, 11, 18, 39, 86, 199, 201, 205, 207; on Muhammad, 122, 123, 125, 126; and archbishopric, 182; work on *The Living God*, 192
Apologetics, 39, 40, 43
Appasamy, Aiyadurai Jesudasen, 179, 183, 184
Aulén, Gustaf, 100, 178, 181, 197, 201, 202

Babel und Bibel debate, 109, 110
Bartholomae, Christian, 41
Baur, Ferdinand Christian, 103, 135
Berggrav, Eivind, 174, 189, 207
Bergson, Henri, xx, 95, 123, 124, 191
Berlin, 133, 137, 138, 145
Bertrand, Ernest, 37, 67
Bhagavad Gita, 157, 194
Billing, Einar, 164, 165
Billing, Gottfrid, 36
Björck, Albert, 64, 66, 67
Blume, Laurentius Ribe, 3, 4
Bohlin, Torsten, 202
Bonney, Charles Carroll, 65
Bousset, Wilhelm, 88, 89, 103, 104
Boutroux, Émile, 124
Brandon, Samuel George Frederick, 86
Brilioth, Yngve, xv, 243 (n. 76)
Bring, Ragnar, 178

Brun, Lyder, 101, 143
Buddha/Buddhism: compared with Christ/Christianity, 85, 130, 164; and prophecy, 99; and mysticism, 112; last Leipzig lecture on, 148; Mahayana, 194

Cairns, David Smith, 130, 131
Carlyle, Thomas, 60, 68, 128, 129
Casartelli, Louis Charles, 57
Catholic Modernism, 153–54, 213
Chantepie de la Saussaye, P. D., 36, 57, 58, 67, 96, 117
China, 180, 181, 182
Christian Socialism. *See* Social Christianity
Comparative religion: in Uppsala, 38, 39; Moulton and, 42, 99; in Paris, 48, 52; Harnack on, 96–97; church and, 98–99; in *Religionsproblemet*, 156–57
Congresses on history of religion: Stockholm 1897, 53, 63–70, 233 (n. 40); Basel 1904, 118–20; Oxford 1908, 129–30
Constantinople Conference of the World's Student Christian Federation (1911), 130–32
Coussanges, Jacques de. *See* Quirielle, Barbe de
Cumont, Franz, 147–48

Danell, Hjalmar, 33, 90, 146
Darmesteter, James, 41, 47, 49, 51–52
Deissmann, Gustav Adolf, xvii, 129

Delitzsch, Friedrich, 107, 109, 110, 113
Deussen, Paul, 118–19
Durkheim, Émile, 170–71

Ecumenism, 31, 189, 190
Edsman, Carl-Martin, xii, xiii, 204
Ehnmark, Erland, 157–58
Eidem, Erling, 177, 182
Eklund, Johan Alfred, 77, 90, 146
Ekman, Johan August, 27, 37–38, 76, 145
Engnell, Ivan, 203
Eschatology: Söderblom's introduction to, 5; as possible Iranian influence on Bible, 37, 42; dissertation on, 48, 50; and Sermon on the Mount, 71; and Kingdom of God, 73; absolute, not accepted, 74, 76; comparative, in *La Vie future*, 79, 83–85; in *Babel und Bibel* debate, 110; and Bergson, 124
Eucken, Rudolf, 95, 129

Fairbairn, Andrew Martin, 95, 128
Farquhar, John Nicol, 130, 131
Fehr, Fredrik: early career of, 24; and "Family Bible," 25; and group around Söderblom, 26, 32–34, 41, 50; death of, 53–54; controversy surrounding, 55; biography by Samuel Fries, 56; and Ritschlianism, 208
Ferré, Nels, 178
Francis of Assisi, Saint, 82, 83, 95, 154, 240 (n. 9)
Frazer, James George, 42, 108, 129, 131, 191
Freidenfeldt, Samuel, 18, 78
Fries, Karl, 19, 29, 130
Fries, Martin, 202
Fries, Samuel Andreas: orthodox radicalism of, 16; background and study of Wellhausen, 23, 28; and Rudin, 27; and Fehr, 32–33, 55–57; *Israels historia*, 34–35; as organizer of Stockholm congress (1897), 64–67; academic rejections of, 77, 89, 101; edits *Beiträge zur Religionswissenschaft*, 140; and archbishopric of Uppsala, 145; final illness and death of, 147, 176

Gabrielsson, Samuel, 127
Genius, 20, 23, 31, 168
Gifford Lectureship, 128, 191
Goldziher, Ignaz, 123
Göransson, N. J., 18, 43, 47, 49, 53, 54, 57, 61, 66, 76, 78, 92, 95, 101, 106, 117, 118, 121, 146, 148
Gunkel, Herman, 102, 103, 104

Hammarskjöld, Dag, 200
Harnack, Adolf von: influence on Söderblom, xviii, 21, 104; and Fehr, 24–25; and *Religionsgeschichtliche Schule*, 85; and comparative religion in theology faculties, 96–98, 135
Hartman, Sven S., 79, 86, 205
Hauck, Albert, 129, 132, 135, 136
Hebert, Gabriel, xvii
Hedenius, Ingemar, 202
Heiler, Friedrich, 153, 178–79, 184, 201
"High gods": Lang on, 107–8, 160; Aryan, 119; "Producers," 163, 236–37 (n. 33)
History: Harnack's role in Söderblom's appreciation of, xviii, 21; scientific principle in, xix; in student years, 26; uses of evidence, 85; in inaugural lecture, 97; and pan-Babylonians, 119; and rev-

elation, 196; and method in study of religion, 219–22
Hjärne, Harald, xx, 21, 101, 113, 146
Holiness: experience of, 44–45, 155, 157, 161; Söderblom's *Encyclopaedia of Religion and Ethics* article, 125, 169–70; and *mana*, 160; as key to understanding phenomenology of religion, 211
Holmström, Folke, 192
Hügel, Friedrich von, 153, 154
Hultkrantz, Åke, 205, 230
Hume, David, 142, 144

Ihmels, Ludwig, 135
Inaugural lecture (1901), 95–100, 215–18
India, 182–87
Iran, Iranian studies: and biblical eschatology, 37; in 1890s, 40–42; Moulton on, 43–44; Söderblom begins, 44; in Paris, 52; de Harlez and Casartelli on, 57; Lehmann on, 58; Söderblom's first publications, 59; and *Fravashis*, 78–79; *La Vie future*, 83–86; in *The Living God*, 194–95
Islam, 125, 126, 177
Israels historia (Samuel Fries), 34–35

Jeremias, Alfred, 110, 119

Kant, Immanuel, 72, 142, 155
Karlström, Nils, 175
Kierkegaard, Søren, 27, 83, 85, 100, 155, 157, 200
Kingdom of God: in Ritschlianism, 22; and "Social Gospel," 60, 63; debate in 1890s, 71; in Sermon on the Mount, 72–75; Johannes Weiss on, 104; discussion at Stockholm conference (1925), 190. *See also* Social Christianity
Kittel, Gerhard, xvii, 129, 136, 137
Kittel, Rudolf, 135–36
Klein, Rabbi G., 64, 67, 89, 90, 93
Kristensen, William Brede, 67, 91, 92, 117

Lang, Andrew, 13, 107, 108, 128, 132, 133, 160, 163, 191, 213
Leeuw, Gerardus van der, xi, xv, xx, 47, 150, 201, 203, 211
Lehmann, Edvard: contacts Söderblom, 58; admires *La Vie future*, 88; and Leiden chair, 91–92; supports Söderblom, 117; humor of, 121, 129; delivers first Olaus Petri lecture, 128, 129; in Berlin, 133, 137, 138; leaves Berlin for Lund, 145
Leiden, 91–92
Leipzig, 92, 132, 134–49
Life and Work conference (1925), 189, 190, 204, 207
Lindblad, Anna, 127–29
Lindroth, Hjalmar, 166, 178
Loisy, Alfred, 153–54
Luther, Martin, 14, 62, 75, 82, 83, 135, 154, 155, 157, 164, 165, 177, 213

Mana, 160, 163, 178
Marett, Robert Ranulph, 115, 129, 160
Ménégoz, Eugène, 52, 53, 119–20
Missions, 17, 19–21, 180–82
Moody, Dwight L., 29, 30, 31, 34, 62, 113
Mott, John R., 30, 31, 130, 131, 180, 231 (n. 44)
Moulton, James Hope, 41, 42, 43, 59, 88, 195, 210

256   Index

Muhammad, 123, 125, 126, 177
Müller, Friedrich Max, xi, 67, 102, 107, 128, 143, 144, 164, 191
Music: Söderblom's proficiency at, 4, 17, 32, 173; at Northfield 1890, 31; in Paris, 51; as analogy in study of religion, 98; at funeral, 198
Mysticism: studied by Rudin, 27; Samuel Fries and, 34; attitudes of Ritschl and Schleiermacher toward, 82, 103; two types of, 112, 158, 168–69; as vogue, 113–15; "of life," 156; in Luther, 165; in Sundar Singh, 183–84; Söderblom's difficulties with living visionaries, 188–89; in Buddhism, 194; in Socrates, 195; reevaluated, 206; *Mystik/Mystizismus*, 237 (n. 46)

Natural religion/theology: discussed in trial lecture, 81; contrasted with experiential religion, 82; extended discussion of in *Natürliche Theologie*, 139–44
Naumann, Friedrich, 61, 62, 68
Nietzsche, Friedrich, 41, 60, 164
Nobel, Alfred, 191
Nobel Peace Prize (1930), xvii, 148, 191, 207
Nyberg, Henrik Samuel, 79
Nygren, Anders, 178, 202

Olaus Petri Foundation, 127–29, 181
Origins of religion, 159–61
Otto, Rudolf, xi, xxii, 45, 80, 83, 114, 115, 129, 155, 179, 211

Pettersson, Olof, 178
Phenomenology of religion: Söderblom pioneer of, according to van der Leeuw, xv, 150, 167, 203, 211; differs from Husserlian phenomenology, xvi, xx, 151; importance of "reality" to, 47, 143; Söderblom's lecture topics concerning, 94; relation of subject to object in, 156; claims to seek *Verstehen*, 201; phenomenology and history, 202; phenomenology and theology, 209. *See also* History; Reality
"Producers." *See* "High gods"
Prophetic religion, 156, 165, 209, 213

Quirielle, Barbe de [pseud. Jacques de Coussanges], 83, 144

Reality, xix, xx, 143, 209, 213, 220. *See also* Phenomenology of religion
Reichelt, Karl Ludvig, 129, 180–81, 208
Reitzenstein, Richard, 104
Religionsgeschichtliche Schule, 36, 40, 85, 88, 97, 102–6, 116
Religionsgeschichtliche Volksbücher, 116, 137
Revelation: unique to Hebrew people, 43; general and special, 99, 105, 107, 110–11, 143–44; evidence for must be investigated, 113; continued, through genius, 131–32; and comparative religion, 157; and history, 195–96
Ritschl, Albrecht, and Ritschlianism, xx, 19, 24, 25, 32, 33, 37, 43, 53, 54, 55, 72, 74, 82, 83, 85, 103, 104, 106, 111, 112, 114, 135, 208
Rosenstock-Huessy, E., 239 (n. 33)
Rudin, Waldemar, 27, 28, 31, 34, 67,

Index   257

89, 231 (n. 32)
Rupp, E. Gordon, 164
Rydberg, Viktor, 13, 18, 26, 41

Sabatier, Auguste, xx, 31, 52, 53, 54, 67, 77, 87, 89, 90, 91, 106, 113, 147, 154, 210
Sabatier, Paul, 88, 154, 240 (n. 9)
Saint, Söderblom's definition of, 31, 196, 197, 212
Samfundet Fritt ur Hjärtat, 18, 23, 50, 57, 117, 176
Schleiermacher, Friedrich, 56, 72, 80–83, 103, 104, 113, 114, 115, 135, 139, 142, 144
Schmidt, Wilhelm, 108, 160
Schomerus, Hilko W., 178
Science, xx, xxiii, 66, 67, 70, 97, 108
Sermon on the Mount, 63, 71–76, 86, 93
Social Christianity, 8, 51, 56, 59–63, 67, 69, 70, 72, 75, 86, 233 (n. 29)
Sociology of religion, 170, 171
Socrates, 85, 95, 195, 243 (n. 67)
Söderblom, Anna (née Forsell): and Fehr, 25; and Rydberg, 26; and Nathan's travel diary (1890), 30; meets Nathan, 32; visits Fehr, 41; and Nathan's "numinous" experience, 44; marries Nathan, 49–50; and Nathan's illness (1906), 121; and Olaus Petri Foundation, 128; returns from Leipzig to Sweden, 147; on *Religionsproblemet*, 153; and Nathan's publications, 172; and Nathan's library, 198; and Nathan's letters and papers, 199; death in 1955, 201
Söderblom, Jonas, 1, 3, 5, 6, 9, 10, 29, 31, 76, 87, 92, 93, 147, 148, 223–24
Söderblom, Nathan, major works discussed: *Les Fravashis* (1899), 78–79; *Gudstrons uppkomst* (1914), 158–63; *Herdabref* (1914), 174–75; *Humor och melankoli* (1919), 164–68; *Jesu bärgspredikan* (1898), 71–76; *The Living God* (1933), 191–97; *Naturlig religion* (1914), 139–44; *Religionsproblemet* (1910), 153–58; *Uppenbarelsereligion* (1903), 110–13; *La Vie future* (1901), 83–87
Söderblom, Sophie, 1, 3, 4
Stöcker, Adolf, 61, 68, 82
Strauss, David Friedrich, 60, 135
Streeter, Burnett Hillman, 179
Studentmissionsföreningen, 17, 19
Sundar Singh, Sadhu, xiii, 179, 180, 182–89, 192
Sundberg, Anton Niklas, 47, 48, 49
Sundén, Hjalmar, 205
Sundkler, Bengt, xi, xiii, xx, 26, 28, 54, 84, 94, 101, 146, 166, 199, 203, 204
Swedenborg, Emanuel, 64, 65, 67, 186, 187, 188

Tagore, Rabindranath, 182, 187
Tiele, Cornelius Petrus, 36, 57, 58, 88, 91, 92, 96, 106, 117, 120, 128, 133, 191
Troeltsch, Ernst, 95, 103
Tylor, Edward Burnett, 107, 108, 128

Uppsala, Uppsala University: Söderblom as student at, 12–34; Reformation celebrations at, 45–47; chair application and trial lecture at, 79–83; professional appointment at, 89–90; returns to from Paris (1901), 93; professorial period (1901–12), 94–133; appointment as archbishop (1914),

172; visit of Sundar Singh, 184–86; reacts against Söderblom, 202; "Uppsala school," 203; World Council of Churches assembly at (1968), 203

Van Veen, J. M., 86
Verheule, Anthonie F., 103
Vivekananda, Swami, 64, 182, 194

War, 10, 174–76
Wellhausen, Julius, 22, 23, 24, 25, 28, 33, 54, 60, 103, 230 (n. 23)

Westman, Karl Gustaf, 146, 190
Westman, Knut Bernhard, 181–82
Widengren, Geo, 86, 203, 205, 242 (n. 17)
Wilder, Robert P., 29, 130
World's Parliament of Religions (Chicago 1893), 64–65, 182

Zarathustra/Zoroaster/Zoroastrianism, 40, 41, 42, 44, 59, 99, 194–95, 241 (n. 46). *See also* Iran, Iranian studies

www.ingramcontent.com/pod-product-compliance
Lightning Source LLC
Chambersburg PA
CBHW021357290426
44108CB00010B/280